The *Carole* of the Shepherds at the Nativity
Bodleian Library, MS. Douce 93, f. 28r. Lower Rhineland, fifteenth century

Â SELECTION OF
ENGLISH CAROLS

Edited with an Introduction, Notes
and Glossary by
RICHARD LEIGHTON GREENE

GREENWOOD PRESS, PUBLISHERS
WESTPORT, CONNECTICUT

Library of Congress Cataloging in Publication Data

Greene, Richard Leighton, ed.
   A selection of English carols.

   Reprint of the 1962 ed. published by Clarendon
Press, Oxford, in the Clarendon medieval and Tudor series.
   Includes bibliographical references and indexes.
    1. English poetry--Middle English, 1100-1500.
2. Carols, English--Texts. I. Title.
[PR1195.C2G73 1977]   821'.1'08   77-13760
ISBN 0-313-20002-5

ERRATA

p. [v], line 19. *After* No. 7 *insert* and No. 68
p. [ix], line 12. *For* Brown *R. L. 15 C. read* Brown *R. L. 14 C.*
p. 39, line 24. *For* Reigendlieder *read* Reigenlieder
p. 46, line 32. *For* Domini *read* Domino
p. 107, No. 46, line 5. *For* Allelyua *read* Alleluya
p. 122, No. 61, line 24. *For* peril *read* pepil
p. 171, line 34. *After* Manfred F. *insert* Bukofzer

Greene: "English Carols"

Reprinted in 1978 by Greenwood Press, Inc.,
51 Riverside Avenue, Westport, CT. 06880

Printed in the United States of America

A SELECTION OF
ENGLISH CAROLS

Edited with an Introduction, Notes
and Glossary by
RICHARD LEIGHTON GREENE

OXFORD
AT THE CLARENDON PRESS
1962

PREFACE

THIS edition of one hundred Middle and Early Modern English carols is designed as a representative selection from the whole preserved corpus of about five times that number. The carols here printed are not 'the hundred best', but are chosen in the hope of giving the reader an adequate idea of the range of subjects, verse-forms, and styles to be found in the carols as a whole. The book is in part an abridgement of the editor's collection published in 1935, *The Early English Carols*, and in part a presentation of new material. The English carols in British Museum MS. Egerton 3307, discovered since the publication of the earlier work, are here first given complete publication in unmodernized language. A considerable amount of information which the editor has acquired since 1935 is incorporated in the Introduction and Notes, and in the list of sources the provenance of various carol manuscripts is given fuller treatment than it has previously had. Passages from the introduction and notes of *The Early English Carols* have been freely used without change when improvement through change has seemed unlikely.

All the texts except No. 7 have been newly compared with the original manuscripts or printed sources or, in a few cases, with photographic reproductions. They are printed in the original spelling except that þ and ȝ are transliterated into their modern equivalents, and i and j and u and v are printed according to modern usage. Punctuation and capitalization follow modern usage and are editorially supplied. Manuscript abbreviations are silently expanded, and supplied letters and words are in square brackets. In general only one text of a carol is published; in a few cases of special interest one or more variants are included. The Glossary aims at practical usefulness for readers with limited command of Middle English.

To the general editor of this series, Dr. J. A. W. Bennett, I owe and gladly pay my hearty thanks for generous encouragement, hospitality, and criticism. For various helpful suggestions I am grateful to Dr. Frank Ll. Harrison of Merton College, Oxford; Mr. J. Lawson of the University, Hull; and Dr. John Stevens of Magdalene College, Cambridge.

R. L. G.

Wesleyan University
Middletown, Connecticut
August 1961

CONTENTS

ABBREVIATIONS USED
IN INTRODUCTION AND NOTES

Anal. Hym.	Dreves, Guido Maria, and Clemens Blume, eds., *Analecta Hymnica Medii Aevi.* Leipzig, 1886– .
Archiv.	*Archiv für das Studium der neueren Sprachen und Litteraturen.* Elberfeld, 1846–9, Brunswick, 1849– .
Babees Book.	Furnivall, F. J., ed. *The Babees Book.* Early English Text Society, Original Series, No. 32, London, 1868.
Balliol	Balliol College, Oxford.
Bliss	Bliss, Philip, ed., *Bibliographical Miscellanies.* Oxford, 1815.
B.M.	British Museum.
Bodl.	Bodleian Library.
Brown, *R.L. 15 C.*	Brown, Carleton, ed., *Religious Lyrics of the XIVth Century.* 2nd ed., Oxford, 1952.
Brown, *R.L. 15 C.*	Brown, Carleton, ed., *Religious Lyrics of the XVth Century.* Oxford, 1939.
B.–R.	Brown, Carleton, and Rossell Hope Robbins, eds., *The Index of Middle English Verse.* N.Y., 1943.
Br. Sar.	Proctor, Francis, and Christopher Wordsworth, eds., *Breviarium ad Usum Insignis Ecclesiae Sarum.* Cambridge, 1879–86.
Bukofzer	Bukofzer, Manfred F., *Studies in Medieval and Renaissance Music,* New York, 1950.
C. & S.	Chambers, [Sir] E. K., and Frank Sidgwick, eds., *Early English Lyrics, Amorous, Divine, Moral, and Trivial.* London, 1926.
Chambers, *M.S.*	Chambers, [Sir] E. K., *The Mediaeval Stage.* Oxford, 1903.
Child	Child, Francis James, ed., *The English and Scottish Popular Ballads.* Boston and New York, 1882–98.
C.U. Lib.	Cambridge University Library.
Dyboski	Dyboski, Roman, ed., *Songs, Carols, and Other Miscellaneous Poems.* Early English Text Society, Extra Series, No. ci. London, 1908.
E.B.M.	Stainer, Sir John, ed., *Early Bodleian Music.* London, 1901.

E.E.C.	Greene, Richard Leighton, ed., *The Early English Carols.* Oxford, 1935.
E.E.T.S.	Early English Text Society.
facs.	Reproduced in facsimile.
Fuller Maitland	Fuller Maitland, J. A., and W. S. Rockstro, eds., *English Carols of the Fifteenth Century.* London, [1891].
G. & C.C.	Gonville and Caius College, Cambridge.
Guide	Dean-Smith, Margaret, *A Guide to English Folk Song Collections, 1822-1952.* Liverpool, 1954.
Hunt. Lib.	The Huntington Library, San Marino, California.
Hym. S.	*Hymnarium Sarisburiense.* London, 1851.
Kaiser	Kaiser, R., ed., *Alt- und mittelenglische Anthologie.* Berlin, 1955.
J.A.M.S.	*Journal of the American Musicological Society.*
J.F.S.S.	*Journal of the Folk-Song Society.*
MacCracken	MacCracken, Henry N., ed., *The Minor Poems of John Lydgate,* Parts I, II. Early English Text Society, Extra Series, No. cvii, Original Series, No. 192. London, 1911, 1934.
Mayer	[Mayer, L. S.], ed., *Music Cantelenas Songs Etc.* London, privately printed, 1906.
M.L.R.	*The Modern Language Review.* Cambridge, 1906–
Nat. Lib. Scot.	The National Library of Scotland.
Nat. Lib. W.	The National Library of Wales.
New Ser.	New Series.
O.B.C.	Dearmer, Percy, R. Vaughan Williams, and Martin Shaw, eds., *The Oxford Book of Carols.* London, 1928.
O.E.D.	Murray, Sir James A. H., *et al.,* eds., *A New English Dictionary on Historical Principles* [*The Oxford English Dictionary*]. Oxford, 1888-1928.
Padelford	Padelford, Frederick Morgan, 'English Songs in Manuscript Selden B. 26', *Anglia,* xxxvi (1912).
Patterson	Patterson, Frank A., ed., *The Middle English Penitential Lyric.* Columbia University Studies in English. New York, 1911.
pr.	printed.
P.R.O.	The Public Record Office.
P.S.	*Percy Society Publications.* London, 1840–52.
Rel. Ant.	Wright, Thomas, and J. O. Halliwell[-Phillipps], eds., *Reliquiae Antiquae.* London, 1841-3.
repr.	reprinted.

Rickert	Rickert, Edith, ed., *Ancient English Christmas Carols*. London, 1914.
Robbins, *Historical Poems*	Robbins, Rossell Hope, ed., *Historical Poems of the XIVth and XVth Centuries*. New York, 1959.
Robbins, *Secular Lyrics*	Robbins, Rossell Hope, ed., *Secular Lyrics of the XIVth and XVth Centuries*. 2nd ed., Oxford, 1955.
S.T.S.	Scottish Text Society.
Sandison	Sandison, Helen E., *The 'Chanson d'Aventure' in Middle English*. Bryn Mawr College Monographs, Monograph Series, xii. Bryn Mawr, Pennsylvania, 1913.
Sandys	Sandys, William, ed., *Christmas Carols, Ancient and Modern*. London, 1833.
Sar. Miss.	Wickham Legg, J., ed., *The Sarum Missal*. Oxford, 1916.
Stevens	Stevens, John, ed., *Mediaeval Carols*. Musica Britannica, iv. 2nd ed., London, 1958.
St. J.C.	St. John's College, Cambridge.
Stud. Phil.	*Studies in Philology*.
T.C.C.	Trinity College, Cambridge.
T.C.D.	Trinity College, Dublin.
Utley	Utley, Francis Lee, *The Crooked Rib*. Ohio State University Contributions in Language and Literature, No. 10. Columbus, 1944.
V.C.H.	*The Victoria County History*.
Whiting	Whiting, Ella Keats, ed., *The Poems of John Audelay*. Early English Text Society, Original Series, No. 184. London, 1931.
Wright, *P.S.* iv 'Christmas Carols'	Wright, Thomas, ed., 'Specimens of Old Christmas Carols, etc., *Percy Society Publications*, iv. London, 1841.
Wright, *P.S.* xxiii	Wright, Thomas, ed., 'Songs and Carols of the Fifteenth Century', *Percy Society Publications*, xxiii. London, 1847.
Wright, *Wart. Club*	Wright, Thomas, ed., *Publications of the Warton Club*, iv. London, 1856.
Zupitza	Zupitza, Julius, ed., 'Die Gedichte des Franziskaners Jakob Ryman', *Archiv für das Studium der neueren Sprachen und Litteraturen*, lxxxix (1892).

INTRODUCTION

THE carol is now universally accepted as one of the important forms of Middle English poetry. It is generally recognized on the basis of musical as well as literary and historical evidence that in England in the fourteenth to sixteenth centuries the word 'carol' denotes a poem for singing, on whatever subject, in uniform stanzas and provided with a burden, a choral element which is sung at the beginning of the piece and repeated after every stanza. The acceptance of this definition results in the recognition of a well-defined corpus of some five hundred preserved carols, of which many are found in more than one version and about a quarter are provided with written music. Within this general verse-form many variations occur, but one formula is particularly prominent, that of a couplet burden rhyming with the last line of a tail-rhyme stanza of the form a a a b and with four measures to the line, as in this example (*E.E.C.*, No. 27B):

> Mane, be glad in halle and bowre;
> This time is bore oure Saviour.

> Al on this tyme God hath ows ysent
> Hys oune Son on a present,
> To dwell wyt ous in verement,
> To be owre help and oure socoure.

It is this metrical form, rather than, as in modern usage, a content in some way or other connected with the Christmas season, that is the mark of the carol for the Middle Ages, as is clearly shown by the concluding stanzas of some of the poems of the fifteenth-century chaplain John Audelay, for example, a piece invoking a blessing on the young Henry VI (*E.E.C.*, No. 428):

> I pray youe, seris, of your gentre,
> Syng this carol reverently,
> Fore hit is mad of Kyng Herre;
> Gret ned fore him we han to pray.

Since songs of this form were sung more frequently at Christmas festivities than at any other single time of year, the word 'carol' comes, after the simplifying of public religious life at the Reformation and the contemporary passing out of high fashion of this verse-form, to mean 'any song for Christmas', as it does to most people at the present day.

The etymological origin of the word 'carol' has been the subject of much discussion, but the important thing for understanding the texts here presented is that it is a direct borrowing of the Old French *carole*, which means a round dance in which the participants provide their own music by singing an alternation of a choral part, a burden, and uniform stanzas assigned to a soloist who leads the dance, the 'ring-leader', in fact. Though in French the word *carole* alone nearly always means this combination of dance and song, the latter alone being called *chanson à carole*, in English the single word comes to be used for any song in a form suitable for such a dance, whether or not actually performed in a prancing circle. The attempt of Dr. Margit Sahlin to derive the French word from the Greek exclamation of the Latin liturgy, *Kyrie eleison*, has not met with the general approval of Romance philologists, and an ultimate derivation from Greek *choraules*, flute-player, through the Latin is still regarded as the most probable.[1]

The limitation of the term 'carol' before about 1550 to the meaning just described involves denying the title to a few pieces, but only a few, that have often borne it. The narrative song of St. Stephen, found in a carol manuscript, which begins 'Seynt Stevene was a clerk in kyng Herowdes halle' is in every respect a ballad, correctly included in Child's collection (No. 22). The exquisite lyric 'I sing of a maiden' is not in true carol-form, and indeed is not a Nativity piece at all, as it has often been taken to be; it is a song of the Annunciation and needs no other label.[2] 'Carol' is best reserved, in the medieval period, for 'those lyrics which bear in their regularly repeated burdens the mark of their descent from the dancing circle of the *carole*'.[3]

[1] *Étude sur la carole médiévale* (Uppsala, 1940).
[2] Leo Spitzer, '*Explication de Texte* applied to Three Great Middle English Poems', *Archivum Linguisticum*, iii (1951), 152–63; see also Stephen Manning, 'I Syng of a Myden', *PMLA*, lxxv (1960), 8–12.   [3] *E.E.C.*, p. xxiv.

One of the earliest uses of the word in Middle English literature
comes in the *Cursor Mundi* of about 1300, where the meaning is
explicitly that of Old French *carole*, a dance in which the participants themselves sing the accompanying music:

> To ierusalem þat heued bare þai.
> þer caroled wiues be þe way.
> of þair carol suche was the sange.
> atte þai for ioy had ham amange.[1]

In the fourteenth-century *Stanzaic Life of Christ* the word 'ring'
is used to indicate a closed round dance. This word persists for at
least four centuries as the regular term for a circle of carollers.
A passage from St. Bernard, who represents Christ as speaking
contrasts the stretched arms of the dancers with his own:

> Thow in þo rymg of carolyng
> spredis þin armes furth from the.
> And I on croice have hom spredyng
> schamely, as men movn see.[2]

It occurs in Lydgate's poem 'The Order of Fools':

> The tenthe fooll may hoppe vpon the ryng,
> Foote al afforn, and lede of riht the daunce.[3]

One of the most sustained pieces of context for the word
'carol' in the fifteenth century is the rhymed ecclesiastical calendar written, or possibly only reworked, by Lydgate.[4] It presents
the whole company of saints listed in it as engaged in dancing a
carole, 'al on a rowe', and the petition of the faithful is to be
taken into that heavenly dance, and to 'escape þe wikked fendes
braule (Fr. *branle*, round dance)'. It is no church procession that is
in the poet's mind here, but a 'mery' *carole* like that of lovers with
their 'valentines', in which the 'heuenly lepars' 'both hoppe and
syng', to instrumental minstrelsy and the poet prays, 'Seynt
Apollinaire, teche me 3oure games', and asks SS. Margaret,

---

[1] R. Morris, ed., E.E.T.S., Or. Ser., Nos. 59, 62, 1875-6, p. 438, Fairfax Text,
ll. 7599–602.

[2] Frances A. Foster, ed., E.E.T.S., Or. Ser., No. 166, 1926, ll. 5937–40.

[3] ll. 25–26, MacCracken, part ii, p. 450.

[4] MacCracken, part i, pp. 363–76. Two MSS. weaken the dance-imagery here
and there by minor verbal changes.

Praxed, and Magdalene to let him bear their trains. The calendar
ends with a prayer to Christ that He will

> Graunt us for to be with Thomas of ynde,
> A curyous [in some manuscripts 'careles'] caral þis Crystemasse
> As to syng nowel when þat we hens passe,

and with a change of the figure of the *carole*, naturally enough, to
that of a feast:

> That we may sitte at Innocentes borde.[1]

A persistent piece of misinformation is that the English carol
is derived from, or at least closely related to, the French *noël*. The
only antidote is for the reader to remember that a *noël* is by
definition a French Christmas song. A May-carol can be a
delightful reality, but a 'May-*noël*' is an impossible contradiction
in terms. The *noël*, moreover, is later than the carol in making its
appearance. It is not found as a recognized type until the late
fifteenth century, a hundred years after the English carol has
become well established.[2] There has yet to be a demonstration of
any significant relation between an early *noël* and an English
carol. *Noëls* differ in favouring long stanza-forms, rare in the
carols, and they often lack both burden and refrain. The word
'*noël*' itself, to modern notions inseparable from songs of Christmastide, was in the fifteenth century not merely the name of the
Feast of the Nativity, but also a cry much like 'Hurrah!', always
in season, as when the maidens chanted it in London streets to
welcome home the victor of Agincourt.[3] Sometimes in English it
means 'news', *nouvelles*, as in the beginning of the traditional 'The
First Nowell', which means: 'The first piece of news the angels

---

[1] Many more examples could be given. It seems worth while to cite a few
because of the amazing conclusion of Dr. Margit Sahlin (op. cit., p. 34) that '. . .
tous ces examples de caroles arrondies n'assurent guère que le mouvement circu-
laire fût un élément constitutif de la "carole", et les définitions de la "carole"
comme "danse en rond", que donner tant de savants, manquent de fondement
réel'.
[2] See Amédée Gastoué, *Le Cantique populaire en France* (Lyon, 1924), pp. 109–
30 and 231–321.
[3] A. Brachet, *Dictionnaire étymologique de la langue française* (Paris, 1868), s.v.
'Noël'; Étienne Pasquier, *Les Recherches de la France* (Paris, 1643), bk. iv, chap. xvi;
Du Cange, *Glossarium Mediae et Infimae Latinitatis* (Niort, 1883–7), s.v. 'Natale'.

did tell.' It does not occur in Middle English with the meaning
which it acquires in French of 'Christmas song'.

One of the earliest specific pieces of evidence for the carol as a
dance-song with a burden, and perhaps the most important of all,
is the famous legend of the cursed carollers of Kölbigk in Saxony.
This story, well known throughout Western Europe, has been
discussed until its interpretation has become a literature in itself.
In Middle English it is well told in Robert of Brunne's *Handlyng
Synne*, but a very brief summary of its contents can best be made
from the Latin version recorded by Goscelin, a monk of Wilton
and of St. Augustine's Canterbury, in his *Life of St. Edith*.[1] It is
there told in the first person by the pilgrim Theodoric, who was
one of the carollers:

On Christmas Eve [in 1020 or thereabout] twelve of us gathered at
the church of St. Magnus in Kölbigk. Gerleuus was our leader, and the
others were Maeinoldus, Odbertus, Bovo, Gerardus, Wetzelo, Azelinus,
Folpoldus, Hildebrandus, Aluuardus, Benna, Odricus. The two girls
Mersuind and Wibecyna seized and brought from the church Ava, the
priest's daughter. We joined hands and danced in the churchyard,
Gerleuus, as *Vorsänger*, gave out the fatal song:

> Equitabat Bouo   per siluam frondosam;
> Ducebat sibi   Mersuindem formosam:
> Quid stamus?   Cur non imus?

When the priest called to us to stop dancing and come to the service, we
refused, and the priest invoked the wrath of God through the influence
of St. Magnus. The curse took effect, and we found that we could not
break the circle or stop dancing for a whole year. The priest's son Azo
attempted to pull his sister Ava out of the ring but only tore away her
arm, which did not bleed.

Meanwhile we danced and leapt and clapped, mocking our own pain
with the refrain of our song, 'Quid stamus? Cur non imus?' We neither
ate nor drank nor slept, and our hair and nails did not grow. People
flocked to see us, and the Emperor Henry attempted to have a shelter
built over us, but each night the work was thrown down. Finally on the
next Christmas Eve the curse was lifted, and we went into the church and
slept three days, but Ava died and her father soon after. Now we wander
separately through all countries, marked by the agitation of our limbs.

[1] André Wilmart, ed., 'La Légende de Ste Édith en prose et vers par le moine
Goscelin', *Analecta Bollandiana*, lvi (1938), 5–101, 265–307.

The importance of this story is twofold. It shows that as early as 1080 in England a Flemish-born monk who had lived in France could present to an English audience, without feeling the need of any explanation, the text of a *carole* (whether translated into Latin from French or not really does not matter much) divided into stanza and burden, the burden expressing in its very words the change from rest to motion which comes with the choral part. He writes not at all as if the *carole* were an unknown foreign phenomenon, and there is no reason to doubt that secular dance-song with a burden was known in England immediately after the Norman Conquest, if not before. Dom Wilmart has demonstrated that Goscelin's version of the legend is the nearest to the presumed common original of all its English, French, and German recordings and has the fullest account of the fatal *carole*. He explains why, in this part of the *Handlyng Synne*, Robert abandons the poorer version found in the *Manuel des Pechiez*, the French original for most of his work, and utilizes a version like that of Goscelin. In reporting the event, the fourteenth-century English poem consistently uses 'carol' for both the dance and its song. The carol-text is thus translated:

'By þe leued wode rode Beuolyne,
wyþ hym he ledde feyre Merswyne;
why stonde we? why go we noght?'[1]

The occurrence in the song of the names of the dancers themselves has been given various interpretations, but it is not a difficulty. Game-songs in which the actual names of participants are inserted are still sung by children.

R. H. Robbins attempts to dismiss this bit of song as 'not valid evidence for fifteenth-century England', for it is a serious embarrassment to his thesis of the carol's origin in processional hymns, but he follows Paul Verrier in declaring it to be 'a translation of twelfth-century French' and ignores Dom Wilmart's conclusive criticism of Verrier.[2] There can be no serious question that in England in the late eleventh century and in the fourteenth, let

---

[1] Frederick J. Furnivall, ed., E.E.T.S., Or. Ser., No. 119, 1901–4, p. 285, ll. 9049–51.
[2] *Stud. in Phil.*, lvi (1959), 577, referring to Verrier, 'La plus vieille citation de carole', *Romania*, lviii (1932), 380–421.

alone the fifteenth, a song divided into burden and stanza was recognized as what could be sung in a *carole*, and that carolling in its origin had no odour of sanctity, but the reverse. The matter would seem to be settled by Robert's proceeding to make it explicit that his English listeners need the warning. Moreover, he emphatically locates the episode in England itself:

And fyl þys chauncë yn þys londe,
Yn Ingland, as y vndyrstonde;
Yn a kynges tyme þat hyght Edward.[1]

The social dance known as the *carole* was beyond all question the favourite dance of the Middle Ages; it persisted for centuries and is by no means defunct in some parts of the world today.[2] It was well known to the ancient Greeks under the name of *Molpê* and was danced around altars and springs and on threshing-floors, a bard 'starting' the song which the dancers then took up, in chorus.[3] The essential form of the *carole*, established by many passages in medieval literature and by many representations in manuscript illumination and other painting, consists of a chain of dancers, with joined hands, which can be open in a line or closed in a circle and pass instantly from one to the other, all the dancers moving to the accompaniment of their own voices, with or without support from instruments. There must be a leader, *coryphée* or *Vorsänger*, who sings the stanzas of the song in alternation with the burden or chorus which is sung by the whole company. The melody is repeated for each stanza, and all repetitions of the burden use one melody. There may or may not be a close relation between the two melodies. The usual procedure is for the ring or chain to mark time in place during the stanza (or 'standing') and to revolve (always to the left or sunwise) during the general singing of the burden. It is obvious that only the leader need know all the verses of the song, and equally obvious that the *carole* is an ideal setting for improvised additions to keep the dance going. Often the

[1] Furnivall, op. cit., p. 283, ll. 9011-13
[2] A good account of the present-day *caro es* in central and south-east Europe is given in Violet Alford and Rodney Gallup, *The Traditional Dance* (London, 1935), chap. iv.
[3] Gilbert Murray, *The Classical Tradition in Poetry* (Cambridge, Massachusetts, 1927), chap. ii.

burden is linked to the stanzas by a definite cue, sometimes only by rhyme with the last line of the stanza, sometimes not at all. That the same group of dancers would form now a processional chain and now a ring (which should be obvious to anyone who has taken part in a lancers) is neatly shown by two successive stanzas of the ballad *The Earl of Errol* (Child No. 231 Aa) in the familiar formula of incremental repetition:

> (Edinburgh, 1658)
>
> (St. 16) There were four-and-twenty maidens
> A' dancing in a ring.
> (St. 17) There were four-and-twenty maidens
> A' dancing in a row.

This division into stanza and burden is the absolute essential of the *chanson à carole*, and it is found in many medieval French lyrics which were used in the dance, as well as in German *Reyenlieder* and notably in the Italian *ballata*, the verse-form most favoured by the followers of St. Francis for use in their missionary *laude*.[1] The basic scheme of the *ballata* is as follows:

> B B (*ritornello*) a a a b (stanza) B B (*rit.*) &c.

This rhyme-scheme is identical with that of many early French dance-songs and becomes in time the most characteristic arrangement of the English carol. One early *ballata* may be quoted as an example of the early appearance of the convivial theme alongside the amorous one which dominates the French *chansons à carole*:

> (*Rit.*) Pur bèi del vin, comadre, e no lo temperare:
> ché lo vin è forte, la testa fa scaldare.
> (St. 1) Gièrnosen le comadri 'ntrambe ad una masone,
> cercòr del vin sotile se l'era de sasone,
> bèvenon cinque barili et erano desone,
> et un quartier de retro per bocca savorare.
> (*Rit.*) Pur bèi del vin, comadre, e no lo temperare:
> ché lo vin è forte, la testa fa scaldare.[2]
> (&c.)

---

[1] On the *ballata* see F. Brittain, *The Medieval Latin and Romance Lyric to A.D. 1300.* 2nd ed. (Cambridge, 1951), pp. 47–49.

[2] Francesco Flamini, *Notizia Storica dei Versi e Metri italiani* (Livorno, 1919), p. 24.

Wherever the *carole* goes the initial and repeated burden goes with it. This applies to many Latin *cantilenae* which derive their form and sometimes their matter from this most popular of all recreations.

The exact amount of indebtedness of the English secular carol to the continental is difficult to state—the dance itself was completely international, and the travels of soldiers, merchants, friars, and other churchmen ensured that the songs of the *carole* as sung in France or Flanders would be brought to England in their tunes if not often in their words. Direct borrowing for translation seems rare, but such themes as the *mal mariée*, the lament of the betrayed girl, and the *pastourelle*, the successful or unsuccessful wooing of a country maid by a knight or a clerk, appear in English as they do in French folk-song to the present day.

The carol in its open or processional form is strikingly preserved into our own time in the May-day celebration of the Hobbyhoss at Padstow, Cornwall.[1] As the man inside the elaborately and traditionally decorated hobby-horse progresses with many caperings and sallies through the streets of the town, accompanied by a troupe who sing parts of both the 'Morning Song' and the 'Day Song', he and his companions stand still during the singing of stanzas and advance when the change to the burden is made. This change is followed without visible signal by the whole surrounding crowd, and when asked the reason for the procedure a young participant assured the present writer with some scorn that it had always been done that way. That the Padstow dance-and-song is a survival of a round dance as well as of an open procession is clear from the first lines of the chorus of the 'Morning Song':

With the merry ring, adieu the merry spring.

That the observance goes back at least to the time of the Battle of Agincourt is shown by such lines in the verses as these:

Where is St. George, where is he O [?]
He is out in his long-boat all on the salt sea O,

---

[1] This is described in A. K. Hamilton Jenkin, *Cornish Homes and Customs* (London, 1934), pp. 211–16; Claude Berry, *Cornwall* (London, 1949), pp. 178–85; *Devon and Cornwall Notes and Queries*, xii (1922), 145–52; and elsewhere. As is to be expected, the text of the songs varies somewhat in different accounts.

and

> Where are the French dogs that make such boast O [?]
> They shall eat the grey goose feather,
> And we will eat the roast O,

though St. George is now likely to emerge as 'King George' and the second stanza quoted is currently out of favour.[1] The *carole* is very much alive at Padstow.

The popularity of the *carole* with the lay public of Europe, rustics and city-dwellers and courtiers alike, was equalled only by its unpopularity with the higher authorities of the Church. A formidable series of denunciations and prohibitions was issued over several centuries. It is obvious that they failed to persuade the people to give up entirely a custom that had strong pre-Christian roots, associations that seemed to the churchmen to be diabolical and in the highest degree dangerous to the soul. These fulminations have a great sameness in their phrasing, and the necessity of renewing them is the best possible evidence of the failure of this frontal attack. A typical early expression of this disapproval is found in the eighth-century missionary handbook *Dicta Abbatis Pirminii* and may be thus translated:

> Flee wicked and lecherous songs, dancings, and leapings as the arrows of the Devil, nor should you dare to perform them at the churches themselves, nor in your own houses, nor in the open spaces, nor in any other place, because this is a remnant of pagan custom.[2]

It was a special cause of concern that the people liked to hold their *caroles*, as did the young folk of Kölbigk, in the central and convenient flat space of the churchyard itself. Particular prohibitions of this practice are frequent. Ralph Baldock, Bishop of London, in April 1308 issued a strong rebuke to the people of Barking, who had held dances and wrestlings and lascivious sports in the cemetery and even in the parochial and conventual churches, to the scandal of the Church and to the peril of souls.[3]

[1] *Padstow Hobby Horse* (pamphlet) (Padstow, 1903), pp. 1, 2.

[2] Quoted by L. Gougaud, 'La Danse dans les églises', *Revue d'histoire ecclésiastique*, xv (1914), 5–22, 229–45. Gougaud cites many such denunciations as does also Joseph Balogh, 'Tänze in Kirchen und auf Kirchhöfen', *Niederdeutsche Zeitschrift für Volkskunde*, Jahrgang 6, Heft 1 (1928), 1–14.

[3] *Registrum Radulphi Baldock*, Canterbury and York Society, Canterbury and York Series, vii (1911), 73–74.

Nor was it altogether an idle fear that the fun of the *carole* might lead to violence. One example must suffice. On Midsummer Eve, a favourite time for the sport, in 1306 the tailors and other townsfolk of Oxford held a wake all night, with much instrumental music. After midnight they held their dances in the High Street itself, and there one Gilbert de Foxlee tried to break up the dance with drawn sword. Thomas de Bloxham gave him a dagger-wound in the back, William de Claydon one in the head, and Henry de Beaumont a sword-cut in the right arm. Then William de Leye 'with a certain axe called spar-axe' inflicted such a wound in the left leg that Gilbert died of it after lingering for eight weeks.[1]

The activity of the *carole* was drawn upon for many *exempla* and brief illustrations in sermons. The *Summa Praedicantium* of the Dominican John Bromyard, for instance, offers passages like these:

> In which service of the Devil [the *carole*] he who begins the song holds the place of the priest; those who take up the song indeed assume the place of the other clerks; and those take the place of the parishioners. . . . For the circle of the dancers is the snare of the Devil. . . . [He] proceeds like a swineherd who, wishing all the swine to come together, causes one of them to squeal. So the Devil causes one to begin the song which he himself has dictated.[2]

'Lewd' songs for the dance were among the pitfalls against which Peter Idley warned his son in a passage that shows both how carols were thought of as forming one of the *genres* related to the dance and how there were pitfalls in the sport for maidens as well as youths:

> Also vse not to pleye at dyes and tables
> Ne no manner of games vppon the holy dayes;
> Vse no tauernes wher be gestis and fables,
> Synggyng of lewde baladis, rondelettes, and verelaies,
> [in another manuscript 'carolleys'],
> And erly on the morow also to fette hom fresshe maijs—
> That maketh maidens stomble and falle in the breris,
> And afterward they telle her counceill to the freres.[3]

---

[1] Oxford Coroners' Rolls, in J. E. Thorold Rogers, *Oxford City Documents Financial and Judicial, 1268–1665* (Oxford, 1891), pp. 165–6, translated by G. G. Coulton, *Life in the Middle Ages* (Cambridge, 1954), ii. 75–76.

[2] Translated from *Summa Praedicantium* (Basel, *c.* 1485), s.v. 'Chorea'.

[3] Charlotte D'Evelyn, ed., *Peter Idley's Instructions to His Son* (Boston, 1935), p. 124, book ii, ll. 1028–34.

There were certainly many songs which justifiably disturbed the guardians of Christian flocks. Naturally most of this kind are not preserved, but we have a few specimens, such as a precious pair in Cambridge University Library MS. Addit. 5943[1] and the 'Crystemes songe' which the enemies of Mankind with Nought as their leader sing in the Macro morality play of *Mankind*,[2] not to mention two of Kele's *Christmas carolles* of about 1550 (*E.E.C.*, Nos. 460, 461). It is plain that the denunciations were not merely the puritanical objections of the ascetic or ultra-squeamish. Christmas was the time when such songs were most often heard, and this prevalence provides another good reason for the dominance of the Christmas theme among religious carols. Wycliffe complains that at Christmas men 'pleie a pagyn of þe deuyl, syngynge songis of lecherie, of batailis and of lesyngis', but he admits that 'ȝonge wymmen may sumtyme daunsen in mesure to haue recreacion and liȝtnesse, so þat þei haue þe more þouȝt on myrþe in heuene & drede more & loue more god þerby, & synge honeste songis of cristis incarnacion, passion, resurexion & ascencion, & of þe ioies of oure ladi, & to dispise synne & preise vertue in alle here doynge'; a permission that includes a very fair summary of the principal themes of the religious carols.[3] It is to be noticed that in Wycliffe's time such songs are associated with the dance in a completely matter-of-fact way.

The whole movement of replacing such songs with pious ones, in which Franciscans were prominent, resembles the proceedings of the early Wesleyan hymn-writers and of the later Salvation Army in its purpose of supplanting songs that were worldly or worse with religious pieces in the same musical idiom or even with the very same melodies. The carol manuscripts which are preserved and the remnants of this type of Christian song in modern oral tradition show in what large measure the friars and other reforming religious succeeded in this substitution, a process that a cynical modern reader might think, without the evidence, unlikely to the verge of impossibility.

[1] *Pr.* Robbins, *Secular Lyrics*, pp. 26–28.

[2] Frederick J. Furnivall and Alfred W. Pollard, eds., *The Macro Plays*, E.E.T.S., Ex. Ser., No. xci, 1904, p. 13.

[3] F. D. Matthew, ed., *The English Works of Wyclif Hitherto Unprinted*, E.E.T.S., Or. Ser., No. 74, 1880, p. 206.

The Italian *lauda* is particularly associated with the earliest missionary followers of St. Francis, and the custom of using religious song in the vernacular and with verse-form and music already familiar to the people long persisted in the activities of his order in other countries, notably France, Germany, and England. The friars were outspoken in their denunciation of the 'dishonest' songs and dances of the simple folk and about their purpose of replacing these songs with sacred parodies or substitutes. No other nation can show a Franciscan so distinguished in this sort of poetry as Jacopone da Todi in Italy, but there were not wholly unworthy practitioners.[1] Jehan Tisserant, theologian and confessor to Queen Anne of Brittany and the first known author of *noëls*, is the great exemplar in France. Some of his songs, written in the fifteenth century, survived in living use into recent times.[2]

In fourteenth-century England the Anglo-Norman friar Nicholas Bozon followed the continental Franciscan practice of including in his sermons stanzaic verses in the vernacular. The important 'Honnd by honnd' (No. 6), still the earliest known 'Christmas carol' in English, is found very pertinently worked into the sermon notes of an anonymous English Franciscan. Friar-poets who work in the genre of the 'popular by destination' appear soon after the first landing of the Franciscans in England in 1224 and their rapid conquest of the country's religious life. Friar Thomas of Hales wrote 'A Luue Ron' about 1275, sending it to a maiden in place of the amorous song she had requested.[3]

A more prolific Franciscan writer was William Herebert, who died in 1333. One of his poems, 'Make Ready for the Long Journey', a free translation of an Anglo-Norman poem by Bozon, has a three-line 'burden' after each stanza, but an independent couplet at the beginning. He also translated Latin hymns, antiphons, and other portions of the service and is hence an honourable figure in the development of preachers' use of vernacular verse, but he does not appear to have much of an ear for song, and

[1] See *Annales Minorum*, xiv. 230, 397.
[2] Gastoué, op. cit., p. 86; for a biography see *Études franciscaines*, vii. 538-44.
[3] Carleton Brown, ed., *English Lyrics of the XIIIth Century* (Oxford, 1932), pp. 68-74.

claims for him as a 'developer' of the carol-form are dubious.[1] Certainly very little of Herebert's verse is really singable.

Franciscan friars in Ireland about 1300 produced the famous Kildare collection of Anglo-Irish poems, of which the one with most significance for the carol is the lullaby in long couplets with a recurring 'Lullay, lullay, little child', in the last couplet of each stanza.[2] Friar Johan de Grimestone, the compiler in 1372 of National Library of Scotland MS. Advocates 18. 7. 21, records a similar lullaby with the human child replaced by the infant Jesus and also a carol which uses the same phrase in its burden (No. 43). The great fourteenth-century Bishop of Ossory, Richard de Ledrede, was a Franciscan trained at Canterbury, and in his replacement of popular worldly holiday songs by sacred Latin pieces to the same tunes he was applying the Franciscan missionary poetic to the more learned group of vicars and minor clergy at Kilkenny. And most prolific of all known carol-writers is Friar James Ryman of Canterbury.

Even without this external evidence we should recognize the influence of St. Francis and his sincere early followers in the general tone of many carols. The emphasis on the humanity of Christ and on the sufferings of his human body, similar to that in the best-selling *Meditationes Vitae Christi*, wrongly attributed to St. Bonaventure and actually by an anonymous Franciscan, and the great interest in the helpless Child in the manger are highly characteristic of the Franciscan stress on that part of religion which makes the most appeal to the unlearned Christian. Although none of the later carol manuscripts except Ryman's can be established as of Franciscan provenance, they show the spirit of Jacopone and his method of sacred imitation of secular poetry in full measure. It will not do, moreover, to suppose that the relations between friars and monks were only those of rivalry and enmity, as the casual student of Chaucer and of medieval satire is in some danger of doing. Good fellowship in a context of carolling is shown by entries in the Journal of Prior William More of

[1] Brown, *R.L. 14 C.*, pp. xiv, 15–29; R. H. Robbins, 'Friar Herebert and the Carol', *Anglia*, lxxv (1957), 194–8.
[2] B.M. MS. Harley 913, *pr.* W. Heuser, *Die Kildare-Gedichte*, Bonner Beiträge zur Anglistik, xiv, (1904), 174–5.

Worcester which imply that the friars of the local houses were made welcome at the annual Christmas feasts of the Abbey. It is tempting to conjecture from the fact that entries of 'rewards' for carollers and friars are recorded in immediate succession that the friars themselves had some carols to offer the mixed company of clergy and city fathers.[1] Nor is there any sustained suggestion in the carols of the feud between clerk and layman which informs so much of the Goliardic Latin poetry. It is as if with the adoption of the vernacular lyric the pride of learning is laid aside and replaced by an emphasis that Francis himself would have approved on the equality in Christ, as in the Christmas feasting, of 'more and lesse'.

Concern on the part of church authorities over the sin of wanton dancing and singing was by no means roused only by the sports of lay folk. There are many records of disapproval and discipline directed at the clergy, both regular and secular, who indulged in such recreation. Two illustrations must stand for what could be a long anthology of such citations.

Statutes promulgated in 1338 by the Dean and Chapter of Wells alleged: 'Moreover [the Canons, in addition to hurrying through the psalms in church], are present personally, hunting, fowling and fishing; caring nothing for the clerical state; they take part in dances and masques and day and night prowl round the streets and lanes of the city leading a riotous existence, singing and shouting (*cum cantu et tumultu*). . . .' At Salisbury in 1418: 'Not only were the Canons and Vicars chatting in service time, but the Vicars were actually singing "balades and cantalenes in their Divine Services".'[2]

Even nuns were known to succumb to the attractions of the convivial dance. Dame Isabel Benet of the Cistercian priory of Catesby in the diocese of Lincoln was a 'receiver' or purchasing

---

[1] For example, 1518: 'Item rewarded for carralls 4*d*. 4*d*. 2*d*. 1*d*. 4*d*. 2*d*. 2*d*. [apparently to successive singers]/Item rewarded to ye grey fryurs 12*d*.' and 1521: 'Item to syngers of carralls 14*d*./ 8*d*./ 8*d*./ Item to ye grey fryurs 12*d*. to ye blake fryurs 12*d*./ to ye hunt 12*d*.' (ed. Ethel S. Fegan, Worcestershire Historical Society, 1914, pp. 76, 145).

[2] Aelred Watkin, *Dean Cosyn and Wells Cathedral Miscellanea*, Somerset Record Society, lvi (1941), 23; Dora H. Robertson, *Sarum Close* (London, 1938), p. 97.

agent of her convent and doubtless had marketing or other affairs to transact in Northampton, but, as with some modern business people, these did not consume all her time:

> [In 1442] Also the said dame Isabel on Monday last did pass the night with the Austin friars at Northampton and did dance and play the lute with them in the same place until midnight, and on the night following she passed the night with the friars preachers at Northampton, luting and dancing in like manner.[1]

In some writing about the medieval lyric the assumption is made that secular songs, especially if not 'literary', were the property of lay people alone. This can never have been the case. One must remember that every monk or nun or other professed religious was a boy or girl before joining the clergy, and no matter how edifying and scrupulous reading and conversation may have become thereafter, the monk or nun had a memory filled with non-religious ditties learned in childhood, just as has every modern clergyman. Even if a boy became a 'little clergeon' at an early age, we may be sure that his repertory was not limited to what he learned on the form of the song-school or in the choir, as that of today's choir-boys most definitely is not. It is as dangerous an inference to assign the performance of non-religious songs to lay people alone as to assume that religious songs would not be sung at secular gatherings.

The highly interesting documents published by Anna Jean Mill in her *Mediaeval Plays in Scotland* provide abundant testimony to the vigorous survival of the medieval Scottish *carole* into the seventeenth century.[2] A number of them record the attempts of the authorities to suppress carols along with other vanities, and some of them show that Protestant reformers, who regarded carols as lingering remnants of Papistry, found them no less difficult to put down than had the older Church in more southerly lands and earlier centuries. The association, real or feared, of the *carole* and its songs with sexual misbehaviour appears to have

---

[1] A. Hamilton Thompson, ed., *Visitations of Religious Houses in the Diocese of Lincoln*, ii, part i, The Canterbury and York Society, Canterbury and York Series, xxiv (1919), p. 50.
[2] London, 1927.

been as strong in the new order of things as in the old. This is the sort of evidence which the records offer:

> In 1552 Archbishop Hamilton of St. Andrews condemned in his catechism 'carreling and wanton synging in the kirk, and all uther vice quhilk commonly hes bein maist usit on the sunday'.[1]

> 1574, Aberdeen Kirk Session Records:
> Fourteen women were charged for 'plaing, dansin and singin off fylthe carrolles on Yeull Day, at evin, and on Sonday, at even, thairefter'.

Similar proceedings against offenders and prohibitions of carolling are found at Haddington in 1588, Errol in 1593 and 1594/5, and Elgin in 1618.[2]

The modern reader of these denunciations is likely to become sceptical of their validity. 'Surely', he says to himself, 'some carolling must have been quite innocent recreation. Are not these churchmen too free with their mention of the Devil as the patron of carollers?'

Without acquitting all the medieval clergy of narrow-mindedness or of hostility to the idea of young people enjoying themselves in their own way, we must yet recognize an aspect of the song-accompanied ring-dance which few, if any, previous writers on the carol have noticed. That is its supposed association with actual witchcraft. It is not necessary to commit oneself to any particular view of what history records as witchcraft to understand how this association would impair the moral standing of any and all *caroles* in a time and place of concern about witches' activities.

It is quite clear that the usual dance of the witches was the *carole*, in both its round and processional forms, or rather a perversion of it. An often reproduced title-page of 1639, that of *Robin Good-fellow, his mad prankes and merry iests*, printed by Thomas Cotes in London, shows a ring of men and women dancing in a circular track to the music of a piper, behind the large ithyphallic figure of Robin himself.[3] But the distinctive and damning feature

---

[1] T. G. Law, ed. (Oxford, 1884), p. 68, quoted by Mill, p. 86.
[2] Mill, op. cit., pp. 162, 253, 243, 242.
[3] Margaret Alice Murray, *The God of the Witches* (London, 1956), plate 11.

of the witches' *carole* was that the dancers faced outwards instead
of inwards and hence, by stepping to the left, moved *widder-
shins* or counter to the sun's motion, instead of sunwise as in all
ordinary mortals' *caroles*.[1] This, like saying a sacred formula back-
wards, is a sure sign of black magic.

Carolling was often among the activities confessed by accused
persons in the witchcraft persecutions of Scotland in the sixteenth
and seventeenth centuries, when, as we shall see elsewhere, the
carole was still very much alive. As in Kölbigk centuries before,
the churchyard itself was a favoured venue. It is reported that in
North Berwick in 1590 Barbara Napier joined the local covens
at the church, 'where she danced endlong the kirkyard, and Gelie
Duncan played on a trump, John Fian masked led the ring, Agnes
Sampson and her daughters and all the rest following the said
Barbara to the number of seven score persons'.[2]

It has often been said that carols were sung by 'minstrels'.
Many unlearned and some learned statements to the contrary, it
is necessary to say that there is no record at all of the vocal performance of any of the English carols by any professional enter-
tainer of the kind to which the term 'minstrel' was applied in the
fourteenth, fifteenth, and early sixteenth centuries. The evidence
that by 'minstrel' was then understood an instrumental musician
playing for pay of one kind or another is simply overwhelming, as
Ritson realized a century and a half ago in the midst of his annoy-
ance with Bishop Percy. A few significant references only will be
quoted here. The key verb is regularly 'play', not 'sing'.

When in 1324 in Cornhill a dealer in skins named Thomas de Lenne
was so angered at the music of a minstrel named Thomas Somer that he
struck him with a door-bar and pursued him to kill him, only to be
stabbed to death himself by the said Somer, it was playing and not singing
that moved him to such violent criticism.[3]

Froissart records a musical incident when King Edward III was on
board ship before the Battle of Winchilsea. Sir John Chandos had

---

[1] Often recorded; see Christina Hole, *Witchcraft in England* (London, 1945),
p. 31; Murray, *The Witch-cult in Western Europe* (Oxford, 1921), pp. 130–5.
[2] Robert Pitcairn, *Criminal Trials* (Edinburgh, 1833), i, part ii, pp. 245–6, quoted
by Murray, *The God of the Witches*, p. 107.
[3] Edith Rickert, *Chaucer's World* (New York, 1948), p. 17.

brought back from Germany a piece called a 'dance'. The King had his minstrels play the accompaniment, but Chandos himself did the singing.[1]

In the mumming presented at Kennington for Richard II by the commons of London just before Candlemas of 1377 there was 'great noyse of mynstralsye, trumpets, cornets and shawmes'. After dicing and gift-giving wine was brought, 'and they dronk with great joye, commanding ye minstrels to play and ye trumpets began to sound and other instruments to pipe, &c.'[2]

Nothing could be more explicit than the Black Book of Edward IV with its prescriptions for the smallest details of the King's household establishment. The section beginning 'Mynstrelles, xiij,' is self-explanatory:

whereof one is veriger that directeth them all in festiuall dayes to theyre stacions, to blowinges and pipinges, to suche offices as must be warned to prepare for the king and his houshold at metes and soupers, to be the more redy in all seruyces, and all thies sitting in the hall togyder, whereof sume vse trumpettes, sume shalmuse and small pipes.[3]

No reference whatever appears to singing by minstrels.

During the coronation feast of Queen Elizabeth, wife of Henry VII, on 25 November 1487:

At the second course 'as the high bourde was servid, the kings mynstrells played a song before the queene, . . . [followed by ceremonies of thanking and Garter's triple cries of *Largesse*]. Then played the queenes mynstrells, and after them the mynstrells of other estates.'[4]

The references in the works of Chaucer and in the metrical romances likewise make it plain that minstrels were instrumentalists and minstrelsy instrumental music.

The recorded names of minstrels, where they signify the skills or specialties of the bearers, show that they are instrumentalists, e.g. John of Gaunt's minstrels 'Hankyn piper' and 'Jacobe Bumbepiper', both of whom received grants in 1380,[5] and the 'Mene-

[1] Clair C. Olson, 'The Minstrels at the Court of Edward III', *PMLA*, lvi (1941), 611–12.   [2] Chambers, *M.S.* i. 394, n. 4.
[3] A. R. Myers, ed., *The Household of Edward IV* (Manchester, 1959), p. 131.
[4] Ives, *Coronacion of Queene Elizabeth*, p. 120, quoted by Arthur Taylor, *The Glory of Regality* (London, 1820), p. 278.
[5] Eleanor C. Lodge and Robert Somerville, eds., *John of Gaunt's Register, 1379–1383*, Camden Society Publications, 3rd ser., lvi, lvii (1937), 113, 301.

strallis' who received rewards at the English court at Pentecost
of 1306, including 'Janin le Lutour', 'Gillotin le Sautreour', 'Baudec
le Tabourer', and others.[1]

Not merely documentary evidence, but carvings in stone con-
firm the same conclusion. For example, in Beverley, where there
was a famous guild of minstrels, the well-known pillar which was
their gift to St. Mary's Church shows four instrumentalists but
no singers, and in the nave of the Minster itself the superb series of
realistic sculptures in the north aisle represents all the figures in
minstrels' dress in possession of instruments. The series includes
one duo of vocalists, who, as if to make the point clear, wear choir
vestments and hold a scroll on which are carved the words of their
sacred song, 'Te deum laudamus'.

Two matters of common sense may be mentioned in passing.
Most of the instruments used by minstrels were of such a nature as
to preclude any vocal performance by their players: bagpipes,
trumpets, and other wind instruments, and viols, and related
stringed instruments. Only harpers, lute-players, and taborers
could sing while playing, and such evidence as there is indicates
that the harp was used to accompany narrative rather than lyric
poetry. The other point, rarely if ever remarked, is that in the
usual arrangement of the medieval hall the musicians' or minstrels' gallery was located at the opposite end of the hall from
the high table on floor or dais, and therefore at a distance quite
suitable for instrumental music during dinner but ill-adapted
to song in an age when the words counted for as much as the
music and a singer needed to be near his audience.[2]

Around the year 1550, with the simultaneous coming of the
English Reformation and of strikingly new fashions in music,
dance, and poetry led by the court, the carol of the Middle Ages
undergoes a sudden decline, though not a complete disappearance.
The monks and friars who appear to have been the chief pro-
pagators of the religious carol vanish totally from the scene, and
the monastic refectories are as bare and ruined as the monastic
choirs, no longer echoing to feasts like those of Prior More at

---

[1] *Manners and Household Expenses of England* [&c.], Roxburghe Club, 1841, 141,
from Exchequer Roll, reprinted by Chambers, *M.S.* ii. 234–8.
[2] See Glynne Wickham, *Early English Stages* (London, 1959), i. 222–3, 245.

Worcester. The non-religious carol goes out of fashionable favour, though a likeness to its form may be seen in the ayres and balletts which, with the totally different madrigal, come to dominate the vocal recreation of the upper class. The simple ring-dance gives way to a variety of more formal and elaborate figures mostly imported from France. Then, in a very natural semantic change, the word 'carol', by way of the stereotyped phrase 'Christmas carol', which is emphasized by the preservation of Christmas almost alone as an important general holiday, comes to mean primarily, as it still does to most people, 'a song in any form designed to be sung at Christmas'.

Nevertheless, the old burden-and-stanza form, usually in a context of humble life, crops up here and there, in broadside songs like the fantastically popular 'Greensleeves' and among the songs of the Tudor drama. 'Back and side go bare', a true carol and a worthy successor to 'Bring us in good ale', is inserted into *Gammer Gurton's Needle*, and no less than five carols are sung in the crude play of *Tom Tyler and His Wife* of about 1558. *The Compleat Angler* represents a carol as sung in regulation solo-and-chorus fashion by a band of strolling beggars, and an occasional moral piece echoes the late medieval treatment of death and judgement. A diligent search of manuscripts and early prints reveals only a few more than sixty specimens from the century after 1550, most of them quite unblessed by any real poetical quality. And of the life of the carol in the oral tradition of the remoter countryside, a life which undoubtedly existed, we have almost no record at all from this period.

At first glance things appear to be much the same in Scotland. Few carols are recorded from north of the Border before 1550, none of them distinguished except Dunbar's two, his plea to the King for a Christmas gift of new clothing with the burden

> 'Schir, lett it nevir in toun be tald
> That I suld be an Yuillis yald',

and his account of the better love that comes with the cooling of Dame Venus's brand with the burden

> Now cumis aige quhair yewth has bene
> And trew luve rysis fro the splene.

A few carols are among the religious parodies of worldly songs in the *Gude and Godlie Ballatis* of the brothers Wedderburn (1567) and then the form undergoes the general eclipse of Scottish popular verse that lasts until the eighteenth century and does not pass fully away until the work of Burns. Among the songs that Burns collected and edited and imitated are many with the initial burden long disused in England and as closely associated with the dance as their medieval prototypes. So frequent is the form that we realize that there has been something like a retreat to survival across the Border on the part of the carol. That story must be told elsewhere. It is enough to point out here that the healthy survival of the Scottish carol into the nineteenth century is an important piece of testimony to the popularity and wide circulation of the non-religious carol in places far removed from the English court, London literary circles, and the new learning of the universities, so resolutely opposed to all that was either rustic or 'monkish'.

Only a very few carols are found both in manuscripts earlier than 1550 and in any kind of traditional survival in actual modern vocal use. The first and simplest case is that of the famous Boar's Head Carol still sung each year at the Queen's College, Oxford (No. 33). It is unique in its almost unchanging text and in the circumstances of its performance. Its stability is easily explained by its long use in a restricted and highly self-conscious society alert to prevent change.

The second instance is that of the Corpus Christi Carol (No. 67), discussed at more length in the notes. This is the most complex of all and the one that has naturally aroused the greatest interest.

There seems to be only one medieval manuscript carol which has survived to the twentieth century in outright oral tradition. This is *E.E.C.*, No. 80, a carol which has become well known in its medieval text but with supplied music not found in the manuscript, British Museum, Harley 5396. The volume is a typical monastic miscellany, apparently owned in 1455 by someone in the Midlands, probably Northamptonshire, who used its blank spaces for commercial accounts. The Harley text begins:

Christo paremus canticam:
'Excelsis gloria.'
When Cryst was born of Mary fre
In Bedlem, in that fayre cyte,
Angellis songen with myrth and gle,
'In excelsis gloria.'

Shortly before 1909, Alice E. Gillington heard this carol sung
by a gipsy in the south of England and recorded it without
recognizing its medieval origin. Margaret Dean-Smith, in her
admirable *Guide to English Folk Song Collections*, rightly calls the
gipsy version a 'vulgarization'. It begins:

Christ is born of maiden fair;
Hark, the heralds in the air,
Thus, adoring, descant there:—
'In Excelsis Gloria'.[1]

It is plain that there has been some influence here from modern
evangelical hymnody: we recognize the herald angels of Wesley
and Whitefield.

There are only three medieval manuscript carols which have
been found in modern unlearned use. One appears most surprisingly in D'Urfey's *Pills to Purge Melancholy*, set to music 'by
Mr. Tenoc'. Its text is in the medieval carol-form with an initial
burden, though the burden is printed without separation from
the stanzas. It begins:

It is my Delight both Night and Day,
To Praise the Women as much as I may;
Three things be glorious,
I'll tell you if I can,
The Sun, an Angel, and a Woman.
(Burden repeated)

The seventh stanza runs:

Three things will be a Chattering,
I'll tell you if I can,
A Pye, a Popinjay, and a Woman.
(Burden repeated)[2]

[1] *Old Christmas Carols of the Southern Counties* (London, 1910), p. 15.
[2] Ed. of 1707, ii. 127; *repr.* John S. Farmer, *Merry Songs and Ballads Prior to the
Year 1800* (privately printed, 1897), iv. 149–51.

This is clearly in direct descent from the jingle in the carol manuscript Bodleian Library Eng. poet. e. 1, the first two lines of which
were not interpreted as a burden in the editing of *The Early English
Carols* and which was consequently excluded.[1] R. H. Robbins has
taken the lines as a burden and listed the piece as a carol.[2] The
medieval piece appears to be another instance of verses in another
form made into a carol, for in the earlier Brome MS. it appears as
a set of puzzle-verses involving a simple cipher: a 'Christmas
game'[3]

The other two appear in more than one text as late as the
nineteenth century. While their history, told elsewhere more
fully, cannot be detailed here, it establishes a point of some
importance, the refutation of the older folk-lorists' idea of
the complete isolation from one another of oral and written
transmission. They are No. 39 in the present collection and
E.E.C., No. 152.[4]

The distinction between the medieval carol and the traditional
narrative ballad as clearly different genres of English poetry is now
easier to make than it once was, and it need cause little, if any,
confusion. That this distinction was well understood in the Middle
Ages is plain from the extreme rarity of the occurrence of carols
and ballads in the same manuscript and, in fact, from the general
scarcity of ballad-texts in manuscripts of the fourteenth and

[1] Pr. Wright, *P.S.* xxiii. 4–5.
[2] 'The Middle English Carol Corpus: Some Additions', *Modern Language Notes*,
lxxiv (1959), 200.
[3] Lucy Toulmin Smith, ed., *A Common-place Book of the Fifteenth Century*
(London: privately printed, 1886), pp. 12–13.
[4] Richard L. Greene, 'The Traditional Survival of Two Medieval Carols',
ELH, vii (1940), 223–38. Only here and there can as much as a whole line of
modern traditional song be recognized as actually surviving from a medieval
carol. One striking example is the second line of the couplet burden of *E.E.C.* No.
163, a lament of Mary over her crucified Son:

> For to se my dere Son dye, and sones have I no mo.

The line appears in stanza 7 of the Shropshire version of the folk-song 'The Seven
Virgins' as
> While I do see my own son die
> When sons I have no more.

(*J.F.S.S.* v (1918), 22). An almost identical phrasing in a Manx version is recorded
ibid. vii (1924), 283.

fifteenth centuries. Of preserved manuscripts, the only one to record ballads in neighbourhood to carols is British Museum Sloane 2593, which contains two, *Robyn and Gandelyn* (Child No. 115) and '*St. Stephen and Herod*' (Child No. 22, the story of Stephen and the roasted cock which crew). It is especially remarkable that Richard Hill, who cast so wide a net, included no ballads in his fine commonplace book, Balliol College, Oxford, MS. 354.

The three principal points of difference between the pieces in Child's *English and Scottish Popular Ballads* and those here collected concern method of transmission, narrative quality, and metrical form. The ballad is by definition a narrative song: with those combinations of ellipsis and repetition which characterize its peculiar style, it tells a tale and there makes an end. The interest is in the tale; none is diverted to the emotions of the teller or his hearers, or to his relations with them. The objectivity of the ballad is one of the touchstones of its authenticity. Now neither complete objectivity nor narrative content is essential or even usual in the carol, although both may be present. The narrative quality of the carol is typically that of a known story entirely lacking in suspense and that of a story told for a purpose, religious, moralizing, satirical, or occasional, quite foreign to the ballad. Nor are the carols the product, like the ballads, of a sustained process of oral transmission impinged upon here and there in later centuries by multiplied and widely circulated broadside or chapbook copies. The third point of difference, that of metrical form, though it still presents some unsolved questions, is yet clear enough to serve in practice as a valuable means of distinction. The key to the difference lies in that important member of the whole structure, the burden.

Where any choral element is found in the ballads, as it is in less than one-fourth of the 1,250 versions in Child's basic collection, it is almost always an internal refrain, a very different thing from the initial and external burden of the carol and indeed from the characteristic refrain of carol-stanzas, which is a repeated *last line* of the stanza. The form of refrain most usual in the English ballad consists of a pair of lines, usually rhyming together, inserted in alternation after the lines of a narrative couplet so that the whole

stanza contains four lines and four musical units in conformity
with the most usual melodic structure, For example:

> One king's daughter said to anither,
> *Brume blumes bonnie and grows sae fair*
> 'We'll gae ride like sister and brither.'
> *And we'll neer gae down to the brume nae mair.*[1]

The same type of internal refrain is often extended to fill out
longer stanzas in ballads. It is common in ballads and folk-songs
of other countries and is found in many pieces which were certainly connected with a dance. A famous instance from English
history is the song reported by Fabyan as sung in the caroles of
the exulting Scots after Bannockburn:

> Than the Scottis enflamyd with pryde, in derysyon of Englysshe men,
> made this ryme as foloweth.

> Maydens of Englonde, sore maye ye morne.
> For your lemmans ye haue loste at Bannockisborne,
>   With heue a lowe.
> What wenyth the kynge of Englonde,
> So soone to haue wonne Scotlande
>   With rumbylowe.

> This songe was after many dayes sungyn, in daunces, in carolis of ye
> maydens & mynstrellys of Scotlande, to the reproofe and dysdayne of
> Englysshe men, w[i]t[h] dyuerse other which I ouer passe.[2]

But it will be seen at once that it requires a different pattern of
dance, though the ring of linked dancers and the alternation of
solo and chorus may very well have been the same. What is
most striking is the extreme scarcity of the carol-type of burden in
the texts of Child ballads. Of all the 1,250 only the merest handful
show the initial and external burden, as do *The Elfin Knight*
(No. 2A) and *Captain Car* (No. 178A). Ballad texts collected
since Child's work show only a slightly higher proportion, and,
while it is undoubtedly true that careless editorial practices have
sometimes obscured the evidence of external burdens, there are
not enough cases to invalidate the distinction. The singers and

---

[1] Child No. 16E, stanza 1.
[2] Robert Fabyan, *The New Chronicles of England and France* (London, 1811,
after Pynson's edition of 1516), p. 420.

listeners of the Middle Ages obviously felt decisively the difference between the narrative ballad and the lyric carol, a difference that corresponds to that between the 'disours' of tales and romances and the 'singing men', amateur or professional, who led a company in the sociable carol.

Beyond all question the principal use of the kind of carol which predominates in this collection was at celebrations involving feasting or social dining. The chief habitat of the manuscript carol was the hall, whether of a castle or manor house or of a monastery or cathedral. This was the place above all others where religious and laity, men and women, and, within limits, great and humble most frequently met to form a common audience, and to indulge a taste in lyric entertainment that varied less from group to group than is often thought. Since these gatherings were more concentrated in the twelve days of Christmas than at any other time of year, it is only to be expected that a very large number of carols will deal directly with the Nativity and with the events and personages connected with the other feast days that conclude with the Epiphany. This close connexion with holiday feasting may well be the explanation of the strikingly small number of carols dealing with Easter as a holiday or with the Resurrection. There was less feasting at Eastertide for one excellent practical reason which, obvious as it is, seems rarely to be mentioned: the lack of available provisions for lavish meals at the end of the long winter, when any establishment was lucky if its larder had no shortage of everyday food.

Out of an abundance of evidence for the singing of carols at dinners and feasts a few specially interesting records may be noticed. The royal court knew them well.

In the Black Book of Edward IV there is a special note at the end of the section concerned with 'Chapleyns and Clerkes of Chapell':

MEMORANDUM that the king hath a song before hym in his hall or chambre vppon All Halowen-day at the later graces, by some of thes clerkes and children of chapell, in remembraunce of Cristmasse, and so of men and children in Cristmasse thorowoute; but after the song on All Halowen-day is don, the steward and thesaurer of household shall be warned where hit likith the king to kepe his Cristmasse.[1]

[1] A. R. Myers, op. cit., p. 136.

At the Twelfth Night feast of Henry VII in 1487 'at the Table in the Medell of the Hall sat the Deane and those of the Kings Chapell, which incontynently after the Kings furst Course sange a Carall'.[1]

Many passages in the romances and other literature make it plain that carols, sung both in the dance and apart from it, were an expected feature of feasts in hall. One of the most interesting is the account in the North Midland romance of about 1400 of Sir Cleges' sadness on Christmas Eve as he recollects how he has spent all his estate on the great feasts that he held at Christmas, where he would reward generously all the minstrels who came. He has a vision in a kind of walking swoon:

> Sore syȝthyng, he hard a sovne
> Of dyvers mynstrelsé:
> Of trompus, pypus, and claraneris,
> Of harpis, luttis, and getarnys,
> A sitole and sawtré,
> Many carellys and gret davnsyng;
> On euery syde he harde syngyng,
> In euery place, trewly.[2]

Carols are prominent in the festivities of *Sir Gawain and the Green Knight*, both those at Arthur's court and those at the castle of the Knight himself. Four mentions of the word clearly designate dancing of knights and ladies, as on St. John's Day.[3] But one passage shows the carols being sung at supper and around the fire, without dancing.[4]

---

[1] *Joannis Lelandi Antiquarii de Rebus Britannicis Collectanea* (London, 1770), iv. 237. See notes on No. 17.

[2] *Sir Cleges*, ll. 98–106, ed. Walter Hoyt French and Charles Brockway Hale, *Middle English Metrical Romances* (New York, 1930), pp. 880–1; see also ll. 481–98, pp. 892–3.

[3] J. R. R. Tolkien and E. V. Gordon, eds. (Oxford, 1925), ll. 1025–6. The other passages are ll. 41–43, 471–3, 1885–8.

[4] Ibid., l. 1652–5. The 'coundutes' mentioned were *conducti*, Latin part-songs of a sophisticated kind which were old-fashioned at the time that the romance was written. Their special use at Christmas is mentioned in *The Owl and the Nightingale*:

> & hure & hure to cristes masse.
> Hwenne riche & poure. more & lasse.
> Singeþ cundut. nyht & day.
> (Jesus text, ll. 481–3)

J. H. G. Grattan and G. F. H. Sykes, eds., E.E.T.S., Ex. Ser., No. cxix, 1935, p. 15. It is not quite accurate to call the carols their 'direct descendants', as does Leonard Ellinwood, 'The *Condustus*', *Musical Quarterly*, xxvii (1941), 188.

A vivid impression of the kind of feast that an officer of a large monastic house would hold in the holiday season is given by the matter-of-fact accounts of disbursements contained in the journal of William More, last Prior of Worcester, who gave a Christmas feast each year to officials of the city of Worcester.[1] Among the most frequent items of expense in the years 1518 to 1532 are malmsey and other wines, minstrels and other entertainers, and singers of carols. It is plain that all of these are regarded as regular components of a large holiday dinner for which a whole ox was bought, and it is equally plain that 'minstrels' and 'singers of carols' are quite separate people, as witness two entries of 1527:

> Item for syngyng of carrolls on cristmas day &
>   to mynstrells 2 *s.* 6 *d.* 16 *d.*
> Item to mynstrells & syngers of carralls 12 *d*/4 *d.*

Carol-singers are also distinguished from a lute-player who sang (and was not paid for some reason) and from players at the Christmas season of 1520:

> Item rewards for caralls on cristmas day
>   dynar 14 d./ at supper 8 *d*
> Item to carrolds a pon seynt Johns Day 8*d.* 2*d.*/8*d.*
> Item rewarded to William ye Lewter for his syngyng &
>   pleyng in ye cristamas wycke nil hic
> Item rewarded to iiij pleyers of glowceter a pon
>   sonday when ye balyffs & ye xxiiij[ti] dyned
>   with me in ye grete hall   3*s.* 4*d.*

There were songs and dances and minstrelsy in the spring as well, when Prior More was enjoying country life at the Abbey's manors of Battenhall and Crowle.[2] Those who would put churchmen and popular merry song into separate worlds are advised to look further into these good times at Worcester Abbey, not to mention the entertainments paid for through many decades at Selby Abbey in Yorkshire, Winchester College, and Magdalen College, Oxford, and through almost three centuries at Durham Priory.[3]

[1] Ethel S. Fegan, ed., Worcestershire Historical Society, 1914.
[2] Ibid., pp. 367, 373, 385.
[3] Glynne Wickham, op. cit. i. 332–9; Chambers, *M.S.* ii. 246–50, 240–4.

The feasting known as a 'Grand Christmas' in the Temple continued into Elizabethan times the same sort of proceedings. The custom was to hold a 'parliament' on the eve of St. Thomas the Apostle (20 December) and, if the celebration was decided upon, to mark it by a speech in the hall from 'the eldest Butler', who announced to the whole society the names of the appointed officers; 'and then in token of joy and good-liking, the Bench and company pass beneath the harth, and sing a carol, and so to boyer'. The custom indicated in No. 4 of calling for a carol from each guest in turn was observed from Christmas Eve through the Twelve Days: 'The antientest Master of the Revels is, after dinner and supper, to sing a caroll or song; and command other gentlemen then present to sing with him and the company; and so it is very decently performed.'[1]

It is interesting to see the same custom at Christmas dinner in the hall after Mass insisted upon by Squire George Gamwell of Gamwell Hall, Notts., in the ballad *Robin Hood's Birth, Breeding, Valor and Marriage* (Child No. 149a, stanzas 15, 16; text from 1716):

> And in comes the squire, and makes a short speech,
> It was, Neighbours, you're welcome all.

> But not a man here shall taste my March beer
> Till a Christmas carrol he sing:
> Then all clapt their hands, and they shouted and sang
> Till the hall and the parlour did ring.

There are many other carols which are shown by the internal evidence of their own texts to be designed for convivial use, especially at holiday feasting. It is well to remember that monasteries and bishops' palaces held many such celebrations and that there is no reason to be surprised at the frequency of such lyrics in connexions which a modern reader would classify as 'religious'. Among the examples in this collection are Nos. 4, 5, 13, 17, 26, 27, 33, 34, 38, 64, 70, 87, 88. Many of the references are very explicit, for example: Others of the same kind are numerous in

No. 70, 'Good men that stondyn and syttyn in this halle.'

---

[1] John Nichols, *The Progresses and Public Processions of Queen Elizabeth*, new ed. (London, 1823), i. 136, 138.

E.E.C., e.g. Nos. 6, 13, 24, 126, 134, 135, 137, 256, 350, 420, Appendix iii.

A conclusion with a form of prayer, found in a great many carols, is not a sign that the piece is designed for use in church rather than for a social gathering in a hall. A benediction or a prayer for salvation of the company is the standard conclusion for a piece of medieval poetry of almost any kind, narrative as well as lyric, and often for a song or tale of completely secular or even coarse nature. It usually implies no connexion whatever with a church service. A good example is No. 84. The matter needs emphasis because of such astonishing statements as those of Dr. Margit Sahlin that 'les plus anciens *carols* sont souvent de véritables litanies populaires' and 'Ces *carols* ne sont souvent que des litanies populaires, destinées, nous semble-t-il, à être chantées aux processions et au danses sacrées des fêtes ecclésiastiques.'[1] It is well to point out once for all that there is only one carol out of the five hundred to which the term 'litany' can with any real accuracy be applied, *E.E.C.*, No. 309a, which adds to the one-stanza prayer 'Jhesus, for thi holy name', found entirely dissociated from any carol in some nine other manuscripts, a burden and eight stanzas which follow in general the list of saints in a York litany. The carol does not resemble the litany in its form and is found only in Bodleian Library MS. Eng. poet. e. 1, of which the convivial character is obvious. As a carol it is definitely a 'sport' and in no sense typical.

Neither does a burden in the form of a prayer imply that the carol is intended for a choir rather than a dining hall, e.g. No. 8:

> To blis God bryng us all and sum,
> Christe redemptor omnium.

The mixture, completely congruous to a medieval Christian, of devotional sentiment and 'mirth' in its special sense of 'cheerfulness resulting from the knowledge of one's salvation', is one secret of the carol's special nature, and attempts at interpretation of the 'religious' carol which are not based on an understanding and

[1] Op. cit., pp. 203, 56, cited with approval by R. H. Robbins, *Stud. in Phil.*, lvi (1959), 571: Ryman's carols to the Virgin are in content something like a litany of Mary, but the regular carol-form is used (*E.E.C.*, Nos. 220–6). He mentions only *E.E.C.*, No. 309a.

acceptance of this mixture lead to strange results. A grace before and another after meat do not make of a meal a religious service, nor in a Christian household do they impair the merriment and good fellowship of the table.

Two of the most familiar and most picturesque customs of the Christmas season, the ceremonial bringing in of the boar's head as a prelude to the feast and the decking of houses, churches, and sometimes streets with the holly and ivy that still flaunt their deep green in midwinter, are the subjects of deservedly well-known carols. The Boar's Head Carol used to this day at the Queen's College, Oxford, is sung in a procession which preserves the old carolling custom of advancing during the burden and remaining in place for the stanzas. It is, of course, an observance for the dining hall and not for the chapel, let alone for a church. There were many other similar celebrations at similar banquets and No. 34, for example, implies singing during the entry of the boar's head, as does *E.E.C.*, No. 135, which is probably derivative from the version used by the Queen's College. A boar's head carol in Bodleian Library MS. Eng. Poet. e. 1, on the other hand (*E.E.C.*, No. 134), suggests by its content no procession but rather the kind of singing carols in rotation that is even more clearly indicated by No. 5. Any idea that boar's head carols were related to processions in the liturgical services of the Church is quite without foundation.

No traditional carol is sung today with more spirit and gaiety than 'The Holly and the Ivy', and though no version of this particular song has been found in a medieval source, its theme is the same as that of one of the most interesting groups of the older carols. Some of the medieval pieces resemble the traditional one in assigning a Christian significance to these plants which obviously owe their favour to much older pre-Christian associations. One carol in praise of the holly alone implies some opposition to it at a banquet and attaches an 'Alleluia' burden to a completely secular stanza text that begins (*E.E.C.*, No. 137):

> Her commys Holly, that is so gent;
> To pleasse all men is his intent.

Two others partisan to the ivy make of it a symbol of the Virgin, one with the refrain from the Song of Songs, 'Veni, coronaberis', the other with a typically medieval acrostic which makes the letters I V E stand for 'Jesus', 'Virgin', and 'Emmanuel' (*E.E.C.*, Nos. 138, 139).

Behind these rather artificially 'moralized' carols stand a number of others which clearly betray an association of holly with the male and ivy with the female. Almost as clearly No. 34 implies that the two evergreens were the respective emblems of the men and the women in some kind of barring-out game that involved rivalry between the sexes. Such a use is even more explicit in a little song not in carol-form but included in the carol manuscript Bodleian Library Eng. poet. e. 1:

> Holvyr and Heyvy mad a gret party,
> Ho xuld have the maystre
> In londes qwer thei goo.[1]

There is undoubtedly some relation here to the unluckiness of a woman or other female creature as the 'first foot' on Christmas or New Year's morning.[2] This sexual association is confirmed by a number of well-known folk customs, such as the Shrovetide burning in East Kent of two effigies known as the 'Holly-boy' and the 'Ivy girl', the latter as variation of the widely-used 'harvest-may' or 'corn dolly', the last sheaf of a harvest shaped or dressed like a girl and brought home in state on the last load.[3] Often cited and still significant, are the reference in a seventeenth-century work, *The Twelve Months*: 'Great is the contention of holly and ivy, whether master or dame wears the breeches', and the Oxfordshire custom that a man had to supply a maid with ivy to keep her from stealing his breeches.[4] A holly twig is the instrument of mastery over a wife in the folk-song 'On Monday Morning I Married a Wife'.[5]

The survival in these customs of a primitive fertility rite is

---

[1] f. 30 r. and v.; *pr.* Wright, *P.S.*, p. 44.

[2] As a precaution some holly was laid outside the door in Holderness to be brought in as the 'first foot' (*Notes and Queries*, 6th. Ser. x (1884), 482).

[3] *Gentleman's Magazine*, xlix (1779), 137; W. C. Hazlitt, ed., *Faiths and Folk-lore* (London, 1905), ii. 319.

[4] By M. Stevenson, quoted by John Brand, *Popular Antiquities of Great Britain and Ireland* (London, 1841), i. 269; *Folk-Lore*, xxviii (1917), 421.

[5] James Reeves, *The Idiom of the People* (London, 1958), p. 164.

obvious, and eager commentators have not been lacking. Margaret Dean-Smith points out, however, that 'the holly-and-ivy metaphor of the male and female principle...is rare in folk-song, despite its continuing prevalence in active Christmas custom'.[1] It is indeed noticeable that holly and ivy occur oftener in modern traditional song as euphonious and irrelevant refrain-words than as symbolic referents, e.g.:

> Holly and ivy,
> Mistletoe bough,
> Give me an apple,
> And I'll go now,[2]

and

> My father left me an acre of land,
> *There goes this ivery(?)*
> My father left me an acre of land,
> *And a bunch of green holly and ivery.*[3]

It is probably such a carefree refrain that appears (? as an indication of tune) at the beginning of No. 7, replacing the holly-ivy burden with the same number of syllables in the Latin words of the great 'Laetabundus' prose.

The more careful and literary praise of ivy found in No. 36 is wholly secular and refers to the plant's remaining green in a north of England winter and to its physical qualities as good medicine and as a preservative of masonry. No mention of mistletoe, which pagan associations kept out of all churches except York Minster, is found in any medieval carol. But ivy was used in England as a substitute for palm-branches in Palm Sunday processions and undoubtedly gained some additional sanctity thereby.[4] Both holly and ivy were among the plants most disliked and shunned by Scottish witches.[5]

---

[1] *Guide*, p. 74; see also p. 57. A direct use of ivy as a fertility charm is reported from Worcestershire and Herefordshire, where a little of the ivy that had hung in church was given to ewes to make them bear twin lambs (*Notes and Queries*, 5th ser. xi (1879), 206).

[2] *Folk-Lore*, xiv (1903), 177, reported as current about 1825.

[3] *J.F.S.S.* ii (1906), 212, Child No. 2.

[4] Theodor Erbe, ed., *Mirk's Festial*, i, E.E.T.S., Ex. Ser., No. xcvi, 1905, p. 115.

[5] F. Marian McNeill, *The Silver Bough* (Glasgow, 1957), i. 82, 84.

Any reader who meets the medieval carols for the first time is struck at once by the frequency with which lines of Latin verse appear in combination with the Middle English texts. A little over two-fifths of the carols preserved from before 1550 contain Latin lines or phrases, and, as would be expected, these are mostly pieces of a religious or moralizing nature, although there are some interesting exceptions, e.g. Nos. 81 and 98 in this collection.[1] Careless or ignorant writers on the carol have often dismissed this Latin content by saying merely that the lines are 'taken from old hymns' and that they give 'a true medieval flavour' to the carols. More serious, because more misleading, are the assumptions that carols are frequently translations of medieval Latin hymns and that the form itself is directly derived from the characteristic hymns of the Office as they are found in the old breviaries. Though anything like a full treatment of the subject is impossible here, a few of the important and corrective points should be made.

In the first place, some of the carols are truly macaronic, that is, maintaining a continuous sense in a patterned alternation of the two languages, the Latin parts, like the English, being composed for their particular places and not quoted from another poem. An occasional cliché or scriptural phrase does not alter this basic character. Friar James Ryman is especially given to this kind of verse, and the best known of all the boar's head carols (No. 32) concludes each stanza with it. Other good examples are Nos. 24 and 74.

A more usual procedure is to use whole lines of Latin as the repeated elements of a carol, as the burden or as the refrain, or both. In this case the line or lines chosen have usually an exclamatory or sententious character, maintaining by repetition the central theme of the piece and summarizing its content. These burdens or refrains are often not exactly fitted to the syntax of the adjoining lines as in fully macaronic verse, but rarely are they irrelevant or inappropriate. Lines which are very familiar, even to the unlearned

[1] More detailed discussion and tables of borrowings will be found in chapter iii of the Introduction to *E.E.C.* The sources of the Latin lines in the carols in this collection, as far as they are known to the editor, are recorded in the notes to the several pieces.

Christian, are naturally put to this use in many carols, e.g. 'Gloria
tibi, Domine', 'Gloria in excelsis', 'Alma redemptoris mater',
'Puer natus est nobis'. As a rule their introduction does not impair perfect regularity of metre. While this free use of Latin is
rightly taken as a sign of the clerical authorship of most of the
carols that we have, we must not assume that it made the carols
unintelligible to lay people. There is no reason to suppose that
medieval listeners were any less intelligent than modern ones;
there is much reason to believe that they were more attentive and
blessed with better aural memories. Most churchgoers must have
known a great deal of Latin by rote and its meaning by context,
even without a day's schooling.

Of the many types of Latin verse composition for singing in
church services to which the term 'hymn' is applied, there are
four which contribute an appreciable number of Latin lines to the
carols: the hymn of the Office, the prose or sequence used in the
Mass, the antiphon of various kinds and uses, and the *cantilena*, or
non-liturgical song in stanzas. By far the most important is the
hymn proper, the poem in stanzas of identical form, usually
though not always rhymed in the same pattern, and sung to a
melody which is repeated for each stanza. The medieval use of
these hymns is not in the Mass but in the Office sung at the canonical hours in communal establishments such as monasteries,
cathedrals, and secular colleges, so that their text would be only
less familiar to professed religious than that of the psalms. The
negligible amount of quotation from the Latin psalms in the
carols is very striking. It is easy to account for: the psalms are in
rhythmic prose, while hymns, like carols, are in metre and for the
most part in lines of four measures. To call the antiphonal singing
of such prose with a repetend 'carol-wise', as R. H. Robbins does,
is as misleading as to call free verse the ancestor of metrical verse.[1]
Nevertheless there is not a single carol that is known to be a full
translation of a Latin hymn. Ryman paraphrases hymns in some
of his carols, but it should be noted that when he actually translates one he follows the form of the Latin, which has no burden,
and does not use the carol form, which he knows so well. The
usual procedure of a carol-writer was to take a line he wanted

[1] *Stud. Phil.* lvi (1959), 570.

wherever he found it. An extreme instance is No. 12, which uses lines from eight different Latin hymns for various occasions in the course of its twenty lines of stanza-text. No carol uses more than five lines from any one hymn: *E.E.C.*, No. 52, a Nativity carol, borrows that many from the great Christmas hymn of Sedulius, 'A solis ortus cardine'. The same kind of borrowing of lines from earlier hymns is found in countless Latin hymns contemporary with the carols. It represents a considerable contribution of content to the carols but does not signify an influence of the hymn on the carol-form in particular cases.

The prose or sequence, an addition to the Mass which grew out of the practice, from the eighth century on, of fitting words to the long *melisma* or *sequentia* originally sung to the last 'a' of 'Alleluia', differs radically from the carol in its metrical and musical structure, though a plain verbal text of a sequence may suggest a likeness which is deceptive. The essential procedure of the sequence is the antiphonal singing of its strophes *in pairs*, the music being the same for both strophes of a pair. These strophes may be in unrhymed prose, as in the early 'Notkerian' type, or in metre and rhyme, as in later specimens like the famous 'Victimae paschali laudes', or even in uniform strophes which look, when printed without their music, like the stanzas of a hymn or of a carol, as do those of the 'regular' proses associated with Adam of St. Victor, such as the renowned 'Verbum bonum et suave'. Some proses have a single strophe to be sung at the beginning by both choirs, usually balanced by a similar final strophe. This may look like the burden of a Latin carol, but it is entirely different: it is not repreated after each strophe, or indeed at all. The prose, in fact, is metrically and musically without any close relationship to the carol, and the half-dozen carols which incorporate lines from well-known proses show no influence at all from the form of these chants in paired strophes which are designed not for leader and chorus, but for antiphonal choirs.

A special word is needed about the 'Laetabundus', attributed to St. Bernard of Clairvaux, perhaps the finest and most popular of all medieval proses. As a magnificent musical ornament of the Christmas season, much imitated and parodied in other Latin proses, we should expect it to have left its mark on the carols. So it has, but only by contributing some of its Latin lines to one of the loveliest of all (No. 46) and by providing the whole content (a rather clumsy English paraphrase, with the *cauda* of each stanza left in the Latin) of No. 7. As if to prevent us from misunderstanding the relation of prose and carol, Bodleian Library MS. Arch. Selden B. 26 includes among its carols an English translation of the 'Laetabundus' which preserves the forms and metre of the Latin strophes and has the true musical form of the sequence, a different melody for each pair of strophes, and, of course, no burden.[1] In the course of his metrical experimentation James Ryman twice translates the 'Laetabundus', leaving the tags in Latin, once in uniform strophes of two lines plus the tag, and once in stanzas of three lines, made by adding a weak and redundant line to each.[2] But Ryman knows that he is not here making a carol: there is again no burden.

The term 'antiphon', from which modern 'anthem' is derived, is applied in the first instance to the verses which were chanted before and after the psalms to plain-song melodies similar to those of the psalms themselves. These are passages of more or less rhythmical prose, not in metre, and have no influence upon the form of the carols in which they are quoted. For instance, the first two carols in *E.E.C.* paraphrase in their English stanzas the sense of two of the famous Advent antiphons beginning with 'O', 'O radix Jesse' and 'O clavis David', but the Latin burdens which begin with these phrases drastically change the rest of the texts of the antiphons into the metrical form (here a quatrain) which a carol requires. Only about a dozen phrases from these regular antiphons appear in all the carols, and of these two are used irreverently and derisively in a nonsense carol (*E.E.C.*, No. 474).

[1] f. 19 v., *pr.* Padelford, p. 105; *E.E.C.*, pp. lxxviii–lxxix; with music, *E.B.M.*, Nos. lxx, lxxi; Latin text, *Anal. Hym.*, liv. 5; *E.E.C.*, p. lxxviii.

[2] C.U.L. MS. Ee. 1. 12, ff. 35v., 76v., *pr.* Zupitza, pp. 201, 276. There is another rendering of the prose into macaronic English and Latin in a London manuscript of the fifteenth century, Bodl., Ashmole 189 (ff. 104 v., 105 r.; *pr. E.E.C.*, p. lxxxi), which in part follows the metrical form of the original and in part deviates from it. It is not a carol. Neither is the fine Anglo-Norman drinking song which imitates the form of the 'Laetabundus' and keeps its Latin tags: 'Or hi parra:' (*pr.* Alfred Jeanroy and A. Långfors, *Chansons satiriques et bachiques du XIIᵉ siècle*, Paris, 1921, p. 78, and frequently elsewhere).

The four Antiphons of the Blessed Virgin Mary, which came to be used separately from psalms, are in rhyme and metre, and contribute another ten lines to various carols, including their opening lines 'Alma redemptoris mater', 'Regina coeli, laetare', and 'Salve regina, mater misericordiae'. The fourth, 'Ave, regina coelorum', is represented only at second hand, by way of another antiphon with the same first line but continuing 'Mater regis angelorum', This had various uses, as a bidding prayer in connexion with the *Ave Maria*, as a grace after meat, and, most interestingly, in the services on the vigils of the five feasts of the Virgin in the University Church of St. Mary the Virgin at Oxford, attendance at which was compulsory for scholars living in the various halls.[1] The antiphon has six lines, and to arrive after the beginning of the fifth brought a fine of a farthing. A change of only half the lines of this composition produced the antiphon in honour of St. Edmund, 'Ave, rex gentis Anglorum', which is quoted in the burden of the only known carol to this saint (No. 63) and which was in frequent use at his monastery in Bury. No influence whatever on the carol-form results from these antiphons, which rhyme all six lines in -*um*.

A much closer relationship exists between the English carol and the non-ritual extra-liturgical *cantio* or *cantilena*, which is often identical in metrical form with the vernacular *carols*, *chansons à carole*, *Reigendlieder*, or *ballate*. It is significant that the same Latin word *cantilena* is applied in many documents to both 'dissolute worldly songs', including those actually sung in the dance, and the festive religious songs in Latin which show similar form, e.g. the decree of a council at Avignon in 1209: 'amatoria carmina, vel cantilenae'; a thirteenth-century Franciscan *exemplum* from Ireland: 'in suis tripudiis, in suis fatuis cantilenis'; the life of Thomas Becket translated by Laurence Wade, monk of Christ Church, Canterbury, who matches the phrase of the Latin heading, 'cantilenas dissolutas sive ad lascivia pertinentes', by the line 'Off al maner off karolles and songes dissolute'.[2] A fine example is the

---

[1] Frank Ll. Harrison, *Music in Medieval Britain* (London, 1958), p. 85.
[2] Quoted by L. Gougaud, op. cit., p. 12; A. G. Little, ed., *Liber Exemplorum ad Usum Praedicantium*, British Society of Franciscan Studies, i (Aberdeen, 1908), 111; Corpus Christi College, Cambridge, MS. 298, f. 20 v., text from manuscript.

'Ecce quod natura', technically a *virelai*, which is found with musical settings in three manuscripts.[1] In all three it appears in company with English carols, and it was known to James Ryman, who borrows its burden for two of his nativity carols and paraphrases the burden in the first stanza of each.[2] A few others are found in carol manuscripts, for example the first piece in Bodleian Library Eng. poet. e. 1. 'Angelum misit suum Deus omnipotens', which has a 'nowell' burden,[3] and a number in British Museum MS. Egerton 3307, e.g. 'Alleluia: Diva natalicia'. The largest collection of such pieces is in volumes xx and xxi of *Analecta Hymnica*, and even a quick survey of this anthology shows the reader that the favourite subjects for Latin stanzaic pieces with burdens were the Nativity and its following feasts and the praise of the Virgin, exactly as with the carols.

This close similarity between Latin *cantilena* and vernacular carol is not hard to explain, for they have common ancestors, the secular songs, often dance-songs, of the countries from which they come. Sometimes a mention of the dance is made in the Latin text, as in the last stanza of a Nativity *cantilena* which is one of a baker's dozen with burdens in a late thirteenth-century antiphoner from Bobbio:

> Ergo nostra concio,
> Psallat cum tripudio
> Nato Dei Filio.
> Per gratiam.[4]

The second line of the burden rhymes with the *cauda* of the stanzas as in innumerable dance-songs:

> Hodie fit regressus
> ad patriam.

Even without any explanation we should recognize the imitation

---

[1] Bodl. Ashmole 1393 and Arch. Selden B. 26, B.M. Egerton 3307. See Stevens, pp. 26, 32, 51; *E.B.M.* ii. 63, 154; Bukofzer, pp. 117, 152, 170. The words are also found with different music in *Piae Cantiones*, the famous book of *cantilenae* printed in Finland in 1582.

[2] No. 14; *E.E.C.*, No. 65.

[3] Wright, *P.S.* xxiii. 1–2; Stevens, pp. 56–57.

[4] *Anal. Hym.*, xx, No. 158, p. 124.

of vernacular dance-song in this Nativity piece from the 'Mosburg Gradual' of 1360:

> Verbum patris humanatur,
> O, O,
> Dum puella salutatur,
> O, O,
> Salutata fecundatur
> Viri nescia.[1]

The burden goes:

> Ey, Ey, Eya,
> Nova gaudia!

Explicit acknowledgement that some of his Latin *cantilenae* were written to the tunes and in the verse-form of secular and vernacular lyrics is made by the grammar-master of the school at Saint-Denis who produced for the use of his scholars the twenty-seven pieces in Bibliothèque Nationale MS. 15131 of the late thirteenth century. Three of the songs have prefixed lines in French which identify the worldly songs from which the tunes and forms are borrowed. In one case we have the entire burden of the French song on the favourite subject of the nightingale:

> Joi te rossignol
> Chantez de sus i rain,
> Viar dinet namie
> De sus laure florie.

After the rubric 'Contra in Latino: Sancti Nicolai etc.' comes the burden of the Latin carol:

> Sancti Nicolai
> vacemus titulis
> Cum summa laetitia
> Pangentes Alleluja.[2]

These instances from the Continent (and there are others) are, of course, parallel to the case of the Red Book of Ossory, now in the Bishop's Palace at Kilkenny, in which are written sixty Latin

---

[1] Ibid., No. 121, pp. 104–5.
[2] *Anal. Hym.*, xxi, No. 121, pp. 82–83.

lyrics, some, but not all, composed by the great fourteenth-century Franciscan Bishop of Ossory, Richard de Ledrede. The Latin memorandum at the foot of the first page of the songs must be cited once again here. In English translation it says:

> Be advised, reader, that the Bishop of Ossory has made these songs for the vicars of the cathedral church, for the priests and his clerks, to be sung on the important holidays and at celebrations, in order that their throats and mouths, consecrated to God, may not be polluted by songs which are lewd, secular, and associated with revelry, and since they are trained singers, let them provide themselves with suitable tunes according to what these pieces require.

Before some sixteen of the Latin *cantilenae*, which are in many different verse-forms including several variations of the carol, are written scraps of varying length of English and French songs, obviously secular. It is plain that these are the incipits of the songs of which the tunes and verse-forms are being followed by the bishop. One which is twice used in this way is an English song of the nightingale:

> 'Do, do' nyghtyngale
> synges wel mury,
> 'Shal Y nevre for thyn
> love lenger karie.'

The burden of the Latin piece goes:

> Regem adoremus
> Superne curie;
> Matri iubilemus
> Regine glorie.

Most telling of all is the case which went unnoticed until a few years ago, a Latin *cantilena* to the Virgin which is marked 'mayde yn the moore lay'.[1] The exquisite fourteenth-century lyric which begins with this line is miraculously one of the only set of English vernacular songs of that date to be preserved, in Bodleian Library MS. Rawlinson D. 913 on an isolated half-leaf probably

---

[1] Richard L. Greene, ' "The Maid of the Moor" in the *Red Book of Ossory*', *Speculum*, xxvii (1952), 504–6; see p. 504, n. 5, for earlier accounts of the Red Book's lyrics.

from the neighbourhood of Coggeshall, Essex. The English and Latin are alike in ryhme and verse-form, in this case a variation of the *rondel* which is found nowhere else in English and, as far as can be discovered, nowhere else in Latin. No clearer evidence of English secular song as the model followed by a writer of Latin *cantilenae* could be imagined. Richard 'of Leatherhead', like his clerkes, was wholly English and a product of the same Franciscan friary at Canterbury that James Ryman was to inhabit a century later.

There are interesting correspondences, too, between English carols and the kind of poetry called Goliardic, the student songs of love and spring and wine and satire of one's worldly superiors. These must go unexplored here, but it may be noted that the most famous of them all, 'Meum est propositum in taberna mori', is in British Museum MS. Sloane 2593, and another not much inferior, 'O potores exquisiti', one of the famous *Carmina Burana* from Benediktbeurn in Bavaria, is in Egerton 3307, congenial neighbours to English carols both devout and convivial. And about this sort of learned and jovial lyric, as about the religious *cantilena* 'it is important', in the words of F. J. E. Raby,

to remember one obvious thing. The peoples of Europe did not live without song, and for thousands of years they had had their songs of love and of death, their drinking-catches and their ballads. It is the continued flow of this stream of popular poetry, which has now perished as though it had not been, that must be taken into account in any attempt to obtain a reasonable view of the Latin lyric. The vernacular song was always there, whatever might happen to its learned counterpart.[1]

From the large number of sacred but extra-liturgical *cantilenae* there can be found only a half-dozen borrowings of exact phrasing in the English carols, and most of these are so trite and obvious that one cannot be sure of a single source. But the kinship is obvious to anyone with an ear and enough Latin to read aloud with. Both carol and *cantilena* owe their form to the immemorial structure of the unlettered people's dance-song: burden, stanza, burden, often linked by rhyme. From the solemn hymn of the Office written by Ambrose and his successors, sung antiphonally

[1] *A History of Secular Latin Poetry in the Middle Ages*, 2nd ed., (Oxford, 1957), ii. 326–7.

by opposed and facing choirs (which are quite different things from a soloist and a chorus) and naturally without a burden but with a last stanza sung by all as a doxology, both carol and *cantilena* show a fundamental difference which must have made them variations in the life of monk or vicar-choral or choir-boy as welcome as the Christmas or saint's-day feast itself.

Some recent attempts to derive the English carol from the specifically processional hymn of the medieval church and to regard the carols themselves (with a wholly artificial distinction between 'religious' and 'non-religious') as hymns performed in liturgical processions into and within the church need no long consideration.[1] The processional hymns for use in the services were very definitely prescribed and were invariably in Latin. Professor Frank Ll. Harrison delivers the verdict of musicology on this point very succinctly: 'The theory . . . that carols were sung in ritual processions is untenable, since the ordinals laid down the chants to be sung for processions throughout the year.'[2] There is no piece in the entire body of English carols which is marked with the rubric *ad processionem* or its equivalent and there is no indication in any known service-book that a carol in English is to be used as a processional hymn. The attempt by Dr. Miller to interpret the headings of British Musuem MS. Addit. 5665 (*In die nativitatis, De innocentibus, In die circumcisionis,* &c.) as implying processional use does not survive comparison with similar rubrics in Audelay's manuscript, Bodleian Library Douce 302.[3] She ignores the presence in the manuscript of pieces like *E.E.C.*, No. 6, with its invitation to the 'company' to drink well and make good cheer, the totally secular *E.E.C.*, No. 348, which praises the mean estate with no religious reference, and *E.E.C.*, No. 133, which is clearly meant to be sung, like the better-known Queen's College carol,

---

[1] For example, Margit Sahlin, op. cit., Catherine Keyes Miller, 'A Fifteenth Century Record of Choir Repertory' (Unpublished dissertation, Yale University, 1948; on B.M. MS. Addit. 5665) and 'The Early English Carol', *Renaissance News*, iii (1950), 61–64; R. H. Robbins, 'Middle English Carols as Processional Hymns', *Stud. Phil.* lvi (1959), 559–82. Bukofzer (pp. 149–150) is very cautious on the point, and recognizes the objections; Stevens (p. xiv) qualifies his statements carefully and has no evidence that can stand against Harrison's verdict.

[2] Op. cit., p. 417, n. 4. See also his important article on the carol in *The Listener*, 27 Dec. 1956, p. 1086.

[3] *Renaissance News*, iii. 63.

by those actually bearing a boar's head into a feast. None of these would by any stretch of assumption be suitable for use in a procession within or into a church service.

The characteristic processional hymn used in England is a Latin one built closely upon the pattern and in the classical quantitative metre of the one great prototype, the *Salve festa dies* attributed to Fortunatus, a cento made from a sixth-century poem on Easter. The unlikeness of its stately measures to the characteristic four-beat accentual line of the carol is apparent to anyone who hears it read or sung, and there is no preserved carol which imitates or even suggests its content.

In the processions of lay-folk, which were a feature of many festivals in medieval England and which, of course, were outside the liturgy, the texts which are referred to as being sung are always in Latin. Neither is there any reliable record of a modern custom of singing Christmas carols processionally in church which can be traced back to the Middle Ages. The artificial association of procession and carol found in recent 'carol services' appears to be entirely a matter of supposed revival influenced by nineteenth-century movements within the English Church.

That carolling and religious processions were recognized in Scotland in 1558 as quite different things is well shown by two neighbouring passages in Sir Richard Maitland's poem 'Of the Quenis Marynge with the Dolphin of France'.

> All burrowis townis euerilk man ȝow prayis
> To mak bainfyris fairseis and clerk playis
> And throw ȝour rewis carrellis danss and sing
>
> .   .   .   .
>
> Preistis and clerkis and men of religioun
> with devote mynd gang in processioun.[1]

It is puzzling that Robbins refers to a single clause of a letter written to the King by Archbishop Cranmer on 7 October 1544 which, if read throughout, shows plainly that English songs had *not* been used in processions before 1544. The 'songs' that Cranmer wants used in processions in English translations are the

---

[1] [Sir] W. A. Craigie, ed., *The Maitland Folio Manuscript*, i, S.T.S. New ser. No. 7, 1919, 28; ll. 19–21, 28–29.

Venite, the *Te Deum*, and so on. 'As concerning the *Salve festa dies*, the Latin note, as I think, is sober and distinct enough; wherefore I have travailed to make the verses in English, and have put the Latin note unto the same. Nevertheless they that be cunning in singing can make a much more solemn note thereto. *I made them only for a proof, to see how English would do in song* [italics mine].'[1] None of the sacred selections referred to is a carol or anything like one, and Cranmer obviously disapproves of such polyphonic music as the important carol manuscripts preserve. One could hardly ask stronger assurance, on higher authority, that the singing of English words in liturgical processions was unknown before this time. Processions in church or churchyard were entirely abolished in 1547.

Robbins does not recognize the one piece in the carol manuscript Eng. poet. e. 1 which is actually a processional hymn:

> Psallimus cantantes
> Domino nova cantica dantes.[2]

Unlike all but one of the carols in the manuscript, it has its music written with it. But this single processional hymn is, as we should expect, in Latin. The burden and first strophe are printed at the beginning of an English song (which Robbins mistakenly calls a carol) by Richard Kele about 1550.[3] The English piece is not a translation of the Latin, but it follows its verse-form and its transfer of the phrase 'Amice Christi Johannes' from its liturgical association with St. John the Baptist to St. John the Evangelist, as in the carols No. 21 (which immediately precedes the Latin hymn in the manuscript) and *E.E.C.*, No. 104 (from the same manuscript).

The one place in the ritual of the Church where it seems likely that carols in English may have been used is not in procession but at the conclusion of the Office during the Christmas season, where 'Benedicamus Domini—Deo gratias' is usually sung. Frank Ll. Harrison has pointed out that so-called 'Benedicamus-

---

[1] John Edmund Cox, ed., *Miscellaneous Writings and Letters of Thomas Cranmer*, The Parker Society (Cambridge, 1846), p. 412.
[2] *pr.* Wright, *P.S.* xxiii. 60–61; with music, *E.B.M.* ii. 182.
[3] Reed, *Christmas Carols Printed in the Sixteenth Century* (Cambridge, Massachusetts, 1932), pp. 28–32.

substitutes' were permitted at this one point and that certain carols, expecially those which contain these Latin phrases, e.g. No. 90, the 'Agincourt' carol, and No. 15, would be suitable for this purpose. But it must be admitted that the carol manuscripts themselves contain no rubric which positively indicates such use.[1]

Unlike the narrative ballads of England and Scotland, which are always anonymous, a considerable number of carols are attributed in the manuscripts to authors who are identified by name. The flexibility of the medieval conscience in matters of literary property makes caution advisable in dealing with these attributions, but a few of them there is no reason to doubt. In quantity of production no carol-writer is known to have excelled James Ryman, a Franciscan friar of the Canterbury house, whose 119 carols and forty-odd other poems are contained in one carefully written manuscript dated 1492, Cambridge University Library MS. Ee. 1. 12. Of Ryman as a person we know only his place and date, but his methods of composition are made plain by the manuscript. He had an interest in trying out different verseforms for the same material and in the reworking of one poem into another that marks him as having the instincts of the true literary craftsman. His lack of any great poetical inspiration has often been remarked, but some of his carols are better than modern commentators have been willing to recognize. It is best to take him in small doses. At any rate it cannot be said that none of his carols gained general circulation, for one piece (No. 18) turns up fifty years after the writing of his manuscript in one of the fragments of the carol-books printed and sold by Richard Kele in London.

The manuscript record of Ryman's 'workshop' methods is valuable evidence of the independence of the carol's characteristic structure from the pattern of the more formal hymn. Ryman translates almost literally some nine Latin hymns, keeping the line-and stanza-structure, and even some Latin lines, of the originals, e.g. 'Crist, that ayene hast made man free' from 'Christe, redemptor omnium' (Zupitza, p. 194). But when he sets about composing a series of twenty variations upon the *Te Deum* (*E.E.C.*, Nos. 285–304), he shows clearly that he is well aware of

---

[1] Op. cit., pp. 416–18; *The Listener*, 27 Dec. 1956, p. 1086.

the various stanzas with and without refrains and the various formulas for combining Latin and English lines which are current in the carols of his time. He is far from unintelligent in his various methods of fitting the content of the original, with which it would be sacrilege to tamper, to one after another of the carol-forms, remaining constant, however, in all but one case, to the couplet-burden which is most characteristic of carols. A study of these twenty pieces will not reveal a great poetical talent, but it will give an insight into the procedure which many another carol-writer must have followed in producing the distinctive blend of orthodoxy with simplicity and informality that is the central literary quality of the carol.

Another cleric who shows more proprietary concern for the carols of his own composition is John Audelay, a chaplain in the house of Augustinian canons at Haghmond, Shropshire. Alone among carol-writers Audelay works his name and some information about himself into the actual text of his pieces, which he must have dictated to a scribe because of his own blindness, deafness, and sickness. We do not know whether Audelay was a member of any regular order, but, as he gives us the only English carol addressed to St. Francis (No. 61), concluding with an exhortation that 'we' pray to Francis 'to save his breder and his covent', and the burden implores him to 'Save thy breder both nyght and day', it is at least possible that Audelay was a grey friar who had found asylum for his triple disability in an Augustinian abbey. More of Audelay's personality than of Ryman's shows through in the carols. It seems churlish to doubt the complete honesty of this benign invalid's claim to original authorship, but the doubt is unavoidable with at least three of the pieces in his manuscript: No. 2, which is also found in MS. Sloane 2593, No. 25, which appears in Trinity College, Cambridge, MS. O. 3. 58 and Arch. Selden B. 26, and *E.E.C.*, No. 122, which is in both the Sloane MS. and Richard Hill's Balliol College, Oxford, MS. 354.

Apart from Ryman and Audelay there are very few verse-writers whom we can name with any confidence as the authors of carols. The single piece by Lydgate (*E.E.C.*, No. 263) was obviously not written by him as a carol, for the burden appears only in the 'Fayrfax' MS. of the sixteenth century out of the fourteen in which the stanzas are found. It may well have been added by the composer of the music, Sheryngham. It is surprising that John Skelton appears to have left only one poem in the true carol-form (*E.E.C.*, No. 459), for there is much in the homely directness of the carol tradition that seems congenial to his spirit. But Sir Thomas Wiat, as if to fulfil his obligation to later text-book-writers by marking the transition from the old medieval to the new Renaissance poetic, wrote at least one carol (*E.E.C.*, No. 467), amorous and lacking in the concrete realism of the truly popular carols, but still less artificial and affected than the extreme aureate verse of about 1500. Another poem attributed to Wiat but certainly not his (*E.E.C.*, No. 468) is closely similar in style, but lacks a burden in one of its two manuscripts. Better than any of these as a lyric for singing is the sure-footed little carol (No. 93) assigned to King Henry VIII in the musical manuscript British Museum Addit. 31922, a gay piece which turns the holly and the ivy from Christmas decorations into symbols of evergreen love. There is no reason to doubt Henry's authorship of the words as well as of the music, in spite of the historical irony involved.

In all other cases where the name of a person is attached to the words of a carol it is not safe to assume that it belongs to the original author rather than to a recorder or transcriber. Examples are 'Wylyam northe of yorke' (*E.E.C.*, No. 36b), 'per me thomam henry persone' (*E.E.C.*, No. 425), and 'bryan hyf my name iet' (*E.E.C.*, No. 456). These and the few other instances of such colophons do little to impair the generalization, best illustrated by the remarkable anthology compiled by the London grocer Richard Hill, that carols circulated freely as common property in the late Middle Ages, just as did verses of all kinds on penny broadsides from the invention of printing to modern times.

The *carole* and its songs are by no means dead today. It has been danced by millions now alive when they were children and were cheerfully unaware that they were doing something older than even the Middle Ages. The student of children's songs and games in France will find the *carole* flourishing. But there is no need to leave England to find it, and people whose ancestors once left England have taken it with them. The game-song of 'Looby Loo' has been sung and danced by some who will read this book. It is still known across the ocean in the rocky hill-pastures of New England. Mrs. Flanders recorded it in 1930 as sung for her by Mrs. John Anderson, once of Windsor, Vermont, in a text learned from her mother. The song has not only the barest minimum of intellectual content and the repetitive formula which is found in the most primitive songs for the *carole*, but like the burden of the cursed carollers of the eleventh century it takes what little content it has from the accompanying physical action. The first stanza goes:

> I put my right foot in,
> I put my right foot out,
> I shake it a little, a little,
> And turn myself about.

All that we need to know of the other stanzas is that they successively substitute 'left foot, right hand, left hand, head, myself'. The burden is singable, if not profound:

> Oh! here we go looby low
> Here we go looby light
> Here we go looby low
> All on a Saturday night.

And here is the action which goes with the song: 'Join in circle and dance about during chorus, and then stop to put foot in and out of circle. Dance around again during chorus.'[1]

We are back to the bare essentials again. The *chanson à carole*, engaging the limbs as well as the voices of berry-brown Vermont farm children in the nineteenth century, is showing once again its powers of survival when it can stay free of fashion and over-education. Its various developments had their flowering and their withering: the direct religious parody; the use of the tunes and verse-forms for religious song not direct parody; the courtly love lyric like those sung and danced in the *Decameron* or those doggedly ground out by Charles d'Orleans in his light imprisonment; the political panegyric and the political satire; the moral or prudential discourse built around a proverb; even the carefully

---

[1] Helen Hartness Flanders and George Brown, *Vermont Folk-Songs and Ballads*, 2nd. ed. (Brattleboro, Vermont, 1932), pp. 192–3. For many texts and an account of this game-song in Britain see Alice Bertha [Lady] Gomme, *The Traditional Games of England, Scotland, and Ireland* (London, 1894–8), i, 352–61.

contrived nonsense song; the drinking song and the male animal's cry of defiance to woman's sovereignty that fades as he
staggers from ale-house to cottage door; most important and
significant and successful of all, the informal and social song of
Christmas and its accompanying emotions which was sometimes
used as the verbal framework of elaborate polyphonic music. But
underneath all of these has lived their ultimate source of alter-
nating rest and lively motion (the rest a physical necessity for the
motion) and of solo passages which differ and advance in alternation with chorus passages which recur unchanged and with
relentless regularity. The carol is social rather than communal:
its basic pattern calls for a leader who *begins* it as one who is
temporarily superior to the group because he or she knows an old
song well or has a new one to teach the circle but who becomes
less distinguishable from the group as the performance proceeds.
Unlike the offering of the professional artist it demands a partici-
pating audience. The *carole* is both an indoor and an outdoor
recreation in the Middle Ages, but its original site is out-of-doors
and socially unrestricted, a 'common', a market-place, or a field
by a sinister-sacred tree or perhaps one where the fairies have left
the lush green circle of their own *carole*, a *platea*, as the old documents call it. Unlike the medieval drama it did not move from
the church to the churchyard; in a few scattered instances it
reversed that process. Long after the 'Christmas carol' has been
separated from the dance and has lost its initial burden people still
feel it appropriate to sing it outdoors in peripatetic groups in spite
of December weather.

The ultimate origins of the carol long antedate the Christian
Church or the Greek round dances on threshing-floors or even
recorded history; the Church rather reluctantly adopted it and
then made good use of it; it has even regained the ground it once
lost in the Reformed Churches of England and Scotland. Unlike
liturgical texts which admit of no unsanctioned verbal change and
which can be immediately and permanently abolished by a learned
conclave at Rome or even by an amorous and autocratic king,
the Christmas songs, whether in the carol's form or another,
which have lived through generations in penny broadsides and
illiterate memories still assert their occasional independence of

orthodox theology and canonical history. The children's game-songs, in unbroken descent for centuries, preserve the secular carol's joy in combined song and exercise, as the Padstow carolling preserves the joy of greeting another spring. The traditional 'Christmas carol', even when it includes a reminder of that death which has been conquered, still keeps as central its insistence upon 'mirth', joy to the world—and in the world of hearth-fires and boar's-brawn with mustard—*because* the Lord is come.

A SELECTION OF CAROLS

I

Cambridge University Library. M S. Ee. 1. 12.   By James Ryman (?), *c.* 1492
f. 58 v.

Farewele, Advent; Cristemas is cum;
Farewele fro us both alle and sume.

With paciens thou hast us fedde
And made us go hungrie to bedde;
For lak of mete we were nyghe dedde;
    Farewele fro [us both alle and sume.]

While thou haste be within oure howse   5
We ete no puddynges ne no sowce,
But stynking fisshe not worthe a lowce;
    Farewele [fro us both alle and sume.]

There was no fresshe fisshe ferre ne nere;
Salt fisshe and samon was to dere,   10
And thus we have had hevy chere;
    Farewele [fro us both alle and sume.]

Thou hast us fedde with plaices thynne,
Nothing on them but bone and skynne;
Therfore oure love thou shalt not wynne;   15
    Farewele [fro us both alle and sume.]

With muskilles gaping afture the mone
Thou hast us fedde at nyght and none,
But ones a wyke, and that to sone;
    Farewele [fro us both alle and sume.]   20

l. 4. MS. fare wele fro &c.   ll. 8, 12, 16, 20, 36, 40. MS. fare wele &c.

Oure brede was browne, oure ale was thynne,
Oure brede was musty in the bynne,
Oure ale soure or we did begynne;
    Fare[wele fro us both alle and sume.]

Thou art of grete ingratitude   25
Good mete fro us for to exclude;   f. 59 r.
Thou art not kyende but verey reude;
    Farewele [fro us both alle and sume.]

Thou dwellest with us ayenst oure wille,
And yet thou gevest us not oure fille;   30
For lak of mete thou woldest us spille;
    Farewele [fro us both alle and sume.]

Above alle thinge thou art a meane
To make oure chekes bothe bare and leane.
I wolde thou were at Boughton Bleane!   35
    Farewele [fro us both alle and sume.]

Come thou no more here nor in Kent,
For, yf thou doo, thou shallt be shent;
It is ynough to faste in Lent;
    Farewele [fro us both alle and sume.]   40

Thou maist not dwelle with none eastate;
Therfore with us thou playest chekmate.
Go hens, or we will breke thy pate!
    Farewele [fro us both alle and sume.]

Thou maist not dwell with knyght nor squier;   45
For them thou maiste lye in the myre;
They love not the nor Lent, thy sire;
    Farewele [fro us both alle and sume.]

l. 24. MS. fare &c.   ll. 28, 32, 60. MS. fare wele &c.   ll. 48, 52 MS.
fare &c

Thou maist not dwell with labouring man,
For on thy fare no skille he can,   50
For he must ete bothe now and than;
    Fare[wele fro us both alle and sume.]

Though thou shalt dwell with monke and frere,
Chanon and nonne ones every yere,
Yet thou shuldest make us better chere;   55
    Fare[wele fro us both alle and sume.]

This tyme of Cristes feest natall
We will be mery, grete and small,
And thou shalt goo oute of this halle;
    Farewele [fro us both alle and sume.]   60

Advent is gone; Cristemas is cume;
Be we mery now, alle and sume;
He is not wise that wille be dume
    In ortu Regis omnium.

2

Bodleian Library. MS. Douce 302.   By John Audelay(?), XV *cent.*
f. 28 r.

      Welcum, Yole, in glod aray,
      In worchip of the holeday.

    Welcum be thou, Heven Kyng,   f. 28 v.
    Welcum, ibore in hon mornyng,
    Welcum to the now wil we syng;
      Welcum, Yole, for ever and ay.

    Welcum be thou, Mare myld,   5
    Welcum be thou and thi child,
    Welcum, fro the fynd thou us schilde;
      Welcum, Yole, for ever and ay.

      MS. heading: In die natalis domini.

Welcum be ye, Steven and Jone,
Welcum, childern everechone,   10
Wellcum, Thomas, marter allon;
  Welcum, Yole, for ever and ay.

Welcum be thou, good New Yere,
Welcum, the xii days efere,
Welcum be ye all that bene here;   15
  Welcum, Yole, for ever and ay.

Welcum be ye, lord and lady,
Welcum be ye, al this cumpane;
Fore Yolis love now makis mere!
  Welcum, Yole, fore ever and ay.   20

3

Bodleian Library. MS. Eng. poet. e. 1.   XV *cent.*
f. 22 r.

Make we myrth
For Crystes byrth,
  And syng we Yole tyl Candelmes.

The fyrst day of Yole have we in mynd
How God was man born of owr kynd
For he the bondes wold onbynd
  Of all owr synnes and wykednes.

The secund day we syng of St[e]vene,   f. 22 v.
That stoned [was] and steyyd up even   6
To God, that he saw stond in hevyn,
  And crounned was for hys prouesse.

The iii day longeth to Sent Johan,
That was Cristys darlyng, derer non,   10
Whom he betok, whan he shuld gon,
  Hys moder der for hyr clennesse.

The iiii day of the chyldren yong
That Herowd to deth had do with wrong,
And Crist thei coud non tell with tong   15
   But with ther blod bar hym wytnesse.

The v day longeth to Sent Thomas,
That as a strong pyller of bras
Held up the Chyrch, and sclayn he was,
   For he stod with ryghtwessnesse.   20

The viii day tok Jhesu hys name,
That saved mankynd fro syn and shame,
And circumsysed was for no blame
   But for ensample of meknesse.

The xii day offerd to hym kynges iii   25
Gold, myr, and cence, thes gyftes free,
For God, and man, and kyng was he:
   Thus worschyppyd thei hys worthynes.

On the xl day cam Mary myld
Unto the temple with hyr chyld   30
To shew hyr clen that never was fylyd,
   And therwith endyth Crystmes.

4

British Museum. MS. Addit. 14997.   4 October 1500
f. 44 v.

    Hay, ay, hay, ay,
    Make we mere as we may.

    Now ys Yole comyn with gentyll chere;
    Of merthe and gomyn he has no pere;
    In every londe where he comys nere
       Is merthe and gomyn, I dar wele say.

    ll. 17–20. *The entire stanza is struck through in MS.*

Now ys comyn a messyngere   5
Of yore lorde, Ser Nu Yere,
Byddes us all be mere here
   And make as mere as we may.

Therefore every mon that ys here   f. 45 r.
Synge a caroll on hys manere;   10
Yf he con non we schall hym lere,
   So that we be mere allway.

Whosoever makes heve chere,
Were he never to me dere;
In a dyche I wolde he were,   15
   To dry hys clothys tyll hyt were day.

Mende the fyre, and make gud chere!
Fyll the cuppe, Ser Botelere!
Let every mon drynke to hys fere!
   Thys endes my caroll with care away.   20

5

Balliol College, Oxford. MS. 354.   XVI *cent.*
f. 223 v.

   Make we mery, bothe more and lasse,
   For now ys the tyme of Crystymas.

Lett no man cum into this hall,
Grome, page, nor yet marshall,
But that sum sport he bryng withall,
   For now ys the tyme of Crystmas.

Yff that he say he can not syng.   5
Sum oder sport then lett hym bryng,
That yt may please at thys festyng,
   For now ys the tyme of Crystmas.

At end: In die dominica prima post festum sancti Michaelis archangeli anno regis
henrici septimi post conquestum anglie sextodecimo illa res erat scripta primo.

Yff he say he can nowght do,
Then for my love aske hym no mo,   10
But to the stokkes then lett hym go,
   For now ys the tyme of Crystmas.

6

Bodleian Library. MS. Bodley 26.   *c.* 1350
f. 202 v.

   Honnd by honnd we schulle ous take,
   And joye and blisse schulle we make,
   For the devel of ele man haght forsake,
   And Godes Sone ys maked oure make.

A child is boren amo[n]ges man,
And in that child was no wam;
That child ys God, that child is man,
And in that child oure lif bygan.

Senful man, be blithe and glad: 5
For your mariage thy peys ys grad
   Wan Crist was boren;
Com to Crist; thy peis ys grad;
For the was hys blod ysched,
   That were forloren.   10

Senful man, be blithe and bold,
For evene ys bothe boght and sold,
   Evereche fote;
Com to Crist; thy peys ys told,
For the he yahf a hondrefo[l]d   15
   Hys lif to bote.

The repetition of the burden is indicated as follows: stza. 1: honnd by honnd
thannes chulle ous take *et ceterum* quod superius dictum est.   stza. 2: honnd by
honnd thanne schulle ous take *and* joy and blisse schu[lle] we make &c.   stza. 3:
honnd by honnd *et ceterum* quod prius.
   l. 6. your] MS. thour.   l. 15. he] MS. ye.

7

Bridgwater Corporation. Muniments, 123.   XV *cent.*
dorse

Letabundus exultet fidelys chorus,
    Alleluia.

Now well may we myrthys make,
For Jhesu mankynd hath take
Of a mayden withoutyne make;
    Gaudeamus.

A kyng of kynges now forth ys browghth   5
Off a maydyne that synnyd nowghte,
Nether in ded nether in thowghhte,
    Res miranda.

An angell of counsell now ys bore
Off a mayde, as Y sayd before,   10
To saw all that was forlore,
    Sol de stella.

That sonne hath never downe-goyng,
And thys lyght no tyme lesyng;
Thys stere ys evermore scheinyng,   15
    Semper clara.

Ryghht as the stere browghht forght a beme,
Oute of the wych commyghth a marvelose streme,
So dud that mayde withowtyn weme,
    Pari forma.   20

At head: MS. Holy holy holy holy holy *and* yffy yffy.
At end: MS. Holy holy *and* yfy yffy holy yffy Holi.   l. 20. Pari] MS. para.

8

Balliol College, Oxford. MS. 354.
f. 222 v.

XVI *cent.*

> To blis God bryng us all and sum,
> Christe redemptor omnium.

In Bedlem, in that fayer cyte,
A chyld was born of Owr Lady,
Lord and Prynce that he shuld be,
A solis ortus cardine.

Chyldren were slayn grett plente,   5
Jhesu, for the love of the;
Lett us never dampned be.
Hostes Herodes ympie.

He was born of Owr Lady
Withowt wemmb of her body,   10
Godes Son that syttyth on hye,
Jhesu salvator seculi.

As the son shynyth thorow the glas,
So Jhesu in her body was;
To serve hym he geve us grace,   15
O lux beata Trinitas.

Now ys born owr Lord Jhesus,
That mad mery all us;
Be all mery in thys howse;
Exultet celum laudibus.   20

l. 4. solis] MS. solus.   At end: Explicit.

9

British Museum. MS. Egerton 3307.   XV *cent.*
ff. 65 v., 66 r.

Almyghty Jhesu, Kyng of Blysse,
Assumpsit carnem virginis;
He was ever and ever ys
Consors paterni luminis.

Holy Chyrch of hym makyth mynd:
Intravit ventris thalamum;
Fro heven to erth to save mankynd
Pater mandavit Filium.

To Mari com a messenjer   5
Ferens salutem hominum,
And sche answerd with myld steven,
'Ecce ancilla Domini.'

'Thorow the myght of the Holy Gost,
Palacium intrans uteri,   10
Aboun al thing meykness is best
In conspectu Altissimi.'

Thre kynges apon the [twelfth] day,
Stella micante previa,
To seyk Our Lord thai toke the way,   15
Baiulantes munera.

A ster beforn the kinges ay:
Primus rex aurum optulit;
He ys God and Lord verray:
Secundus rex thus protulit.   20

ll. 1, 2 of the burden and l. 2 of each stanza are to be repeated as a chorus. The
second lines of stzas. 1–3 are written again on f. 66 r.

He was namyd the thyrd kyng
  Incensum pulcrum qui tradidit;
He us al to blysse bryng
  Qui cruce mori voluit.

IO

British Museum. MS. Sloane 2593.   XV *cent.*
f. 28 r.

Man, be merie as bryd on berie,
And al thi care let away.

This tyme is born a chyld ful good,
He that us bowt upon the rod;
He bond the devyl, that is so wod,
  Til the drydful domysday.

Quan the chyld of meche myght   5
Wold be born of Mary bryght,
A tokene he sente to kyng and knyght,
  A sterre that schon bothe nyght and day.

The sterre scon as bryght as fer
Ouer al the world bothe fer and ner,   10
In tokene he was withoutyn per,
  And pereles he xal lastyn ay.

The [eighth] day he was circumsise
For to fulfylle the profecye[s];
The profetes with wordes wyse   15
  Hym present with ryche aray.

The [twelfth] day come kynges thre
Out of the est with herte fre;
To worchepyn hym thei knelyd on kne
  With gold and myr and francincens.   20

11

Bodleian Library. MS. Arch. Selden B. 26.   XV *cent.*
f. 14 v.

> Nowel, nowel, nowel,
> Nowel, nowel, nowel!

Owt of your slepe aryse and wake,
For God mankynd nowe hath ytake
Al of a maide without eny make;
    Of al women she bereth the belle.
        Nowel!   5

And thorwe a maide faire and wys
Now man is made of ful grete pris;
Now angelys knelen to mannys servys,
    And at this tyme al this byfel.
        [Nowel!]   10

Now man is brighter than the sonne;
Now man in heven an hye shal wone;
Blessyd be God this game is begonne,
    And his moder emperesse of helle.
        [Nowel!]   15

That ever was thralle, now ys he fre;
That ever was smalle, now grete is she;
Now shal God deme bothe the and me
    Unto his blysse yf we do wel.
        Nowel!   20

Now man may to heven wende;
Now heven and erthe to hym they bende;
He that was foo now is oure frende;
    This is no nay that Y yowe telle.
        Nowel!   25

Now, blessyd brother, graunte us grace
A domesday to se thy face
And in thy courte to have a place,
   That we mow there synge nowel.
    Nowel! 30

I2

Bodleian Library. MS. Arch. Selden B. 26.
f. 15 r.   XV *cent.*

    Make we joye nowe in this fest,
    In quo Christus natus est.
      Eya!

A Patre unigenitus
Thorw a maiden is com to us.
Synge we to here and sey, 'Welcome!
Veni redemptor gencium.'

Agnoscat omne seculum: 5
A bryght sterre thre kynges [made] come
For to seke with here presens
Verbum supernum prodiens.

A solis ortus cardine,
So myghty a lord was none as he, 10
For to oure kynde he hath yeve gryth,
Adam parens quod polluit.

Maria ventre concepit;
The Holy Gost was ay here with.
In Bedleem yborne he ys, 15
Consors paterni luminis.

O lux beata Trinitas!
He lay bytwene an oxe and asse.
Thou moder and maiden fre,
Gloria tibi, Domine. 20

13

Balliol College, Oxford. MS. 354.   XVI *cent.*
f. 230 v.

Wassaill, wassayll, wassaill, syng we
In worshipe of Cristes nativite.

Now joy be to the Trynyte,
    Fader, Son, and Holy Gost,
That on God is in Trynite,
    Fader of Hevyn, of myghtes most.

And joy to the virgyn pure   5
    That ever kepte her undefiled,
Grundid in grace, in hart full sure.
    And bare a child as maydyn myld.

Bethelem and the sterre so shen,
    That shon iii kynges for to gide,   10
Bere witnesse of this maydyn clene;
    The kynges iii offred that tide,

And sheperdis hard, a[s] wretyn is,
    The joyffull songe that ther was songe:
'Glorya in excelsis!'   15
    With angelles voys it was owt ronge.

Now joy be to the blessidfull child,
    And joy be to his moder dere;
Joy we all of that maydyn myld,
    And joy have they that mak good chere.   20

The repetition of the burden is indicated as follows: stza. 1: wassaill &c.
stza. 2: wassayll.   stzas. 3–5: wassaill.

14

Cambridge University Library. MS. Ee. 1. 12.   By James Ryman, *c.* 1492.
f. 23 r.

Ecce quod natura
Mutat sua iura:
Virgo parit pura
    Dei Filium.

Beholde and see how that nature
Chaungith here lawe: a mayden pure
Shalle bere a chielde, (thus seith Scripture)   f. 23 v.
    Jhesus, oure Savyour.

Beholde, the flease of Gedeon   5
Wexed wete, that no dewe fel on;
Beholde, the yerde of Aaron
    Unmoysted bare a floure.

The prophete Isay seith thus:
'A mayde shall bere a childe to us   10
Whose name shall be called Jhesus,
    Oure helpe and our socour.

'A yerde shall goo oute of Jesse rote
Wherof a floure shall ascende full soote.'
This floure is Crist, oure helth and boote,   15
    This yerde, Mary, his boure.

Seynt Mathew seith in the gospell,
'A mayde shall bere Emanuell,
That is to sey, God with us to dwell,
    That lovely paramour.'   20

Forsoth, to us is borne a chielde;
A sonne is yeven to us full myelde
Of virgyne Marie undefielde
    To cease oure grete langoure.

This is the stone cutte of the hille,   f. 24 r.
Criste borne of Marie us vntille   26
Without synne in thought, dede, and wille
    To save us fro dolour.

This chielde shall be the Prince of Peas,
Whose kingdome shall evir encrease,   30
Wherof the peas shall nevir ceas
    But encreace day and houre.

Seint Anselme seith, 'So Criste did pas
Thurgh Marie myelde, as his wille was,
As the sonne beame goth thurgh the glas,   35
    That mayde full of honoure.'

15

British Museum. MS. Egerton 3307.   XV *cent.*
f. 51 v.

    Novo profusi gaudio
    Benedicamus Domino.

Omnes gentes plaudite,
Car nostre Saveyour est ne;
Over all blyssyd he be,
    Rex alpha et O.

A solis ortus cardine,   5
Com le mound est long et le,
Al mankynd makith gle:
    Angeli canunt Deo.

Enixa est puerpera
Que Seynt Espryt en engrossa;   10
Blyssyd be tyme that sche sayd, 'Ya'
    Gabriele nuncio.

        l. 4. O] MS. oo.

Ex illabata virgine
Est nascu le Roy de mageste;
The hyrdes hym se in low degre,   15
    Iacentem in presepio.

Gloria tibi, Domine,
Fortime de grace et de pyte;
Of all thi goodness we thank the:
    Benedicamus Domino.   20

16

Balliol College, Oxford. MS. 354.   XVI *cent.*
f. 224 r.

Can I not syng but hoy,
Whan the joly sheperd made so mych joy.

The sheperd upon a hill he satt;
He had on hym his tabard and his hat,
Hys tarbox, hys pype, and hys flagat;
Hys name was called Joly, Joly Wat,
    For he was a gud herdes boy.   5
        Vith hoy!
    For in hys pype he made so mych joy.

The sheperd upon a hill was layd;
Hys doge to hys gyrdyll was tayd;
He had not slept but a lytill broyd   10
But 'Gloria in excelcis' was to hym sayd.
        Vith hoy!
    For in his pipe he mad so myche joy.

l. 15. degre] MS. do gre.
16. The repetition of the burden is indicated as follows: stza. 1: can I not sing
but hay &c.   stza. 2: can I not syng.   stzas. 3, 6–8: can I not sing but hoy &c.
stza. 4: can I not syng &c.   stza. 5: can I not sing &.   stza. 9: can I not sing.
Stzas. 6 and 7 are transposed in MS., the correction being indicated by the prefixed letters
a *and* b.

The sheperd on a hill he stode;
Rownd abowt hym his shepe they yode;   15
He put hys hond under hys hode;
He saw a star as rede as blod.
  Vith hoy!
 For in his pipe he mad so myche joy.

'Now farwell Mall, and also Will;   20
For my love go ye all styll
Unto I cum agayn you till,
And evermore, Will, ryng well thy bell.'
  Vith hoy!
 For in his pipe he mad so mych joy.   25

'Now must I go ther Cryst was borne;
Farewell, I cum agayn tomorn;
Dog, kepe well my shep fro the corn,
And warn well, warroke, when I blow my horn.'
  Vith hoy!   30
For in hys pype he made so mych joy.

The sheperd sayd anon ryght,
'I will go se yon farly syght,
Wheras the angell syngith on hight,
And the star that shynyth so bryght.'   35
  Vith hoy!
 For in [his] pipe he made so mych joy.

Whan Wat to Bedlem cum was,
He swet; he had gon faster than a pace.
He fownd Jhesu in a sympyll place   40
Betwen an ox and an asse.
  Vith hoy!
 For in his pipe he mad so mych joy.

'Jhesu, I offer to the here my pype,
My skyrte, my tarbox, and my scrype;   45
Home to my fellowes now will I skype,
And also loke unto my shepe.'
  Vith hoy!
 For in his pipe he mad so myche joy.

'Now, farewell, myne own herdesman Wat.'   f. 224 v.
'Ye, for God, lady, even so I hat.   51
Lull well Jhesu in thy lape,
And farewell, Joseph, wyth thy rownd cape.'
  Vith hoy!
 For in hys pipe he mad so myche joy.   55

'Now may I well both hope and syng,
For I have bene a Crystes beryng.
Home to my felowes now wyll I flyng.
Cryst of hevyn to his blis us bryng!'
  Vith hoy!   60
 For in his pipe he mad so myche joy.

17

Bodleian Library. MS. Eng. poet. e. 1.   XV *cent.*
f. 60 r.

  Tyrle, tyrlo,
  So merylye the shepperdes began to blowe.

Abowt the fyld thei pyped full right,
Even abowt the middes off the nyght;
Adown frome heven thei saw cum a lyght.
  Tyrle, tirlo.

Off angels ther came a company   5
With mery songes and melody;
The shepperdes anonne gane them aspy.
  Tyrle, tyrlo.

   l. 45. MS. My scrype my tarbox *and* my skyrte.

'Gloria in excelsis,' the angels song,
And said who peace was present among   10
To every man that to the faith wold long.
   Tyrle, tyrlo.

The shepperdes hyed them to Bethleme
To se that blyssid sons beme,
And ther they found that glorious streme.   15
   Tyrle, tyrlo.

Now preye we to that mek chyld,
And to his mothere that is so myld,
The wich was never defylyd,
   Tyrle, tyrlo,   20

That we may cum unto his blysse
Where joy shall never mysse;
Than may we syng in paradice,
   'Tyrle, tirlo.'

I pray yow all that be here   25
Fore to syng and mak good chere
In the worschip off God thys yere.
   Tyrle, tirlo.

18

Cambridge University Library. MS. Ee. 1. 12.   By James Ryman, *c*. 1492.
f. 38 v.

Be we mery now in this fest,
In quo Salvator natus est.

Now in Betheleme, that holy place,
To bringe man oute of woofull case,
Of virgyn Marie full of grace
   Salvator mundi natus est.

To the sheperdes keping theire folde 5
On Cristemas nyght an aungell tolde
That in Bethelem with bestes bolde
  Salvator [mundi natus est.]

They were compassed all aboute with light,
And they dredde of that hevenly sight. 10
'Drede not,' he seyde, that aungell bright,
  'Salvator [mundi natus est.]

'Beholde, to you grete joye I bringe:
This daye of Mary, that good thinge,
In the citie of David, that king, 15
  Salvator [mundi natus est.]

'And this infant there fynde ye shalle f. 39 r.
In pore clothing in an oxe stalle.'
The aungelles tho lawded God alle;
  Salvator [mundi natus est.] 20

'Glorie to God,' the aungelles songe,
'And peas in erthe good men amonge;
To save mankyende, that had done wronge,
  Salvator [mundi natus est.']

They toke theire way with good entent, 25
And to Bethelem right sone they went,
To see and know what that worde ment:
  'Salvator [mundi natus est.']

They founde Joseph and Mary myelde,
Wyfe, moder, and mayde undefielde, 30
And in a stalle they founde that childe.
  Salvator [mundi natus est.]

Now seke we alle with hert and myende
This yonge infant tille we hym fyende
That of a mayde to save mankyende 35
  De virgine nunc natus est.

    ll. 8, 12, 16, 20, 24, 28, 32. MS. Saluator &c.

19

Bodleian Library. MS. Eng. poet. e. 1.
f. 45 v.

XV *cent.*

Hey now, now, now!

Swet Jhesus
Is cum to us,
   This good tym of Crystmas;
Wherfor with prays
Syng we always,   5
   'Welcum, owr Messyas.'

The God Almyght
And Kyng of Lyght,
   Whose powr is over all,
Gyve us of grace   10
For to purchas
   Hys realme celestyall.

Whe[r] hys aungels
And archangels
   Do syng incessantly,   15
Hys princypates
And potestates
   Maketh gret armony.

The cherubyns   f. 46 r.
And seraphyns   20
   With ther tunykes mery,
The trones al,
Most musycall,
   Syng the hevenly Kery.

The vertues clere   25
Ther tunes bere,

MS. heading: A song in the tune of / and I were a mayd &c.
The burden is first written after stza. 1. The repetition is indicated after each
following stanza save the last by: hey &c.

Ther quere for to repayre,
Whose song to hold
Was manyfold
  Of domynacyons fayer.   30

With on acord
Serve we that Lord
  With laudes and orayson,
The wych hayth sent
By good assent   35
  To us hys onely Sone.

Borne ful porly,
Redy to dey
  For to redeme us all,
In the Jury   40
Of mayd Mary
  In a poore oxes stall.

He taught the sawes
Of Crysten lawes
  To hys apostels twelve;   45
In flome Jordan
Of good Saynt Johan
  He was crystned hymselve.

Hymselfe ded preche   f. 46 v.
And the folke tech   50
  The commaundmentes tene;
He went barfote,
That swete herte rote,
  Example to al mene.

The lame and blynd,   55
Men owt of mynd,
  And the demonyacle,
The deef and dombe,
Men layd in tombe
  Wher hol by hys myracle.   60

The Jewes truly
Had grete envy
 To se hys myght expresse;
Thei ded conspyre
By grete desyre   65
 To deth hym for to dresse.

But by hys myght
Thei had no syght
 To know hys corpolence
Tyll unwysse bold   70
Judas hym sold
 For thyrty golden pence.

Than thei hym tost,
And at a post
 Thei bownd hym lyk a thefe;   75
Thei ded hym bete
With scorges grete
 To put hym to reprefe.

Nakyd and bare
Hys flesch thei tare,   80
 And with a crowne of thorne
Thei ded hym crowne
(The blod rane downe)
 And gave hym a rede in scorne.

With mokkes and mowes,   f. 47 r.
Buffetes and blowes,   86
 And other cursed thewes,
Thei gan to cry
Dyspytously,
 'Al hayle the Kyng of Jewes!'   90

With dredfull othes,
The wych hym lothes,

Thei cryd, 'Crucifige!'
To Calvary
  Thei gane hym hy;   95
    The crosse hymself bar he.

They hym naylyd
And yl flaylyd,
    Alas, that innocent!
Lunges, blynd knyght,   100
With al hys myght
    With a spere hys hart rent.

Watur and blod
Fro hys hart yode,
    And yet that blyssyd Sone   105
Prayd for thosse
That ware hys fose
    To get for them perdone.

Lo, what kyndnesse
In owr dystresse   110
    That Lord ded schow us than,
The deth to tak
Al for owr sake
    And bryng us fro Sathan.

Owr Savyour,   f. 47 v.
Our Creatur   116
    On the crosse deyed ther;
Of newe tourment
We do hym rent
    Whan we hys membres swer.   120

Then let us pray
Both nyght and day
    To hym per omnia
That we may cum
To hys kyn[g]dome   125
    In finis secula.

20

British Museum. MS. Egerton 3307.   XV *cent.*
f. 54 v.

> The holy marter Steven we pray
> To be our socour both nyght and day.

I schal yow tell this ilk nyght
Of Seynt Steven, Godes knyght:
He told the Jewis that it was ryght
  That Crist was born of a may.

Than sayd the Jewis with grett scorn   5
That God Son myght not be born;
Steven than sayd, 'Ye be forlorn,
  And all that leven in that lay.'

Now ys sprong the wel of lyff
Of Mary, moder, madyn, and wyff;   10
Therfor the Jewis fel in stryff,
  Dysputyng with Steven aganys hys fay.

The cursyd Jewys at the last,
Stonys to Steven thei gan cast;
Thei betyn hym and band hym fast   15
  And made hys body in fowle aray.

Into the feld thei led hym tho,
And than hym folowyd many a fo;
Thei greivyd on hym and dyd hym wo;
  Hem thoght thei had a nowbyll play.   20

The Jewys that wer bothe styff and strong,
Thei stonyd hym and dyd [hym] wrong—
Gret stonys abowte hym sprong—
  And sayd, 'Wee thi meyd schall pay.'

The burden is written again at the end: The holy martyr steuen we pray. To be
our socour bothe nyght and day.

21

Bodleian Library. MS. Eng. poet. e. 1. XV *cent.*
f. 40 r.

Pray for us, thou prynce of pes,
Amici Christi Johannes.

To the now, Crystys der derlyng,
That was a mayd bothe old and yyng,
Myn hert is sett for to syng:
Amici Christi Johannes.

For he was so clene a maye, 5
On Crystys brest aslepe he laye;
The privyteys of he[v]yn ther he saye;
Amici Christi Johannes.

Quhen Cryst beforne Pilate was broute,
Hys clene mayd forsoke hym nowte; 10
To deye with hym was all hys thowte;
Amici Christi Johannes.

Crystys moder was hym betake,
Won mayd to be anodyrs make,
To help that we be nott forsake: 15
Amici Christi Johannes.

22

Bodleian Library. MS. Douce 302. By John Audelay, XV *cent.*
f. 28 v.

With al the rever[en]s that we may
Worchip we Childermas Day.

Crist crid in cradil, 'Moder, ba ba!'
The childer of I[s]ral cridyn, 'Wa wa!'
Fore here merth hit was aga
When Erod fersly cowth hem fray.

MS. heading: In die *sanctorum* Innocencium.

Al knave childer with ii yere   5
Of age in Bedlem fere or nere,
Thai chedyn here blod with swerd and spere;
    Alas, ther was a rewful aray!

An hunderd and fourte thousand ther were;
Crist ham cristynd al in fere   10
In eor blod, and were martere,
    Al clene vergyns, hit is no nay:

The crisum childer to Crist con cry:
'We beth slayne fore gret envy;
Lord, venge our blod fore thi mercy,   15
    And take our soulis to the, we pray.'

An hevenle voys answerd ayayn,
'Abyds a wyle, and sofer your payn;
Hent the nowmbir be eslayn
    Of your breder, as I you say.   20

'Fore ye han sofird marterdom   f. 29 r.
For Cristis sake, al and sum,
He wil youe crowne in his kyngdam,
    And folou the Lomb in joy for ay.'

23

British Museum. MS. Egerton 3307   XV *cent.*
ff. 62 v., 63 r.

Seynt Thomas honour w[e],
Thorgh whos blod Holy Chyrch ys made fre.

Al Holy Chyrch was bot a thrall
Thorgh kyng and temperal lordys all,
To he was slane in Cristys hall
    And set all thing in unite:
    Hys deth hath such auctorite.   5

The burden and ll. 1 and 4 of each stanza are to be repeated as a chorus.

The kyng exilyd hym owt of land
And toke hys good in hys hond,
Forbedyng both fre and bond
   That no prayer for hym schuld be,
   So fers he schewyd hys crewelte.   10

Al ben exilyd that to hym lang,
Wemen, chyldryn, old men among,
Yong babys that wepyd insted of song,
   Seynt Thomas said, 'Welcom ye be;
   Ilk lond is now your awen contre.'   15

Sex yer he had povert and wo;
The sevent yer hom he schuld go;
Sum hopyd of pes, sum dyd not so,
   Bot he was welcom to hys se,
   Derly desyryd of ilk degre.   20

The kyng bot lytyl whyl hym sparyd:
Knyghtes in chyrch hys crown of paryd;
Thus the corner-ston was swaryd
   Betwen clergy and temperalte,
   To knytt pes and unite.   25

The corn overcast, the chaff lyght law:
The kyng in hys ost ys overthraw:
The tyler on ground hys brayn hath saw,
   As Crist seyd hym at Pountane,
   'My chyrch with thi blod halowyd schal be.'   30

On Tewsday born, accusyd also,
On Tewsday exilid hys frendes fro,
Comfort of Crist to dreyd no wo,
   Clepyd hom, translate was he—
   Thus seven Tewsdays worschypyd the see.   35

24

British Museum. MS. Sloane 2593.   XV *cent.*
f. 23 v.

A, a, a, a,
Nu[n]c gaudet ecclesia.

Lestenytgh, lordynges, bothe grete and smale:
I xal you telyn a wonder tale,
How Holy Cherche was brow[t] in bale
    Cum magna iniuria.

The greteste clerk of al this lond,   5
Of Cauntyrbery, ye understond,
Slawyn he was [with] wykkyd hond,
    Demonis potencia.

Knytes kemyn fro Hendry Kyng,
Wykkyd men, withoute lesyng;   10
Ther they dedyn a wonder thing,
    Ferventes insania.

They sowtyn hym al abowtyn,
Withine the paleys and withoutyn;
Of Jhesu Cryst hadde they non dowte   15
    In sua malicia.

They openyd here mowthis wonder wyde;
To Thomeys they spokyn mekyl pryde:
'Here, tretour, thou xalt abyde,
    Ferens mortis tedia.'   20

Thomas answerid with mylde chere,
'If ye wil me slon in this manere,   f. 24 r.
Let hem pasyn, alle tho arn here,
    Sine contumilia.'

Beforn his aunter he knelyd adoun;   25
Ther they gunne to paryn his crown;
He sterdyn the braynys up and doun,
    Optans celi gaudia.

The turmentowres abowtyn sterte;
With dedly wondys thei gunne him hurte;   30
Thomas deyid in Moder Cherche,
    Pergens ad celestia.

Moder, clerk, wedue, and wyf,
Worchepe ye Thomeys in al your lyf;
For lii poyntes he les his lyf,   35
    Contra regis consilia.

25

Bodleian Library. MS. Douce 302.   By John Audelay (?), XV *cent.*
f. 29 r.

    What tythyngis bryngst us, messangere,
    Of Cristis borth this New Eris Day?

A babe is borne of hye natewre,
    A Prynce of Pese that ever schal be;
Off heven and erthe he hath the cewre;
    Hys lordchip is eternete.
        Seche wonder tythyngis ye may here: 5
        That God and mon is hon in fere,
            Hour syn had mad bot fyndis pray.

A semle selcouth hit is to se:
    The burd that had this barne iborne
This child conseyvyd in he degre   10
    And maydyn is as was beforne.

MS. heading: In die circu[m]cicionis dom*i*ni.
   The repetition of the burden is indicated as follows: stza. 3: What tythyngis
bryngis thou vt sup*r*a.
   After l. 5. MS. *inserts* What tythyngis bryngis the messangere.

Seche wondur tydyngus ye mow here:
That maydon and modur ys won yfere
And lady ys of hye aray.

A wonder thyng is now befall: 15
  That Lord that mad both se and sun,
Heven and erth and angelis al,
  In monkynde ys now becumme.
      Whatt tydyngus bryngu[st us, messangere?]
      A faunt that is bot of on yere   20
      Euer as ben and schal be ay.

These lovele lade con grete her chylde:
  'Hayle, Sun, haile, Broder, haile, Fader dere!'
'Haile, doghter, haile, suster, haile, moder myld!'
  This haylsyng was on coynt manere.   25
      Seche wo[n]der tythyngis [ye may here:]
      This gretyng was of so he chere
      That mans pyne hit turnyd to play.

That Lord that al thyng mad of noght
  Is mon becum fore mons love,   30
Fore with his blood he schul be boght
  From bale to blys that is above.
      Seche wonder tythyngis [ye may here:]
      That Lord us grawnt now our prayoure,
      To twel in heven that we may.   35

26

Balliol College, Oxford. MS. 354.   XVI *cent.*
f. 223 v.

What cher? Gud cher, gud cher, gud cher!
Be mery and glad this gud New Yere.

'Lyft up your hartes and be glad
  In Crystes byrth,' the angell bad,

25. l. 19.[us messangere]] MS. vt supra. *The line is written at the right of the
stanza.*   l. 22. These] MS. iese.   l. 26. [ye may here]] MS. vt supra.
l. 33. [ye may here]] MS. vt supra.   after l. 35. MS. Seche wonder tythyngis
vt supra.

'Say eche to oder, yf any be sade,
   "What cher?"'

Now the Kyng of Hevyn his byrth hath take,   5
Joy and myrth we owght to make;
Say eche to oder for hys sake,
   'What cher?'

I tell you all with hart so fre,
Ryght welcum ye be to me;   10
Be glad and mery, for charite.
   What cher?

The gudman of this place in fere,
You to be mery he prayth you here,
And with gud hert he doth to you say,   15
   'What cher?'

27

British Museum. MS. Addit. 40166 (C 3).   XV *cent.*
f. 12 v.

   Who wot nowe that ys here
   Where he schall be anoder yere?

Anoder yere hit may betyde
This compeny to be full wyde,
And never onodyr here to abyde;
   Cryste may send now sych a yere.

Another yere hit may befall   5
The lest that is withyn this hall
To be more mastur then we all;
   Cryste [may send now sych a yere.]

This lordis that ben wonder grete,
They threton powre men for to bete;   10
Hyt lendith lytull in hur threte;
   Cryste may send sich a yere.

28

Balliol College, Oxford. MS. 354.   XVI *cent.*
f. 222 v.

Alleluya, alleluia,
Deo Patri sit gloria.

Ther ys a blossum sprong of a thorn
To save mankynd, that was forlorne,
As the profettes sayd beforne;
   Deo Patri sit gloria.

Ther sprong a well at Maris fote   5
That torned all this world to bote;
Of her toke Jhesu flesshe and blod;
   Deo Patri [sit gloria.]

From that well ther strake a strem
Owt of Egypt into Bedlem;   10
God thorowgh his highnes turned yt agayn;
   Deo [Patri sit gloria.]

Ther was iii kynges of dyvers londes;
They thowght a thowght that was strong,
Hym to seke and thanke among;   15
   Deo [Patri sit gloria.]

They cam richely with ther presens,
With gold, myre, and frankynsens,
As clerkys rede in ther sequens;
   Deo Patri sit gloria.   20

The eldest kyng of them thre,
He went formest, for he wold se
What domysman that this shuld be;
   Deo Patri sit gloria.

The medylmest kyng, up he rose;   25
He sawe a babe in armys close;

In medyll age he thowght he was;
    Deo Patri [sit gloria.]

The yongest kyng, up he stode;
He made his offeryng rych and gud   30
To Jhesu Cryst, that shed his blod;
    Deo Patri sit gloria.

Ther shon a star owt of hevyn bryght,
That men of erth shuld deme aright
That this was Jhesu full of myght;   35
    Deo Patri [sit gloria.]

29

British Museum. MS. Sloane 2593.   XV *cent.*
f. 17 r.

    Reges de Saba venient;
    Aurum, tus, myrram offerent;
    Alleluia.

Now is the Twelthe Day icome;
The Fader and Sone togeder arn nome,
The Holy Gost, as they wern wone,
    In fere;
    God send us good Newe Yere.   5

I wil you synge with al myn myght
Of a chyld so fayr in syght;
A maydyn hym bar this ender nyght,
    So stylle,
    As it was his wylle.   10

Thre kynges out of Galylie
Kemyn to Bedlem, that cete,
For to takyn into that se
    Be nyte;
    It was a ful fayr syte.   15

The burden is written again at the end: Reges de Saba venient aurum
tus mirra[m] offer . . .

As they keme forght with here offeryng,
They mette with Herowdes, that mody kyng;
He askyd hem of here comyng
    That tyde,
    And thus to hem he seyde: 20

'Fro qwens come ye, kynges thre?'   f. 17 v.
'Out of the est, as thou mayst se,
To sekyn hym that evere xal be
    Throw ryte
    Lord and Kyng of Myte,'   25

'Quan ye han at that Kyng ibe,
Comit ageyn this weye be me,
And tel me the sytes that [ye] han se;
    I praye,
    Ye gon non other waye.'   30

Of Herowdys, that mody kyng,
He tokyn here leve of eld and yyng,
And for[th] they wente with here offeryng
    In syghte,
    And ther they come be nyte.   35

Into Bedlem thei gunne pas;   f. 18 r.
The sterre gan schynyn in here fas
Brytter than evere schon sunne in glas
    In londe;
    Jhesu with Mari thei fonde.   40

Quan they comyn into that plas   f. 17 v.
Ther Jhesu with his moder was,
Thei made offeryng with gret solas,
    Not ferre,
    With gold, incens, and myrre.   45

As they wern homward iwent,
The Fader of Hevene an aungyl sent

Stza. 8 is written after stza. 13 in MS.

To tho thre kynges that made present
    Or daye,
    And thus to hem gan saye: 50

'My Lord haght warnyd you of your fon,
Be Kyng Herowdes that ye not gon,
For, if ye don, he wil you slon
    And traye;
    Ye gon another waye.'   55

Quan they comyn hom to here cuntre,   f. 18 r.
Blythe and glad they wern alle thre
Of tho sytes that they had se
    Be nyte:
    Jhesu and Mari bryte.   60

With tresoun to us gan he sayn;
He trowid Jhesu to han slayn;
Into Egypt thei went ful playn
    Be syde;
    Josep was here gyde.   65

Kyng Herowdes, he made his vow;
Gret plente of chylderin he slow;
He wende ther xuld a be Jhesu;
    I saye,
    He falyid of his praye.   70

Herowdes was wod in ryalte;
He slow schylderin ryght gret plente
In Bedlem, that fayre cete,
    With stryf;
    Ne left he non on lyf.   75

The chylderin of Israel cryid, 'Wa wa!'
The moderis of Bedlem cryid, 'Ba, ba!'
Herowdes low and seyd, 'Aha!'
    That qwede,
    'The Kyng of Juwys is dede.'   80

Almyty God in mageste,   f. 18 v.
In on God personys thre,
Bryng us to the blysse that is so fre
  In fere,
And send us a good Newe Yere.   85

30

British Museum. MS. Egerton 3307.   XV *cent.*
ff. 55 v., 57 r.

Ave, rex angelorum,
Ave, rexque celorum,
Ave, princepsque polorum.

Hayl, most myghty in thi werkyng,
Hail, thou lord of all thing;
I offre the gold as to a kyng;
  Ave, rex angelorum.

31

British Museum. MS. Egerton 3307.   XV *cent.*
ff. 58 v., 59 r.

Illuminare Jherusalem;
The duke aperyth in Bedlem.

Hys signe ys a ster bryth
That shyneth over hym wyth lyght;
Yt ys nought come bott of hys myth:
  Illuminare Jerusalem.

Thys day iii kynges made oblacion;   5
He gyth to watyr sanctificacion;
He baptym our renovacion:
  Illuminare Jerusalem.

30. The burden is to be repeated as a chorus.
31. The burden is to be repeated as a chorus.

The Holy Gost over hym alight;
The Faders vois was herd on hyght: 10
'This ys my Son; me plese hym ryght'
Illuminare Jerusalem.

32

Balliol College, Oxford. MS. 354.   XVI *cent.*
f. 228 r.

Caput apri refero,
Resonens laudes Domino.

The boris hed in hondes I brynge,
With garlondes gay and byrdes syngynge;
I pray you all, helpe me to synge,
    Qui estis in convivio.

The boris hede, I understond,   5
Ys cheff servyce in all this londe;
Whersoever it may be fonde,
    Servitur cum sinapio.

The boris hede, I dare well say,
Anon after the [Twelfth] Day   10
He taketh his leve and goth away,
    Exivit tunc de patria.

33

British Museum. MS. Addit. 5665.   XV *cent.*
f. 7 v.

Nowell, nowell, nowell, nowell!
Tydynges gode Y thyngke *to telle.   *f. 8 r.

The borys hede that we bryng here
Betokeneth a Prince withowte pere
Ys born this day to bye us dere;
    Nowell, nowelle!

32. MS. marks burden: fote.
33. MS. heading: In die natiuitat*is*.

A bore ys a soverayn beste   f. 7 v.
And acceptab[l]e in every feste;   6
So mote thys Lord be to moste and leste;
  Nowell, [nowelle!]

This borys hede we bryng with song
In worchyp of hym that thus sprang   10
Of a virgine to redresse all wrong;
  Nowell, [nowelle!]

34A

British Museum. MS. Harley 5396.   XV *cent.*
f. 275 v.

Nay, Ivy, nay, hyt shal not be, iwys;
  Let Holy hafe the maystry, as the maner ys.

Holy stond in the hall, fayre to behold;
Ivy stond without the dore; she ys ful sore a-cold.

Holy and hys mery men, they dawnsyn and they syng;
Ivy and hur maydenys, they wepyn and they wryng.

Ivy hath a kybe; she kaght yt with the colde;   5
So mot they all haf ae that with Ivy hold.

Holy hat berys as rede as any rose;
The foster, the hunters kepe hem fro the doo[s].

Ivy hath berys as blake as any slo;
Ther com the oule and ete hym as she goo.   10

Holy hath byrdys, a ful fayre flok,
The nyghtyngale, the poppynguy, the gayntyl lavyrok.

Gode Ivy, what byrdys ast thou?
Non but the howlat, that kreye, 'How, how!'

33. Signature: Smert.
34A. MS. heading (*in later hand*): A Song on the Ivy *and* the Holly.
  The repetition of the burden is indicated as follows: stza. 1: Nay Iuy. stzas. 2,
6: Nay. stza. 3: Nay Iuy noy hyt. stzas 4, 5: Nay Iuy nay hyt. stza. 7: Nay Iuy
nay hyt shalnot.

34B

Balliol College, Oxford. MS. 354.   XVI *cent.*
f. 251 r.

Nay, nay, Ive, it may not be, iwis,
For Holy must have the mastry, as the maner is.

Holy berith beris, beris rede ynowgh;
The thristilcok, the popyngay daunce in every bow.
Welaway, sory Ivy, what fowles hast thow
But the sory howlet, that syngith, 'How, how?'

Ivy berith beris as black as any slo;   5
Ther commeth the woode-colver and fedith her of tho.
She liftith up her tayll, and she cakkes or she go;
She wold not for [a] hundred poundes serve Holy soo.

Holy with his mery men, they can daunce in hall;   f. 251 v.
Ivy and her jentyl women can not daunce at all,   10
But lyke a meyny of bullokkes in a waterfall,
Or on a whot somers day, whan they be mad all.

Holy and his mery men sytt in cheyres of gold;
Ivy and her jentyll women sytt withowt in fold,
With a payre of kybid helis cawght with cold;   15
So wold I that every man had that with Yvy will hold.

35

Bodleian Library. MS. Eng. poet. e. 1.   XV *cent.*
f. 54 r.

Ivy, chefe off treis it is;
Veni, coronaberis.

The most worthye she is in towne—
He that seyth other do amysse—
And worthy to bere the crowne;
Veni, coronaberis.

34B. The repetition of the burden is indicated as follows: stza. 1: na[y]
(*MS. torn*). stzas. 3, 4: nay.   l. 5. slo] MS. sho.   l. 8. [a] hundred
poundes] MS. C libra.   At end: Explicit.

Ivy is soft and mek off spech;   5
  Ageynst all bale she is blysse;
Well is he that may hyre rech;
  Veni, coronaberis.

Ivy is green with coloure bright;
  Of all treis best she is;   10
And that I preve well now be right:
  Veni, coronaberis.

Ivy beryth berys black;
  God graunt us all his blysse,
Fore there shall we nothyng lack;   15
  Veni, coronaberis.

36

British Museum. MS. Egerton 3307.   XV *cent.*
ff. 59 v., 60 r.

    Ivy ys good and glad to se;
    Ivy is fair in hys degre.

Ivy is both fair and gren,
  In wynter and in somer also,
And it is medecinable, I wen,
  Who knew the vertus that long therto;
  Ivy,   5
  It is god and lusty
  And in hys kynd a wel god tre.

Ivy hathe vertues ful good,
  Namely spredyng on the ground;
Wheder it be in town or wod,   10
  It helpyth the sor and maykth sound;
  Ivy,
  In bok is fond ful sekerly
  That gren is gladsom [for] to se.

Stzas. 2, 3 are written again on f. 60 r. The burden, with 'Ivy' prefixed, is to be
repeated as a chorus.   l. 14. for] from text on f. 69 r.

When other treyss most del fail,   15
  Than berith Ivy hys berys ful bold
In gret stormys of snaw and hail;
  It spares for no wedyrs cold,
    Ivy,
  To bryng furth fruit ful properly   20
  To best and byrd ful gret plente.

The farest byrd that flyth be skye
  For gladnesse of that lusty tree
Myght make hys nest in gren Ivy,
  To norrysch hys byrdes fayr and free,   25
    Ivy,
  Ther in ys covert wel privy,
  To comforth hym that ther wyll bee.

Wher it takyth hold it kepyth fast,
  And strenkyth it that is hym bye;   30
It kepyth wall from cost and wast,
  As men may se al day at hye;
    Ivy,
  I kan tel no caus qwy
  Bot we must love that gentyll tre.   35

37

Bodleian Library. MS. Eng. poet. e. 1.   XV *cent.*
f. 38 r.

    Revertere, revertere,
    The quene of blysse and of beaute.

    Behold what lyfe that we ryne ine,
    Frayl to fale and ever lyke to syne
    Thorow owr enmys entysyng;
      Therfor we syng and cry to the:

MS. heading: Of the puryfycacion.
The repetition of the burden is indicated after each stanza by: reuertere &c.

Come hyder, Lady, fayryst floure,   5
And kepe us, Lady, from douloure;
Defend us, Lady, and be owr socoure,
     For we cease not to cal to the:

Torne owr lyfe, Lady, to Goddys luste,
Syne to fle and fleschly luste,   10
For aftur hym in the we trust
     To kep us frome adversyte.

Thys holy day of Puryfycacyon   f. 38 v.
To the temple thou bare owr salvacyon,
Jhesu Cryst, thin own swet Sone,   15
     To whome therfor now syng we:

Farwell, Crystmas fayer and fre!
Farwell, Newers Day with the!
Farwell, the holy Epyphane!
     And to Mary now syng we: 20

38

Balliol College, Oxford. MS. 354.   XVI *cent.*
f. 224 v.

     Now have gud day, now have gud day!
     I am Crystmas, and now I go my way.

     Here have I dwellyd with more and lasse
     From Halowtyde till Candylmas,
     And now must I from you hens passe;
          Now have gud day!

     I take my leve of kyng and knyght,   5
     And erle, baron, and lady bryght;
     To wildernes I must me dyght;
          Now have gud day!

And at the gud lord of this hall
I take my leve, and of gestes all;   10
Me thynke I here, Lent doth call;
    Now have gud day!

And at every worthy offycer,
Merchall, panter, and butler,
I take my leve as for this yere;   15
    Now have gud day!

Anoder yere I trust I shall
Make mery in this hall,
Yf rest and pease in Ynglond may fall;
    Now have gud day!   20

But oftyntymys I have hard say
That he is loth to pert away
That oftyn byddyth, 'Have gud day!'
    Now have gud day!

Now fare ye well, all in fere;   25
Now fare ye well for all this yere;
Yet for my sake make ye gud cher;
    Now hav[e] gud day!

39

St. John's College, Cambridge. MS. S. 54.   **XV** *cent.*
f. 6 v.

            'Lollay, lay, lay, lay,
            My dere modyre, lullay.'
            'Lullay, my chyld.'

        A chyld ys born, ewys,
        That all this word xall blys;
        Hys joy xall never myse,
            For Jhesu ys hys name.

                burden, *after* l. 2. MS. c⁰.

On the good Yowe morne   5
The blyssfull chyld was borne,
To were a crown of thorne,
    [For Jhesu ys hys name.]

Of a madyn so good
He toke both fleche and blod;   10
For us he deyd upon the rode,
    [For Jhesu ys hys name.]

Of a medyn so trew
He toke both fleche and hewe;
For us he deyd on a tre,   15
    [For Jhesu ys hys name.]

On the Estern mo[r]n all blyth
He ros fro deth to lyve
To make us all blyth,
    [For Jhesu ys hys name.]   20

On the Good Fryday at non   f. 7 r.
To the deth he was done;
For us he deyd on tre,
    [For Jhesu ys hys name.]

40

British Museum. MS. Sloane 2593.   XV *cent.*
f. 32 r.

'Lullay, myn lykyng, my dere sone, myn swetyng,
Lullay, my dere herte, myn owyn dere derlyng.'

I saw a fayr maydyn syttyn and synge;
Sche lullyd a lytyl chyld, a swete lordyng.

That eche Lord is that that made alle thinge;
Of alle lordis he is Lord, of alle kynges Kyng.

39. ll. 8, 24. MS. vt su*pr*a.
40. The repetition of the burden is indicated as follows: stza. 1: lull my*n*.
stza. 2: lull*a*y.

Ther was mekyl melody at that chyldes berthe;   f. 32 v.
Alle tho wern in hevene blys, thei made mekyl merth.   6

Aungele bryght, thei song that nyght and seydyn to that chyld,
'Blyssid be thou, and so be sche that is bothe mek and myld.'

Prey we now to that chyld, and to his moder dere,
Grawnt hem his blyssyng that now makyn chere.   10

4I

National Library of Scotland. MS. Advocates 19. 3. 1.   XV *cent.*
f. 210 v.

> This endurs nyght
> I see a syght,
>   A sterne schone bryght as day,
> And ever ymong
> A meden song
>   Was, 'By, by, lulley.'

> This lovely lady sete and song,
>   And tyll hur chyld con say,
> 'My Son, my Lord, my Fadur dere,
>   Why lyus thou thus in hey?
>   Myn one swete bryd,   5
>   What art thou kyd
>   And knowus the Lord of ey?
>   Neverthelesse
>   I will not sesse
>   To syng, "By, by, lulley." '   10

> This chyld ontyll is modur spake,
>   And thus me thowght he seyd:
> 'I am kend for Hevun Kyng
>   In cryb thowgh I be leyd.

The repetition of the burden is indicated as follows: stzas. 1–4, 6, 7: This.
stza. 5. This *endurus* nygh. *After the burden is also written*: This. *Perhaps this is to
indicate that the burden is to be twice sung.*

Angeles bryght   15
Shall to me lyght,
   Ye wot ryght welle, in fey;
Off this behest
Gyffe me yowre brest,
   And syng, "By, by, lolley." '   20

'My aune dere Son, to the I say
   Thou art me lefe and dere;
How shuld I serve the to pey
   And plese on all manere?
     All thi wyll   25
     I wyll fulfyll,
       Thou wottes ryght well in fey
     Nevertheleyse
     I wyll not sesse
       To syng, "By, by, lulley." '   30

'My dere modere, when tyme it be,
   Ye take [me] up on loft,
And sett me ryght apon yowre kne,
   And hondul me full soft.
     In yowre arme   f. 211 r.
     Ye hape me warme,   36
       Both by nyght and day;
     Gyff I wepe
     And will not slepe,
       To syng, "By, by, lulley." '   40

'My aune dere Son, sen it is thus,
   That thou art Lord of all,
Thou shuld have ordent the sum bydyng
   In sum kyngus halle.
     Me thenkus aryght   45
     A kyng or a knyght
       Shuld be in rych arey,
     And yett for this
     I woll not seysse
       To syng, "By and lulley."   50

'My aune dere Son, to the I say,
    Me thynkus it is no laye
That kyngus shuld com so fer to the,
    And thou not to them dray.
        Thow schw[l]n see   55
        Then kyngus iii
            Apon the Twelfe Day,
        And for that syght
        Ye may be lyght
            To syng, "By, by, lolley."   60

'May aune dere Son, sen it is thus,
    At all thyng is at thi wyll,
I pray the grant me a bone,
    Gyf it be ryght of skylle:
        Chyld or man   65
        That will or can
            Be mery on this gud day;
        To hevun blysse
        Grawnt hit us,
            And syng, "By, by, lulley." '   70

42

Balliol College, Oxford. MS. 354.   XVI *cent.*
f. 225 v.

Now synge we with angelis,
'Gloria in excelcis.'

A babe is born to blis us brynge;
I hard a mayd lulley and synge;
She said, 'Dere Son, leve thy wepyng;
    Thy Fader is the Kyng of Blis.

MS. marks burden: fote.
    The repetition of the burden is indicated as follows: stzas. 1, 11: now syg we.
stza. 2: nowe syng.   stzas. 3, 4, 6, 7, 9, 10: now.   stza. 5: now syg.

'Lulley,' she said, and songe also,   5
'Myn own dere Son, whi art thou wo?
Have I not do as I shuld do?
  Thy grevance, tell me what it is.'

'Nay, dere moder, for the wepe I nowght,
But for the wo that shall be wrowght   10
To me or I mankynd have bowght;
  Was never sorow lik it, ywis.'

'Pesse, dere Son, tell me not soo.
Thou art my child, I have no moo;
Shuld I se men myn own Son sloo?   15
  Alas, my dere Son, what menys this?'

'My hondes, moder, that ye may see,
Shall be nayled unto a tree;
My fete allso fast shall be;
  Men shall wepe that shall se this.'   20

'A, dere Son, hard is my happe,
To see my child that sokid my pappe,
His hondes, his fete, that I dide wrappe,
  Be so naylid, that never dide amysse.'

'A, dere moder, yet shall a spere   25
My hart in sonder all to-tere;
No wondre yf I carefull were
  And wepe full sore to thynk on this.'

'A, dere Son, shall I se this?
Thou art my child, and I thy moder, ywis.   30
Whan Gabryell called me "full of grace",
  He told me nothyng of this.'

'A, dere moder, thorow myn here
To thrust in thornes they will not spare;
Alas, moder, I am full of care   35
  That ye shall see this hevynes.'

'A, dere Son, leve thy wepyng;
Thou bryngyst my hart in gret mornyng;
A carefull songe now may I sing;
   This tydynges, hard to me it is.' 40

'A, pece, dere moder, I the pray,
And comforte me all that ye may,
And syng, "By by, lulley, lulley,"
   To put away all hevynes.'

43

National Library of Scotland. MS. Advocates 18. 7. 21.   *c.* 1372.
f. 6 r.

Lullay, lullay, litel child,
   Qui wepest thou so sore?

Lullay, lullay, litel child,
Thou that were so sterne and wild
Nou art become meke and mild
   To saven that was forlore.

But for my senne I wot it is 5
That Godis Sone suffret this;
Merci, Lord! I have do mis;
   Iwis, I wile no more.

Ayenis my Fadris wille I ches
An appel with a reuful res; 10
Werfore myn hertage I les,
   And nou thou wepist therfore.

An appel I tok of a tre;
God it hadde forboden me;
Werfore I sulde dampned be, 15
   Yef thi weping ne wore.

Lullay, for wo, thou litel thing,
Thou litel barun, thou litel king;
Mankindde is cause of thi murning,
    That thou hast loved so yore.   20

For man, that thou hast ay loved so,
Yet saltu suffren peines mo,
In heved, in feet, in hondis to,
    And yet wepen wel more.

That peine us make of senne fre;   25
That peine us bringge, Jesu, to the;
That peine us helpe ay to fle
    The wikkede fendes lore.

44

Bodleian Library. MS. Eng. poet. e. 1.   XV *cent.*
f. 27² r.

'Mary modyr, cum and se:
    Thi Son is naylyd on a tre.

'His body is wappyd all in wo,
Hand and fot; he may not go;
Thi Son, lady, that thou lovyst soo,
    Nakyd is naylyd upon a tre.

'The blyssyd body that thou hast born   5
To save mankynd, that was forlorn,
His body, lady, is al to-torn,
    His hed with thornys, as ye may se.'

Wan Johan this tal began to tell,
Mary wyld not lenger dwell   10
Thyl sche cam to that hyll
    Ther sche myth her owyn Son see.

        l. 4. tre] MS. trer.

'My swet Son, thou art me der;
Qwy have men hang the her?
Thi hed is closyd wyth a brer;   15
    Qwy have men soo doo to the?'

'Johan, this woman I the betake;
Kep this woman for my sake;
On the rod I hyng for mannys sake,
    For synful man, as thou may se.   20

'This game alone me must pley   f. 27² v.
For synfull sowlis that ar to dey;
Ther ys no man that gothe be the wey
    That on my peynis wyl lok and se.

'Fadyr, my sowle I the betake;   25
My body deth for mannys sake;
To hel I go withowtyn wake,
    Mannys sole to make fre.'

Prey we al to that blyssyd Son
That he us help wan we not mon,   30
And bryng us to blys that is abone.
    Amen, amen, amen, for charite.

45

Bodleian Library. MS. Ashmole 1379.   *c.* 1500.
p. 32

There blows a colde wynd todaye, todaye,
    The wynd blows cold todaye;
Cryst sufferyd his passyon for manys salvacyon,
    To kype the cold wynd awaye.

l. 20. thou] MS. the.   l. 21. alone] MS. & loue.

Thys wynde be reson ys callyd tentacyon;
   Yt ravyghth both nyghth and daye.
Remember, man, how the Savyor was slayne
   To kype the colde wyn[d]e awaye.

Pride and presumcyon and fals extorcyon,   5
   That meny man dothe betraye—
Man, cum to contrycyon and axe confessyon
   To kype the colde wynd awaye.

O Mary myld, for love of the chyld
   That dyed on Good Frydaye,   10
Be owr salvacyon frome mortall damnacyon,
   To kype the cold wynd awaye.

He was naylyd, his blode was halyd,   p. 33
   Owre remyssyon for to by,
And for owr synnys all he dronke both eysell and gall, 15
   To kype the cold wynd awaye.

Slowthe, envy, covytis, and lechere
   Bl[e]we the cold wynd, as Y dare saye;
Agene suche pusyn he suffe[r]yd his paysscyon
   To kype the cold wynd awaye.   20

O man, remember the Lord so tender
   Whyche dyed withowte denaye;
Hys hondes so smert laye next to his hart
   To kepe the cold wynd awaye.

Now pray we all to the Kyng selestyall,   25
   That borne he was off mayde,
That we maye love so with other mo,
   To kype the cold wynd awaye.

At the daye of dome when we schall cum   p. 34
   Owr synns not for to denaye,   30
Mary, praye to the Sone that syghthy yn hys trone
   To kype the cold wynd awaye.

At the last ynde, man, thou schalt send
  And kype bothe nyghth and daye;
The moste goodlyst tresyor ys Cryst the Savyor   35
  To kype the cold wynd awaye.

Here let us ynde, and Cryst us defend
  All be the nyghth and be daye,
And bryng us to hys place where ys myrthe and solas
  To kype the cold wynd awaye.   40

46

Trinity College, Cambridge. MS. O. 3. 58.   XV *cent.*
recto

    [T]her is [n]o rose of swych vertu
    As is the rose that bare Jhesu.

    Ther is no ro[se of] swych vertu
    As is the rose that bar Jhesu;
      Allelyua.

    For in this rose conteynyd was
    Heven and erthe in lytyl space,   5
      Res miranda.

    Be that rose we may weel see
    That he is God in personys thre,
      Pari forma.

    The aungelys sungyn the sheperdes to: 10
    'Gloria in excelcis Deo.'
      Gaudeamus.

    [L]eve we al this wordly merthe,
    And folwe we this joyful berthe;
      Transeamus.   15

      l. 35. Cryst] MS. agenyst.

47

Bodleian Library. MS. Eng. poet. e. 1. XV *cent.*
f. 21 r.

Of a rose, a lovely rose,
　　Of a rose I syng a song.

Lyth and lystyn, both old and yyng,
How the rose begane to spryng;
A fayyrer rose to owr lekyng
　　Sprong ther never in kynges lond.

v branchis of that rose ther ben,　　　　　5
The wych ben both feyer and chene;
Of a maydyn, Mary, hevyn quene,
　　Ought of hyr bo[s[um the branch sprong.

The [first] branch was of gret honour:　　　f. 21 v.
That blyssed Mary shuld ber the flour,　　　10
Ther cam an angell ought hevyn toure
　　To breke the develes bond.

The secund branch was gret of myght,
That sprong upon Cristmes nyght;
The sterre shone and lemeghd bryght,　　　15
　　That man schuld se it both day and nyght.

The [third] branch can spryng and spred;
iii kynges than to branch gan led
Tho to Owr Lady in hure chyldbed;
　　Into Bethlem that branch sprong ryght.　　20

The [fourth] branch, it sprong to hell,
The develes powr for to fell,
That no soule therin shuld dwell,
　　The brannch so blessedfully sprong.

The [fifth] branch, it was so swote,　　　25
Yt sprong to hevyn, both croppe and rote,
In every ball to ben owr bott,
　　So blessedly yt sprong.

48

Bodleian Library. MS. Eng. poet. e. 1.   XV *cent.*
f. 25 r.

Of M, A, R, I,
   Syng I wyll a new song.

Of thes iiii letters purpose I,
Of M and A, R and I;
Thei betokyn mayd Mary;
   All owr joy of hyr it sprong.

Withoughten wem of hyr body,   5
M and A, R and I,
Of hyr was borne a Kyng truly
   The Jewys dedyn to deth with wrong.

Upon the mounte of Calvery,   f. 25 v.
M and A, R and I,   10
Ther thei betyn hys bar body
   With schorges that war sharp and long.

Owr der Lady she stod hym by,
M and A, R and I,
And wep[t] water ful bytterly   15
   And terys of blod ever among.

49

British Museum. MS. Egerton 3307.   XV *cent.*
f. 67 r.

Ave, plena gracia,
Dei mater Maria.

Hayle be thou, Mary most of honowr,
Thou bar Jhesu our Saviour,
   Maria,
   Ave, plena gracia.

Hayle be thou, madyn, moder, and wyff,   5
Hayl be thou, stynter of our stryff,
   Maria,
   [Ave, plena gracia.]

Hayle be thou, qwen of paradysse,
Of al wemen thou berys prysse,   10
   Maria,
   [Ave, plena gracia.]

Thow pray for us unto thy Son,
In heven blyss that we may won,
   Maria,   15
   Ave, p[lena] g[racia.]

50

British Museum. MS. Egerton 3307.   XV *cent.*
f. 53 r.

   Novus sol de virgine
   Reluxit nobis hodie.

The holy doghter of Syon,
   Princes of Jherusalem,
This day sprang owt of the alon
   The grane of Jesse in Bedlem.

This day also the bryght ster   5
   That Balam gan to magnifi,
He ros of the to stynt our werr
   And in dirkness us to gy.

Thow ert also abown ilkon
   A moder and a madyn trew,   10
And the yerd ek of Aaron
   That bar this day a burion newe.

The orient lyght of Nazareth
  Thow ert also to stynt our stryff
That broght forth agaynys deth   15
  This day the sothfast Man of Lyff.

Thow ert ek the fleys of Jedeon
  A-dewyd with the Holy Gost,
The chast tempyll of Salamon,
  Cler as cristal in every cost.   20

Thow ert eke the joy of Israel
  To stynt all our old sorowe,
The gate whych Ezechiel
  Saw alway closse, both even and morow.

And thow ert eke the purpyl rose   25
  That whylom grew in Jerico;
The Faders wysdom to enclos
  Thou wer the tempyl and tour also.

Now thow chast lylly flour
  Spriggyng from the Jewis spyn,   30
Be our help and our socour
  Agaynys the venom serpentyn.

                          51

Bodleian Library. MS. Eng. poet. e. 1.   XV *cent.*
f. 45 r.

          A, a, a a,
          Gaude celi domina.

          Mary, for the love of the
          Glad and mery schal we be;
          Whe schal syng unto the
            Tua quinque gaudia.

          MS. heading: Off the 5 joyes of owr lady.

The fyrste joy that came to the   5
Was whan the aungel greted the
And sayd, 'Mary, ful of charyte,
    Ave, plena gracia.'

The secund joye, that was ful good:
Whan Goddes Son tok flesch and blood,   10
Withowt sorow and changyng of mood
    Enixa est puerpera.

The thyrd joy was ful of myght:
Whan Goddes Son on rood was pyght,
Deed and buryed and layd in syght,   15
    Surrexit die tercia.

The fourth joy was on Holy Thursday,   f. 45 v.
Whan God to heven tok hys way;
God and man, withowten nay,
    Ascendit supra sydera.   20

The fyfth joy is for to come
At the dredful day of dome,
Whan he schal deme us, al and some,
    Ad celi palacia.

Mary to serve God gyve us grace,   25
And grete hyr with joys in every place,
To cum afor hyr Sones face
    In seculorum secula.

52

Bodleian Library. MS. Arch. Selden B. 26.   XV *cent.*
f. 23 r.

        Hayl, Mary, ful of grace,
            Moder in virginite.

    The Holi Goste is to the sent
    From the Fader Omnipotent;
    Now is God withyn the went
        While the angel seide, 'Ave.'

Whan the angel 'Ave' byganne,   5
Flesh and blode togedre ranne;
Mary bare bothe God and manne
    Thorwe the vertu of the dignite.

So seith the gospel of Syn Johan:
God and man is made al one   10
In flesch and blode, body and bone,
    O God in personys thre.

And the prophete Jeremye
Telleth in his prophecie
That the Sone of Marie   15
    For us deyde uppon a tre.

Moche joye was us ygraunte
And in erthe pees yplaunte
Whan ybore was that faunte
    In the londe of Galile.   20

Mary, graunte us of the blys
Thereas thy Sonys wonynge ys;
Of that we have ydone amys
    Pray for us pur charite.

53

Bodleian Library. MS. Eng. poet. e. 1.   XV *cent.*
f. 51 v.

'Nowell, nowell!'
This is the salutacion off the aungell Gabriell:

Tydynges trew ther be cum new, sent frome the Trinite
Be Gabriel to Nazaret, cite off Galile:
A clene mayden and pure virgyn, thorow hyre humilite,
Conceyvid the secund person in divinite.

*A later hand has drawn a crude sketch of a cock opposite stza. 5 and has added the
following stanza at the end of the carol:*

    Hayl, blyssyd lade, qwych hays born
      God Son in Trinite;
    In the, laydy, he tuk hys plays
      Qwen the angel sayd, 'Ave.'

Whan he fyrst presentid was before hyre fayer visag,   5
In the most demuere and goodly wys he ded to hyre omag
And seid, 'Lady, frome heven so hy, that Lordes herytag
The wich off the borne wold be, I am sent on messag.

'Hayle, virgyne celestiall, the mekest that ever was;
Hayle, temple off deitie and myrrour off all grace;   10
Hayle, virgyne puer, I the ensure, within full lyty[l] space
Thou shalt receyve and hym conceyve that shal bryng gret solace.'

Sodenly she, abashid truly, but not al thyng dysmaid,
With mynd dyscret and mek spyryt to the aungel she said,
'By what maner shuld I chyld bere, the wich ever a maid   15
Have lyvid chast al my lyf past and never mane asaid?'

Than ageyne to hire certeyn answered the aungell,
'O lady dere, be off good chere, and dred the never a dell.
Thou shalt conceyve in thi body, mayden, very God hymself,
In whos byrth heven and erth shal joy, callid Emanuell.   20

'Not [y]it,' he seid, 'vi monethys past, thi cosyn Elyzabeth,
That was baren, conceyvid Sent Johan; tru it is that I tell.
Syn she in ag, why not in yought mayst thou conceyve
          as well,   f. 52 r.
If God wyl, whome is possybyll to have don every dell?'   25

Thane ageyne to the aungell she answered womanly,
'Whatever my Lord commaund me do I wyll obey mekely.
Ecce, sum humilima ancilla Domini;
Secundum verbum tuum,' she seid, 'fiat mihi.'

54

British Museum. MS. Sloane 2593.   XV *cent.*
f. 10 r.

          Nowel, el, el, el, el, el, el, el, el, el, el, el!
          Mary was gret with Gabriel.

          Mary moder, meke and mylde,
          Fro schame and synne that ye us schyllde,
          For gret on grownd ye gon with childe,
               Gabriele nuncio.

Mary moder, be not adred;   5
Jhesu is in your body bred,
And of your bryst he wil be fed
    Cum pudoris lilio.

Mary moder, the frewt of the
For us was naylid on a tre;   10
In hevene is now his mageste;
    Fulget resurrecio.

Mary moder, the thredde day
Up he ros, as I yow say;
To helle he tok the ryghte way;   15
    Motu fertur proprio.

Mary moder, after thin Sone
Up thou steyist, with hym to wone;
The aungele wern glad quan thou were come
    In celi palacio.   20

55

British Museum. MS. Addit. 5665.   XVI *cent.*
f. 10 r.

    'Mervele noght, Josep, on Mary mylde;
    Forsake hyr not tho she be with childe.'

    'I, Josep, wonder how hit may be,   f. 10 v.
    I, Josep, wonder how hit may be,
    That Mary wex gret when Y and she
    Ever have levyd in chastite;
    Iff she be with chylde, hit *ys not by me.'   *f. 11 r.
      'Mervell not, Joseph;   6
      Merwell noght, Joseph.

burden, l. 1. on] *in words for tenor part* MS. of.   l. 2. tho] MS. they.   l. 4.
tho] MS. thos.
ll. 7, 12, 13, 17, 18, 21. *These lines are to be repeated in singing, as written in stza. 1.*
MS. heading: In die natiuitatis.

'The Holy Gost with mercifull disstens   f. 10 v.
In here hathe entryd withowte offens,
God and man conceyved by hys presens,   10
An[d] she virgyn pure withowte violens.
    Mervell no[t,] Joseph.'

'What the angell of God to me dothe say   f. 11 r.
I, Joseph, muste and will umble obay,
Ellys prively Y wolde have stole away,   15
But now will Y serve here tille that Y day.'
    'Mervell not, Josep.'

'Josep, thow shalt here mayde and moder fynde,
Here Sone redemptor of all mankynde
Thy forefaderes of paynes to unbynde;   20
Therefor muse not this mater in thy mynde;
    Mervell not, [Joseph.']

56

Bodleian Library. MS. Eng. poet. e. 1.   XV *cent.*
f. 47 v.

'Nowel, nowel, nowel,'
    Syng we with myrth;
Cryst is come wel,
With us to dewell,
    By hys most noble byrth.

Under a tre
In sportyng me,
    Alone by a wod syd,
I hard a mayd
That swetly sayd,   5
    'I am with chyld this tyd.

MS. heading: A song vpon (now must I syng &c).
The repetition of the burden is indicated after each stanza by: nowell &c.

'Gracyusly
Conceyvyd have I
   The Son of God so swete;
Hys gracyous wyll   10
I put me tyll,
   As moder hym to kepe.

'Both nyght and day
I wyl hym pray
   And her hys lawes taught,   15
And every dell
Hys trew gospell
   In hys apostles fraught.

'Thys goostly case   f. 48 r.
Dooth me embrace   20
   Withowt dyspyte or mokc;
With my derlyng
Lullay to syng
   And lovely hym to roke.

'Withowt dystresse   25
In grete lyghtnesse
   I am both nyght and day;
This hevenly fod
In hys chyldhod
   Schal dayly with me play.   30

'Soone must I syng
With rejoycing,
   For the tym is all ronne
That I schal chyld,
All undefyld,   35
   The Kyng of Hevens Sonne.'

57

St. John's College, Cambridge. MS. S. 54.   XV *cent.*
f. 9 r.

'Fadyr, my wyll yt is:
Nolo mortem peccatoris.'

'Fadyr, I am thin owyn chyld
And born of Mary mek and myld;
  Fadyr, now my will yt is:
  Nolo mortem peccatoris.

'My hert is sore qwan I bethynk   5
And se mene trespas and in syn synk.
  For all that is done amyse
  Nolo mortem pec[catoris.]

'Thou falce fend, with all thi slent,
Y wyll no more mankynd be schent;   10
  Of hem thou getyst no ryghht, ywys;
  [Nolo mortem peccatoris.']

Now mak we both joy and myrght
In worschyp of Cristys owyn byrtht.
  This is Goddes owyn word, ywys: 15
  ['Nolo mortem peccatoris.']

58

British Museum. MS. Royal 17. B. xliii.   *c.* 1500.
f. 184 r.

Com home agayne,
Com home agayne,
Min owine swet hart, com home agayne;
  Ye are gone astray
  Owt of youer way;
  There[fore] com h[o]me agayne.

l. 8. MS. Nolo mortem &c.   ll. 12, 16. MS. vt. supra.   l. 13. myrght]
MS. myghht.

Mankend I cale, wich lyith in frale;.
   For love I mad the fre;
To pay the det the prise was gret,
   From hell that I ranssomed the.

Mi blod so red for the was shed;   5
   The prise it ys not smale;
Remembre welle what I the tell,
   And com whan I the kale.

Mi prophetes all, they ded the cale;
   For love I mad the free;   10
 .   .   .   .
 .   .   .   .

And I miselfe and mi postels twelfe,
   To prech was all mi thouth
Mi Faders kyngedom both hole and sound,   15
   Which that I so derly bouth.

Therefore refreyne, and torne agayne,
   And leve thyne owene intent,
The which it is contrare, iwos,
   Onto mi commaundment.   20

Thow standest in dout and sekest about
   Where that thow mayst me se;
Idoules be set, mony for to gyt,
   Wich ys made of stone and tre.   f. 184 v.

I am no stoke, nor no payncted bloke,   25
   Nor mad by no mannes hand,
Bot I am he that shall los the
   From Satan the phinnes bonde.

59

British Museum. MS. Egerton 3307.   XV *cent.*
f. 55 r.

Qui natus est de virgine,
Salvum me fac, Domine.

Fader and Son and Holy Gost,
  Gret God in Trinite,
As thou ert lord of myth most,
  Salvum me fac, [Domine.]

As thou ert wysse and ryth wel wost   5
  This world ys bot a vanite,
When [I] schall dy and yeld my gost,
  Salvum me fac, [Domine.]

Wher I slep, wher I wake,
  On lond or water, wer I be,   10
As thou dyd dy for man sak,
  Salvum me fac, [Domine.]

60

Cambridge University Library. MS. Ee. 1. 12.   By James Ryman, *c.* 1492.
f. 50 r.

O, O, O, O, O, O, O, O,
O Deus sine termino.

O Fader withoute begynnyng,
  O Sonne and Holi Goost also,
O iii and One without ending,
  O Deus sine termino.

59. The burden is to be repeated after each stanza as a chorus.

O iii persones in one unyte,
  Beyng but one God and no moo, 6
One in substaunce, essens, and myght,
  O Deus sine termino.

O, whiche hast made bothe day and nyght,
  Heven and erthe rounde like an O, 10
By thy wisdome and endeles myght,
  O Deus sine termino.

O, whiche of nought al thing hast wrought,
  O verbum in principio,
O, without whom is wrought right nought, 15
  O Deus sine termino.

O Prince of Peas, O Heven King,
  O fynall ender of oure woo,
O, whose kingdome hath non ending,
  O Deus sine termino. 20

O maker of eche creature,
  O supplanter of oure foo,
O Sonne of Marie, virgyn pure,
  O Deus sine termino.

We beseche the with alle oure myght, 25
  Or we depart this worlde fro,
Of forgevenes of oure delicte,
  O Deus sine termino.

Criste graunte us grace, that we come may
  To heven blisse, whenne we hens goo, 30
That deyed for us on Good Friday
  Et regnat sine termino.

61

Bodleian Library. MS. Douce 302.   By John Audelay, XV *cent*.
f. 32 r.

> Saynt Frances, to the I say,
> Saue thi breder both nyght and day.

A hole confessoure thou were hone
And levydist on contemplacion,
To thyng on Cristis passioun,
    That sofyrd deth on Good Fryday.

His passion was in the so fervent   5
That he aperd to thi present;
Upon thi body he set his preynt,
    His v wondis, hit is no nay.

Upon thi body thou hem bere
Affter that tyme ful iii ye[re;]   10
To al men syght thai did apere;
    No water myght wasche hem away.

Weder thou schuldist ete ore drenke,
On Cristis passion thou woldist thynke;
In v pertys wes thi pertyng   15
    Of his sustinans, sothe to say.

Crist he grawnt the specialy,
Fore on his passion thou hadist pete,
To feche thi breder out of purgatori,
    That lyin ther in rewful aray.   20

Thou thongis Crist of his swete sonde
And thoghtist to go to the Hole Londe;
Fore dred of deth thou woldist not wond
    To teche the peril thi Cristyn fay.

MS. heading: de sancto fransisco. The repetition of the burden is indicated after
stza. 1 by: Saynt frawnces to the I pray.

Then Crist he knew well then entent   25
And turned the out of that talent
And bede the make thi testament
    And 'Come to me fore ens and ay.

'A, hole Frawnces, now I se
Fore my love that thou woldist dye;   30
Thou schalt have joy perpetual[e],
    Thou hast dyssired mone a day.'

His hole reule of relegiowne
To his breder he wrote anon
And prayd ham, fore Cristis passiowne,   35
    To kepe hit wel both nyght and day.

A sad ensampil here mow ye se,
On Cristis passioun to have pete
And to leve in love and charete;
    Then mere in hert be ye may.   40

His last prayer to Crist this was
Fore al that sustens this hole place:
'Gr[a]cious God, grawnt ham thi grace
    Tofore thi jugement at domysday.'

Pray we to Frawnses, that beth present,   45
To save his breder and his covent,
That thai be never chamyd ne chent
    With wyckid man ne fyndis fray.

I pray youe, seris, pur charyte,
Redis this caral reverently,   50
Fore I mad hit with wepyng eye,
    Your broder, Jon, the blynd Awdlay.

62

British Museum. MS. Egerton 3307.　　　　　　　　　　XV *cent.*
f. 63 v.

Enfors we us with all our myght
To love Seynt Georg, Owr Lady knyght.

Worschip of vertu ys the mede
　And sewyth hym ay of ryght;
To worschip Georg than haue we ned,
　Whych is our sovereyn Ladys knyght.

He kepyd the mad from dragons dred　　　　　　　　5
　And fraid al Fraunce and put to fligh[t]
At Agyncourt, the crownecle ye red:
　The French hym se formest in fyght.

In hys vertu he wol us led
　Agaynys the fend, the ful wyght,　　　　　　　　　10
And with hys banner us oversprede
　Yf we hym love with all our myght.

63

British Museum. MS. Sloane 2593.　　　　　　　　　　XV *cent.*
f. 25 v.

Synge we now, all a[nd] sum,
'Ave rex gentis Anglorum.'

A newe song I wil begynne
　Of Kyng Edmund, that was so fre,
How he deyid withoute synne,
　And bow[n]dyn his body was to a tre.

With arwys scharpe they gunne hym prykke;　　　5
　For non rewthe wold they lete;
As dropys of reyn they comyn thikke,
　And every arwe with other gan mete.

　　　63. burden, l. 2. gentis] MS. ge*n*tes.

And his hed also thei of smette;
 Among the breres thei it kest;   10
A wolf it kepte withoutyn lette;
 A blynd man fond it at the last.

Prey we to that worthi kyng,   f. 26 r.
 That sufferid ded this same day,
He saf us, bothe eld and yyng,   15
 And scheld us fro the fendes fray.

64

British Museum. MS. Sloane 2593.   XV *cent.*
f. 34 r.

 Mak ye merie as ye may,
 And syng with me, I you pray.

In Patras, ther born he was,
The holy buschop Seynt Nycholas,
He wyst mekyl of Godes gras
 Throw vertu of the Trinite.

He reysyd thre klerkes fro deth to lyfve 5
That wern in salt put full swythe
Betwyx a bochere and his wyfve
 And was hid in privyte.

He maryid thre maydenys of myld mod;
He yaf hem gold to here fod;   10
He turnyd hem fro ille to good
 Throw vertu of the Trynyte.

Another he dede sekerly:
He savyd a thef that was ful sly,
That stal a swyn out of his sty; 15
 His lyf thann savyd he.

God graw[n]t vs grace here, eld and yyng,
Hym to serve at his plesyng;
To hevene blysse he us bryng
    Throw vertu of the Trinite.   20

65

Cambridge University Library. MS. Ee. 1. 12.   By James Ryman, *c.* 1492.
f. 49 v.

Ete ye this brede, ete ye this brede,
And ete it so ye be not dede.

This brede geveth eternall lyfe,
Bothe unto man, to chielde, and wyfe;
It yeldeth grace and bateth stryfe;
    Ete ye it so ye be not ded.

It semeth white, yet it is rede,   f. 50 r.
And it is quik and semeth dede,   6
For it is God in fourme of brede;
    Ete ye it so ye be not ded.

This blessed brede is aungelles foode,
Mannes also, perfecte and goode;   10
Therfore ete ye it with myelde moode;
    Ete ye it so ye be not dede.

This brede fro heven did descende,
Us fro alle ille for to defende,
And to geve us lyfe withoute ende;   15
    Ete ye it so ye [be not dede.]

In virgyne Mary this brede was bake
Whenne Criste of her manhoode did take,
Fre of alle synne mankyende to make;
    Ete ye it so ye be [not dede.]   20

l. 16. MS. ete ye it so ye &c.   l. 20. MS. ete ye it so ye be &c.

Ete ye this brede withouten synne;
Eternall blis thanne shall ye wynne;
God graunte us grace to dwell therin!
    Ete ye it so ye be not dede.

66

Balliol College, Oxford. MS. 354.   XVI *cent.*
f. 228 v.

    A blessid byrd, as I you say,
    That dyed and rose on Good Fryday.

On Cristes day, I understond,
An ere of whet of a mayd spronge,
[Thirti] wynter in erth to stond,
    To make us bred all to his pay.

This corn was repyn and layd to grownd,   5
Full sore beten and faste bownd
Unto a piler with cordes rownd;
    At his fyngers endes the blod ran owt that day.

This corn was repyn with gret envye
Upon the mownt of Caluary;   10
Tokyn he shewed on Shere Thursday:
    Mawndy he gaff to his dissiples ther.

Jhesu upon his body the crosse bare;
Water and blode cam from hym ther:
This corn was skorged all in f[e]re   15
    Tyll it wexed blode rede.

A crown of thorn set on his hede,
And he was done on the rode
And betyn till his body was blody rede;
    Thus they bett Jhesu, owr det to pay.   20

          MS. marks burden: fote.

67A

Balliol College, Oxford. MS. 354.   XVI *cent.*
f. 165 v.

Lully, lulley; lully, lulley;
The fawcon hath born my mak away.

He bare hym up, he bare hym down;
He bare hym into an orchard brown.

In that orchard ther was an hall,
That was hangid with purpill and pall.

And in that hall ther was a bede;   5
Hit was hangid with gold so rede.

And yn that bed ther lythe a knyght,
His wowndes bledyng day and nyght.

By that bedes side ther kneleth a may,
And she wepeth both nyght and day.   10

And by that beddes side ther stondith a ston,
'Corpus Christi' wretyn theron.

67B

Traditional version, North Staffordshire.   XIX *cent.*
[No burden]

Over yonder's a park, which is newly begun,
    All bells in Paradise I heard them a-ring;
Which is silver on the outside, and gold within,
    And I love sweet Jesus above all things.

And in that park there stands a hall,
Which is covered all over with purple and pall.

67A. The burden is written again in full after stza. 1. The other repetitions of the
burden are indicated as follows: stzas. 2–5: lully lulley. stza. 6: lully lulley &c.

And in that hall there stands a bed,   5
Which is hung all round with silk curtains so red.

And in that bed there lies a knight,
Whose wounds they do bleed by day and by night.

At that bed side there lies a stone,
Which is our blessed Virgin Mary then kneeling on.   10

At that bed's foot there lies a hound,
Which is licking the blood as it daily runs down.

At that bed's head there grows a thorn,
Which was never so blossomed since Christ was born.

67C

Traditional version, Derbyshire.   XIX *cent.*
[No burden]

Down in yon forest there stands a hall,
    The bells of Paradise I heard them ring,
It's covered all over with purple and pall,
    And I love my Lord Jesus above anything.

In that hall there stands a bed,
It's covered all over with scarlet so red.

At the bed-side there lies a stone,   5
Which the sweet Virgin Mary knelt upon.

Under that bed there runs a flood,
The one half runs water, the other runs blood.

At the bed's foot there grows a thorn,
Which ever blows blossom since he was born.   10

Over that bed the moon shines bright,
Denoting our Saviour was born this night.

67D

Traditional version, Scotland. XIX *cent.*
[No burden]

The heron flew east, the heron flew west,
The heron flew to the fair forest;
She flew o'er streams and meadows green,
And a' to see what could be seen:
And when she saw the faithful pair,   5
Her breast grew sick, her head grew sair;
For there she saw a lovely bower,
Was a' clad o'er wi' lilly-flower;
And in the bower there was a bed
With silken sheets, and weel down spread: 10
And in the bed there lay a knight,
Whose wounds did bleed both day and night;
And by the bed there stood a stane,
And there was set a leal maiden,
With silver needle and silken thread,   15
Stemming the wounds when they did bleed.

68

National Library of Wales. MS. Porkington 10. XV *cent.*
f. 198 r.

Mery hyt ys in May mornyng,
   Mery wayys for to gone.

And by a chapell as Y came,
Mett Y wyhte Jhesu to chyrcheward gone,
Petur and Pawle, Thomas and Jhon,
   And hys desyplys everychone.

Sente Thomas the bellys gane ryng,   f. 198 v.
And Sent Collas the Mas gane syng: 6
Sente Jhon toke that swete offeryng,
   And by a chapell as Y came.

68. The repetition of the burden is indicated after each stanza by: Mery hyt ys.

Owre Lorde offeryd whate he wollde,
A challes alle off ryche rede gollde,   10
Owre Lady the crowne off hyr mowlde;
  The son owte off hyr bosom schone.

Sent Jorge, that ys Owre Lady knyghte,
He tende the tapyrys fayre and bryte,
To myn yghe a semley syghte,   15
  And by a chapell as Y came.

69

British Museum. MS. Egerton 3307.   XV *cent.*
f. 66 v.

I pray yow all with on thoght,
  Amendith me, and pair me noght.

Holy Wret seth—nothing ys sother—
That no man schuld apeir other;
Seth in God I am thi brother,
  Amendyth me, and payr me noght.

The lore in the gospell ilk man may se: 5
Yf thi brother trespas to the,
Betwen us two snyb thou me;
  Amendyth me, and peyr me noght.

Yf thou se I do amysse,
And no man wot bo[t] thou of this,   10
Mak it noght so il as it ys;
  Amend me, and peyr me noght.

God byddes thou schalt no man defame,
No[r] apeyr no mans name,
Bot, even as thou wold han the same,   15
  Amend me, and peyr me noght.

Apeyr thou no man with thi word,
Nother in ernest ne in bowrd;
Lat thi tong, that is thi sword,
    Amend ever and peyr noght.   20

Now to amend God gyf us grace
Of repentaunce and verre space,
In heven ther to se hys face,
    Qwer we schall mend and peyr noght.

70

British Museum. MS. Sloane 2593.   XV *cent.*
f. 30 r.

Kep thi tunge, thi tunge, thi tunge;
    Thi wykyd tunge werkit me w[o.]

Ther is non gres that growit on ground,
Satenas ne peny-round,
Wersse then is a wykkyd tunge
    That spekit bethe evyl of frynd [and] fo.

Wykkyd tunge makit ofte stryf   5
Betwyxe a good man and his wyf;
Quan he xulde lede a merie lyf,
    Here qwyte sydys waxin ful blo.

Wykkyd tunge makit ofte stauns,
Bethe in Engelond and in Frauns;   10
Many a man wyt spere and launs
    Throw wykkyd tunge to ded is do.

Wykkyd tunge brekit bon,   f. 30 v.
Thow the self have non;
Of his frynd he makit his fon   15
    In every place qw[er] that he go.

Good men that stondyn and syttyn in this halle,
I prey you, bothe on and alle,
That wykkyd tunges fro you falle,
    That ye mowun to hefne go.   20

71

Balliol College, Oxford. MS. 354.   XVI *cent.*
f. 231 r.

    He is wise, so most I goo,
    That can be mery and suffer woo.

Be mery and suffer, as I the vise,
Wherever thow sytt or rise;
Be well ware whom thow dispise;
    Thou shalt kysse who is thy foo.

Beware to whom thou spek thy will,   5
For thy speche may greve the yll;
Here and see, and goo than still;
    But well is he that can do soo.

Many a man holdyth hym so stowght
Whatsoever he thynk, he seyth it owt;   10
But if he loke well abowt,
    His tonge may be his most foo.

'Be mery,' now is all my songe;
The Wise Man tawght both old and yonge:
'Who can suffer and hold his tonge,   15
    He may be mery and nothyng woo.'

Yff any man displese the owght,
Suffer with a mery thowght;
Let care away, and greve the nowght,
    And shake thy lappe, and lat it go.   20

The repetition of the burden is indicated after each stanza by: he is wise &c.

72

Cambridge University Library. MS. Addit. 5943.   XV *cent.*
f. 145 v.

Lord, how scholde I roule me,
Of al men ipreysyd to be?

If Y halde the lowe asyse
And take aray of lytel pryse,
Then men wil say, 'He ys nowght wyse;
    He ys a fow; let hym be.'

And yyf I take the mene astate   5
And wyth non man maky debat,
Than men wil sey, erly and late,
    That I am worth no maner fe.

And yf Y take gryte aray,
Hors and hondes and clothes gay,   10
Than men wel say every day
    That I passe my degre.

Then take thow hede of the oxe;
Go nowght to lowe for the foxe,
Nether to hey tyl thow be wox,   15
    For the kyte that wolde the sle.

Therfor loke that thow be scley:
For no thyng hew thow tow hey,
Last they falle don into thy ey,
    The spones that above the be.   20

ll. 16, 20. the] MS. they.

73

British Museum. MS. Sloane 2593.   XV *cent.*
f. 26 r.

> Man, be wys, and arys,
>   And thynk on lyf that lestenit ay.

Thynk, man, qwerof thou art wrout;
Powre and nakyd thou were heder browt;
Thynk how Cryst thi sowle haght bowt,
    And fond to servyn hym to pay.

Thynk, man, on the dere yeres thre: 5
For hunger deyid gret plente,
Powre and ryche, bond and fre,
    Thei leyn dede in every way.

Thynk, man, on the pestelens tweye:
In every cuntre men gunne deye;   10
Deth left neyther for lowe ne heye,
    But lettyd hem of here pray.

Deth is wonder coveytous:
Quan he comit to a manys hous,
He takit the good man and his spows   15
    And bryngit hem in powre aray.

After cam a wyndes blast
That made many a man agast;
Stefve stepelys thei stodyn fast;
    The weyke fyllyn and blewyn away.   20

Many merveylis God haght sent
Of lytenyng and of thunder-dent;
At the Frere Camys haght it hent,
    At Lynne toun, it is non nay.

l. 19. thei] MS. that.

Lytenyng at Lynne dede gret harm   25
Of tolbothe and of Fryre Carm;   f. 26 v.
Thei stondyn wol cole that stodyn wol warm;
   It made hem a wol sory fray.

Lok, man, how thou ledyst thi lyf,
And how thou spendyst thi wyttes v;   30
Go to cherche, and do the schryf,
   And bryng thi sowle in redy way.

74

St. John's College, Cambridge. MS. S. 54.   XV *cent.*
f. 10 v.

   Nowell.

This word is falce, I dare wyll say,
And man xalt fade as dose hay,
For as a flour it fallys away;
   Tunc non valebit corpore.

Tell me sothe qwoso canne: 5
Qwan he hys dede, qwat has he wan?
Qw[e]re se ye ony rych dede man?
   Revela mihi hodie.

Thou plesyst hym both nyth and day
And knele to serve hym wyll to pay;   10
He may not hym a good word say
   Cum operitur pulvere.

Hys secutoures, withoute lete,
Yow he wyth cuces owersette;
Thei sey he ouyt so mykyll dette   15
   Non postest solvi integre.

Qwan he is closyd in hys grave,
Than is he ther he may not crave;
As he have done, so xall he have:
   Oblitus prave tempore.   20

And therfor, man, or thou hens wende,
Dele thi good with thi honde,
And thynke wyll dede man have no frond;
   Tu miseretis anime.

Lord, yyf us grace so to do here   f. 11 r.
That, qwan we are broth on bere,   26
Ther take oure sole, that thou both dere,
   Pende[n]s alto arbore.

And gyfe us grace so to spende
The god that thou onto us sende   30
That we may sey at oure last end,
   'Laus summo regule.'

75

Bodleian Library. MS. Eng. poet. e. 1.   XV *cent.*
f. 38 v.

      In what estate so ever I be,
      Timor mortis conturbat me.

    As I went in a mery mornyng,
    I hard a byrd bothe wep and syng;
    Thys was the tenowr of her talkyng:
      'Timor [mortis conturbat me.']

    I asked that byrd what sche ment.   5
    'I am a musket bothe fayer and gent;
    For dred of deth I am al schent;
      Timor [mortis conturbat me.]

    'Whan I schal dey, I know no day;
    What countre or place I cannot sey;   10
    Wherfor this song syng I may:
      "Timor [mortis conturbat me."]

74. l. 30. The] MS. Thou.   l. 31. oure] MS. youre.
75. Last line of all stanzas. MS. timor &c.

'Jhesu Cryst, whane he schuld dey,
To hys Fader he gan sey;
"Fader," he seyd, "in Trinyte,   15
    Timor [mortis conturbat me."]

'Al Crysten pepull, behold and se: f. 39 r.
This world is but a vanyte
And replet with necessyte;
    Timor [mortis conturbat me.]   20

'Wak I or sclep, ete or drynke,
Whan I on my last end do thynk,
For grete fer my sowle do shrynke;
    Timor [mortis conturbat me.']

God graunte us grace hym for to serve   25
And be at owr end whan we sterve,
And frome the fynd he us preserve;
    Timor [mortis conturbat me.]

76

British Museum. MS. Sloane 2593.   XV *cent.*
f. 8 r.

    Bewar, sqwyer, yeman, and page,
    For servyse is non erytage.

If thou serve a lord of prys,   f. 8 v.
Be not to boystous in thin servys;
Damne not thin sowle in non wys,
    For servyse is non erytage.

Wynteris wether and wommanys thowt   5
And lordis love schaungit oft;
This is the sothe, if it be sowt,
    For servyse [is non erytage.]

        l. 8. MS. for seruyse &c.

Now thou art gret, tomorwe xal I,
As lordys schaungyn here baly; 10
In thin welthe werk sekyrly,
    For [servyse is non erytage.]

Than serve we God in alle wyse;
He xal us quityn our servyse
And yevyn us yyftes most of pryse, 15
    Hevene to ben our erytage.

77

British Museum. MS. Sloane 2593.   XV *cent.*
f. 7 r.

    God be with trewthe qwer he be;
    I wolde he were in this cuntre.

A man that xuld of trewthe telle,   f. 7 v.
With grete lordys he may not dwelle;
I[n] trewe story, as klerkes telle,
    Trewthe is put in low degre.

In laydyis chaumberes comit he not; 5
Ther dar trewthe settyn non fot;
Thow he wolde he may not
    Comyn among the heye mene.

With men of lawe he haght non spas;
They lovyn trewthe in non plas; 10
Me thinkit they han a rewly grace
    That tre[w]the is put at swych degre.

In Holy Cherche he may not sytte;
Fro man to man they xuln hym flytte;
It rewit me sore in myn wytte; 15
    Of tre[w]the I have gret pete.

76. l. 12. MS. for &c.

Relygius, that xulde be good,
If trewthe cum ther, I holde hym wood;
They xuldyn hym rynde cote and hood
    And make hym bare for to fle.   20

A man that xulde of trewthe aspye,
He must sekyn esylye
In the bosum of Marye,
    For there he is forsothe.

78

Bodleian Library. MS. Eng. poet e. 1.   XV *cent.*
f. 23 v.

    Man, be ware and wyse indede,
    And asay thi frend or thou hast nede.

Under a forest that was so long
    As I me rod with mekyll dred,
I hard a berd syngyng a song:
    'Asay thi frend or thou hast ned.'

I theran stod and hoved styll,   5
    And to a tre I teyd my sted,
And ever the byrd sang ful shyll,
    'Asay thi frend or thou hast ned.'

Me thought it was a wonder noyse;   f. 24 r.
    Alwey ner and ner I yed,   10
And ever she song with loud voys,
    'Asay thi frynd or thou have ned.'

I behyld that byrd full long;
    She bad me do as I the rede;
'Whether that thou do ryght or wrong,   15
    Asay thi frynd or thou have ned.'

The byrd sat upon a tre;
  With fethers gray than was hyr wed;
She seyd, 'And thou wylt do aftur me,
  Asay thi frend or thou have ned.'   20

Of me I trow she was agast;
  She tok hyr flyghth in lenghth and bred,
And thus she sang when she shan[g] last:
  'Asay thi frend or thou have ned.'

Away full fast she gan hyr hyghe;   25
  God graunt us well owr lyves to led,
For thus she sang w[he]n she gan flyghe:
  'Asay thi frynd or thou have ned.'

79

British Museum. MS. Sloane 2593.   XV *cent.*
f. 6 r.

    Synge we alle, and sey we thus:
    'Gramersy myn owyn purs.'

Quan I have in myn purs inow,
I may have bothe hors and plow,
And also fryndis inow,
  Throw the vertu of myn purs.

Quan my purs gynnyght to slak,   5
And ther is nowt in my pak,
They wil seyn, 'Go, farwil, Jak;
  Thou xalt non more drynke with us.'

Thus is al myn good ilorn
And myn purs al to-torn;   10
I may pley me with an horn
  In the stede al of myn purs.

l. 18. hyr] MS. hys.

Farwil, hors, and farwil, cow;
Farwil, carte, and farwil, plow;
As I pleyid me with a bow,   15
    I seyd, 'God! Quat is al this?'

80

British Museum. MS. Harley 7358.   XV *cent.*
f. 8 r.

Wymmen beth bothe goude and truwe:
Wytnesse on Marie.

Wymmen beth bothe goud and schene,
On handes, fet, and face clene;
Wymmen may no beter bene:
    Wytnesse on M[arie.]

Wymmen beth gentel on her tour;   5
A womman bar oure Sauyour;
Of al thys wor[ld] wymman ys flour:
    W[ytnesse on Marie.]

Wyrchyp we wymmanys face
Wer we seth hem on a place,   10
For wymman ys the wyl of grace:
    W[ytnesse on Marie.]

Love a womman with herte truwe;
He nel chongy for no newe;
Wymmen beth of wordes fewe: 15
    W[ytnesse on Marie.]

Wymmen beth goud, withoute lesyng;
Fro sorwe and care hy wol us bryng;
Wymman ys flour of alle thyng:
    W[ytnesse on Marie.]   20

81

Balliol College, Oxford. MS. 354.   XVI *cent.*
f. 250 r.

Of all creatures women be best,
Cuius contrarium verum est.

In every place ye may well see
That women be trewe as tirtyll on tree,
Not lyberall in langage, but ever in secrete,
And gret joye amonge them ys for to be.

The stedfastnes of women will never be don,   5
So jentyll, so curtes they be everychon,
Meke as a lambe, still as a stone;
Croked nor crabbed fynd ye none.

Men be more cumbers a thowsand fold,
And I mervayll how they dare be so bold   10
Agaynst women for to hold,
Seyng them so pascyent, softe, and cold.

For, tell a woman all your cownsayle,
And she can kepe it wonderly well;
She had lever go quyk to hell   15
Than to her neyghbowr she wold it tell.

For by women men be reconsiled;
For by women was never man begiled;
For they be of the condicion of curtes Gryzell;
For they be so meke and mylde.   20

Now say well by women, or elles be still,
For they never displesed man by ther will;
To be angry or wroth they can no skill,
For I dare say they thynk non yll.

MS. marks burden: Fote.
The repetition of the burden is indicated after each stanza by: Cui*u*s.

Trow ye that women list to smater   25
Or agaynst ther husbondes for to clater?
Nay, they had lever fast, bred and water,
Then for to dele in suche a mater.

Thowgh all the paciens in the world were drownd,
And non were lefte here on the grownd,   30
Agayn in a woman it myght be fownd,
Suche vertu in them dothe abownd.

To the tavern they will not goo,
Nor to the ale-hows never the moo,
For, God wot, ther hartes wold be woo   35
To spende ther husbondes money soo.

Yff here were a woman or a mayd
That lyst for to go fresshely arayed,
Or with fyne kyrchers to go displayed,
Ye wold say, 'They be prowde'; it is yll said.   40

82

British Museum. MS. Sloane 2593.   XV *cent.*
f. 24 v.

How, hey! It is non les:
   I dar not seyn quan che seygh[t], 'Pes!'

Yyng men, I warne you everychon:
Elde wywys tak ye non,
For I myself have on at hom;
   I dar not seyn quan che seyght, 'Pes!'

Quan I cum fro the plow at non,   f. 25 r.
In a reven dych myn mete is don;   6
I dar not askyn our dame a spon;
   I dar not [seyn quan che seyght, 'Pes!']

ll. 8, 12. MS. I dar not &c.

If I aske our dame bred,
Che takyt a staf and brekit myn hed   10
And doth me rennyn under the led;
    I dar not [seyn quan che seyght, 'Pes!']

If I aske our dame fleych,
Che brekit myn hed with a dych:
'Boy, thou art not worght a reych!'   15
    I dar [not seyn quan che seyght, 'Pes!']

If I aske our dame chese,
'Boy,' che seyght, al at ese,
'Thou art not worght half a pese.'
    I dar not sey quan che seyght, 'Pes!'   20

83

Balliol College, Oxford. MS. 354.   XVI *cent.*
f. 252 r.

Hay, hay, by this day,
What avayleth it me thowgh I say nay?

I wold fayn be a clarke,
But yet hit is a strange werke;
The byrchyn twygges be so sharpe
Hit makith me have a faynt harte;
    What avaylith it me thowgh I say nay?   5

On Monday in the mornyng whan I shall rise,
At vi of the clok, hyt is the gise,
To go to skole withowt avise,
I had lever go [twenti] myle twyse;
    What avaylith it me thowgh I say nay?   10

My master lokith as he were madde:
'Wher hast thou be, thow sory ladde?'
'Milked dukkes, my moder badde.'
Hit was no mervayle thow I were sadde;
    What vaylith it me thowgh I say nay?   15

82. l. 16. MS. I dar &c.

My master pepered my ars with well good spede;
Hit was worse than fynkyll sede;
He wold not leve till it did blede;
Myche sorow have he for his dede!
   What vayleth it me thowgh I say nay?   20

I wold my master were a watt,
And my boke a wyld catt,
And a brase of grehowndes in his toppe;
I wold be glade for to se that.
   What vayleth it me thowgh I say nay?   25

I wold my master were an hare,
And all his bokes howndes were,
And I myself a joly hontere;
To blow my horn I wold not spare,
For if he were dede I wold not care.   30
   What vaylith me thowgh I say nay?

84

Gonville & Caius College, Cambridge. MS. 383.   XV *cent.*
p. 41

Hos is to hoth at hom,
Ryd out; it wol agon.

Wan ic wente byyonde the see,
Ryche man for te bee,
Never the betur was me;
   Ic hadde lever han ben at om.

Hammard wanne ic gan drawe,   5
Wyth a ryt hongury mawe,
A lytyl god ic was wel fawe;
   My frendus werun my fulle fon.

84. *Before burden* (*apparently the name of the air*): alone y lyue alone.
  The repetition of the burden is indicated after stza. 5 by: wos is to.

A man that nower nel abyde,
But sech contreys wyde,   10
Ofte tene schal him betyde;
   Myche yerne bryngeth lytel hom.

A man that nower nel groute,
But seche contreys aboute,
Of his thrift he is in doute;   15
   God ne schal he gete non.

God, that is in hevene cler,
And his swete modur derre
And hys halwen al yfere
   Yyf us grace wel to don.   20

85

Bodleian Library. MS. Arch. Selden B. 26.   XV *cent.*
f. 19 r.

   The merthe of alle this londe
   Maketh the gode husbonde
      With erynge of his plowe.

   Iblessyd be Cristes sonde,
   That hath us sent in honde   5
      Merthe and joye ynowe.

   The plowe goth mony a gate,
   Bothe erly and eke late,
      In wynter in the clay.

   Aboute barly and whete,   10
   That maketh men to swete,
      God spede the plowe al day!

   Browne, Morel, and gore
   Drawen the plowe ful sore
      Al in the morwenynge.   15

Rewarde hem therfore
With a shefe or more
        Alle in the evenynge.

Whan men bygynne to sowe,
Ful wel here corne they knowe   20
        In the monnthe of May.

Howe ever Janyver blowe,
Whether hye or lowe,
        God spede the plowe allway!

Whan men bygynneth to wede   25
The thystle fro the sede,
        In somer whan they may:

God lete hem wel to spede
And longe gode lyfe to lede,
        All that for plowemen pray.   30

86

Balliol College, Oxford. MS. 354.   XVI *cent.*
f. 206 v.

        Hoow, gossip myne, gossip myn,
        Whan will we go to the wyne?
        Good gossipes [myn.]

I shall you tell a full good sport,
How gossippis gader them on a sort,
Ther seke bodyes to comforte,
        Whan they mete
        In lane or stret,   5
        God gossipis myn.

But I dare not, for ther dissplesauns,
Tell of thes maters half the substance,

But yet sumwhat of ther gouernaunce
   As ferre as I dare,   10
  I will declare,
    Good gossipis myn.

'Good gossip myn, wher have ye be?
Hit is so long sith I you see.
Wher is the best wyne? Tell you me.   15
   Can ye owght tell?'
  'Ye, full well,
    Good gossippis myn.

'I know a drawght of mery-go-down;
The beste it is in all this town;   20
But yet I wolde not for my gown
   My husbond wyste,
  Ye may me triste,
    Good gossippis myn.'

'Call forth owr gossippis by and by,   25
Elynore, Johan, and Margery,
Margret, Alis, and Cecely,
   For thei will cum,
  Both all and som,
    Good gossippis myn-a.   30

'And eche of them will sumwhat bryng,
Gose or pigge or capons wynge,
Pastes of pigynes or sum other thyng,
   For we muste ete
  Sum maner mett,   35
    Good gossippis myn-a.'

'Go beffore by tweyn and tweyn,
Wisely, that ye be not seen,
For I muste home and cum agayn
   To witt, ywis,   40
  Wher my husbond is,
    Good gossippis myn-a.

'A strype or two God myght send me   f. 207 r.
Yf my husbond myght here see me.'
'She that is aferde, lett her flee,'   45
    Quod Alis than,
    'I dred no man,
        Good gossippis myn-a.

'Now be we in the tavern sett;
A drawght of the best lett hym fett,   50
To bryng owr husbondes owt of dett,
    For we will spend
    Till God more send,
        Good gossippis myn-a.'

Eche of them browght forth ther disshe;   55
Sume browght flesshe and sum fisshe;
Quod Margret meke now with a wisshe,
    'I wold Anne were here;
    She wold mak us chere,
        Good gossippis myn-a.   60

'How say ye, gossippis, is this wyn good?'
'That is it,' quod Elynore, 'by the rode!
It chereth the hart and comforteth the blod;
    Such jonkers amonge
    Shall make us leve long,   65
        Good gossippis [myn-a.']

Anne bade, 'Fill a pot of muscadell,
For of all wynes I love it well;
Swet wynes kepe my body in hele;
    Yf I had it nowght,   70
    I shuld tak thowght,
        Good gossippis myn-a.

'How loke ye, gossip, at the bordes end?
Not mery, gossip? God it amend!

All shall be well; els God defend!   75
  Be mery and glad,
  And sit not so sade,
    Good gossip myn-a.'

'Wold God I had don after your counsell,
For my husbond is so fell   80
He betith me lyke the devill of hell,
  And the more I crye,
  The lesse mercy,
    Good gossippis myn-a.'

Alis with a lowde voys spak than;   85
'Evis,' she said, 'littill good he can
That betith or strikith any woman,
  And specially his wyff—
  God geve hym short lyff,
    Good gossippis myn-a.'   90

Margret meke saide, 'So mot I thryve,
I know no man that is alyve
That gevith me ii strokes but he have v!
  I am not afferd,
  Thowgh he have a berde,   95
    Good gossippis myn-a.'

On cast down her shot and went away.
'Gossip,' quod Elynore, 'what dide she pay?
Not but a peny? Loo, therfor I say
  She shall no more   100
  Be of owr lore,
    Good gossippis myn-a.

'Suche gestes we may have ynow,
That will not for ther shot alowe;
With whom com she? Gossip, with you?'   105
  'Nay,' quod Johan,
  'I com aloon,
    Good gossipis myn-a.'

'Now rekyn owr shot, and go we hens.
What? Cummeth to eche of us but iii [pence]? 110
Perde, this is but a small expens
   For suche a sorte,
   And all but sporte,
     Good gossipes myn-a.

'Torn down the stret whan ye cum owt, f. 207 v.
And we wil cumpas rownd abowt.' 116
'Gossip,' quod Anne, 'what nedith that dowt?
   Your husbondes [be] pleased
   Whan ye be eased,
     Good gossippes myn-a. 120

'Whatsoever any man thynk,
We com for nowght but for good drynk;
Now let us go home and wynke,
   For it may be seen
   Wher we have ben, 125
     Good gossippes myn-a.'

This is the thowght that gossippis take:
Ons in the wek mery will they make,
And all small drynkes thei will forsake,
   But wyne of the best 130
   Shall have no rest,
     Good gossippes myn-a.

Sum be at the tavern [thrise] in the weke.
And so be sum every day eke,
Or elles thei will gron and mak them sek, 135
   For thyngis used
   Will not be refused,
     Go[o]d gossippes myn-a.

Who sey yow, women, is it not soo?
Yes, suerly, and that ye wyll know; 140

ll. 139–50, not in MS. are supplied from Bodl. MS. Eng. poet. e. 1, f. 59 v.

And therfore lat us drynk all a-row
 And of owr syngyng
 Mak a good endyng,
  [Good gossippis myn-a.]

Now fyll the cupe, and drynk to me,   145
And than shal we good felows be,
And off thys talkyng leve will we
 And speak then
 Good off women,
  [Good gossippis myn-a.]   150

87

Balliol College, Oxford. MS. 354.   XVI *cent.*
f. 251 v.

  How, butler, how! Bevis a towt!
  Fill the boll, jentill butler and let the cup rowght.

Jentill butler, bell amy,
Fyll the boll by the eye,
That we may drynk by and by;
 With how, butler, how! Bevis a towt!
 Fill the boll, butler, and let the cup rowght.   5

Here is mete for us all,
Both for gret and for small;
I trow we must the butlar call;
 With how, butler, how! Bevis a towt!
 Fill the boll, butler, and lett the cupe rowght.   10

I am so dry I cannot spek;   f. 252 r.
I am nygh choked with my mete;
I trow the butler be aslepe;
 With how, butler, how! Bevis a towght!
 Fill the boll, butler, [and let the cup rowght.]   15

  l. 15. MS. Fill the boll butler &c.

Butler, butler, fill the boll,
Or elles I beshrewe thy noll;
I trow we must the bell toll;
   With how, butler, how! Bevis a towght!
   Fill the boll, [butler, and let the cup rowght.]   20

Iff the butlers name be Water,
I wold he were a galow-claper,
But if he bryng us drynk the rather;
   With how, butler, how! Bevis a towght!
   Fill [the boll, butler, and let the cup rowght.]   25

88

Bodleian Library. MS. Eng. poet. e. 1.   XV *cent.*
f. 41 v.

Bryng us in good ale, and bryng us in good ale;
Fore owr blyssyd Lady sak, bryng us in good ale.

Bryng us in no browne bred, fore that is mad of brane, f. 42 r.
Nore bryng us in no whyt bred, fore therin is no game,
   But bryng us in good ale.

Bryng us in no befe, for ther is many bonys,
But bryng us in good ale, for that goth downe at onys,   5
   And bryng us in good ale.

Bryng us in no bacon, for that is passyng fate,
But bryng us in go[o]d ale, and gyfe us inought of that,
   And bryng us in good ale.

Bryng us in no mutton, for that is often lene,   10
Nor brynge us in no trypys, for thei be syldom clene,
   But bryng us in good ale.

Bryng us in no eggys, for ther ar many schelles,
But bryng us in good ale, and gyfe us noth[y]ng ellys,   15
   And bryng us in good ale.

      l. 20. MS. Fill the boll &c.   l. 25. MS. Fill &c.

Bryng us in no butter, for therin ar many herys,
Nor bryng us in no pygges flesch, for that wyl mak us borys,
  But bryng us in good ale.

Bryng us in no podynges, for therin is al Godes good,
Nor bryng us in no veneson, for that is not for owr blod,   20
  But bryng us in good ale.

Bryng us in no capons flesch, for that is often der,
Nor bryng us in no dokes flesch, for thei slober in the mer,
  But bryng us in good ale.

89

Bodleian Library. MS. Eng. poet. e. 1.   XV *cent.*
f. 52 r.

    Doll thi ale, doll; doll thi ale, dole;
    Ale mak many a mane to have a doty poll.

Ale mak many a mane to styk at a brere,
Ale mak many a mane to ly in the myere,
And ale mak many a mane to slep by the fyere;
  With doll.

Ale mak many a mane to stombyl at a stone,   5
Ale mak many a mane to go dronken home,
And ale mak many a mane to brek hys tone;
  With doll.

Ale mak many a mane to draw hys knyfe,
Ale mak many a mane to mak gret stryfe,   10
And ale mak many a mane to bet hys wyf;
  With dole.

Ale mak many a mane to wet hys chekes,
Ale mak many a mane to ly in the stretes,
And ale mak many a mane to wet hys shetes;   15
  With dole.

Ale mak many a mane to stombyll at the blokkes,
Ale mak many a mane to mak his hed have knokkes,
And ale mak many a mane to syt in the stokkes;
    With dol.   20

Ale mak many a mane to ryne over the falows,   f. 52 v.
Ale mak many a mane to swere by God and Al-Halows,
And ale mak many a mane to hang upon the galows;
    With dol.

90

Bodleian Library. MS. Arch. Selden B. 26.   XV *cent.*
f. 17 v.

    Deo gracias Anglia
    Redde pro victoria.

    Owre kynge went forth to Normandy
    With grace and myght of chyvalry;
    Ther God for hym wrought mervelusly;
    Wherfore Englonde may calle and cry,
      'Deo gracias.'   5

    He sette a sege, the sothe for to say,   f. 18 r.
    To Harflu toune with ryal aray;
    That toune he wan and made a fray
    That Fraunce shal rywe tyl domesday;
      Deo gracias.   10

    Than went oure kynge with alle his oste
    Thorwe Fraunce, for alle the Frenshe boste;
    He spared no drede of lest ne moste
    Tyl he come to Agincourt coste;
      Deo gracias.   15

    Than, forsoth, that knyght comely,
    In Agincourt feld he faught manly;

The burden is again written in full after stza. 1 and marked: chorus.

Thorw grace of God most myghty
He had bothe the felde and the victory;
   Deo gracias.   20

There dukys and erlys, lorde and barone
Were take and slayne, and that wel sone,
And summe were ladde into Lundone
With joye and merthe and grete renone;
   Deo gracias.   25

Now gracious God he save oure kynge,
His peple, and alle his wel-wyllynge;
Yef hym gode lyfe and gode endynge,
That we with merth mowe savely synge,
   'Deo gracias.'   30

91

British Museum. MS. Addit. 31042.   XV *cent.*
f. 110 v.

The Rose es the fayreste flour of alle
That evermore wasse or evermore schall,
   The Rose of Ryse;
  Off alle thies flourres the Rose berys pryce.

The Rose it es the fairest flour;
The Rose es swetteste of odoure;
The Rose, in care it es comforthetour;
The Rose, in seknes it es salvoure,
   The Rose so bryghte;   5
  In medcyns it es moste of myghte.

Witnesse thies clerkes that bene wysse:
The Rose es the flour moste holdyn in prysse;
Therfore me thynke the Flour-de-Lyse
Scholde wirchipe the Rose of Ryse   10
   And bene his thralle,
  And so scholde other floures alle.

     MS. heading: A Carolle for Crystynmesse.

Many a knyghte with spere and launce
Folowede that Rose to his plesance;
When the Rose bytyde a chaunce,   15
Than fadide alle the floures of Fraunce
        And chaungyd hewe
    In plesance of the Rose so trewe.

92

British Museum. MS. Harley 2253.   XIV *cent.*
f. 72 v.

        Blow, northerne wynd,
            Sent thou me my suetyng;
        Blow, northerne wynd,
            Blou, blou, blou!

    Ichot a burde in boure bryht
    That fully semly is on syht,
    Menskful maiden of myht,
        Feir ant fre to fonde;
    In al this wurhliche won   5
    A burde of blod and of bon
    Neuer yete Y nuste non
        Lussomore in londe.

    With lokkes lefliche and longe,
    With frount and face feir to fonde,   10
    With murthes monie more heo monge,
        That brid so breme in boure,
    With lossom eye, grete ant gode,
    With browen blysfol under hode,
    He that reste him on the rode   15
        That leflich lyf honoure!

    Hire lure lumes liht
    Ase a launterne a-nyht,
    Hire bleo blykyeth so bryht,
        So feyr heo is ant fyn;   20

The repetition of the burden is indicated as follows: stza. 1: blow &c. stza. 2:
Blou &c.

A suetly suyre heo hath to holde,
With armes, shuldre, ase mon wolde,
Ant fyngres feyre for te folde;
   God wolde hue were myn!

Middel heo hath menskful smal,   25
Hire loveliche chere as cristal,
Theghes, legges, fet, and al
   Ywraht wes of the beste;
A lussum ledy lasteles
That sweting is and euer wes;   30
A betere burde never nes
   Yheryed with the heste.

Heo is dereworthe in day,
Graciouse, stout, ant gay,
Gentil, jolyf so the jay   35
   Worhliche when heo waketh,
Maiden murgest of mouth;
Bi est, bi west, by north, and south,
Ther nis fi[th]ele ne crouth
   That such murthes maketh.   40

Heo is coral of godnesse;
Heo is rubie of ryhtfulnesse;
Heo is cristal of clannesse
   Ant baner of bealte;
Heo is lilie of largesse;   45
Heo is paruenke of prouesse;
Heo is salsecle of suetnesse
   Ant ledy of lealte.

To Love, that leflich is in londe,
Y tolde him, as ych understonde,   50
Hou this hende hath hent in honde
   On huerte that myn wes,
Ant hire knyhtes me han so soht,
Sykyng, Sorewyng, and Thoht,
Tho thre me han in bale broht   55
   Ayeyn the poer of Pees.

To Love Y putte pleyntes mo: f. 73 r.
Hou Sykyng me hath siwed so
Ant eke Thoht me thrat to slo
   With maistry, yef he myhte,   60
Ant Serewe sore in balful bende,
That he wolde for this hende
Me lede to my lyves ende,
   Unlahfulliche in lyhte.

Hire Love me lustnede uch word   65
Ant beh him to me over bord
Ant bed me hente that hord
   Of myne huerte hele:
'Ant bisecheth that swete ant swote,
Er then thou falle as fen of fote,   70
That heo with the wolle of bote
   Dereworthliche dele.'

For hire love Y carke ant care;
For hire love Y droupne ant dare;
For hire love my blisse is bare,   75
   Ant al ich waxe won;
For hire love in slep Y slake;
For hire love al nyht ich wake;
For hire love mournyng Y make
   More then eny mon.   80

93

British Museum. MS. Addit. 31922.   By King Henry VIII, XVI *cent.*
f. 37 v.

Grene growith the holy,
So doth the ive,
Thow wynter blastys blow never so hye,
Grene growth the holy.

MS. heading: The. kyng. H. viii.
The burden is written three times, once for each voice.
The repetition of the burden is indicated as follows: stza. 1: grene growth. &c.
stzas. 2–4 vt supra.

As the holy grouth grene   f. 38 r.
   And never chaungyth hew,
So I am, ever hath bene,
   Unto my lady trew.

A[s] the holy grouth grene   5
   With ive all alone
When flowerys cannot be sene,
   And grenewode levys be gone.

Now unto my lady
   Promyse to her I make,   10
Frome all other only
   To her I me betake.

Adew, myne owne lady,
   Adew, my specyall,
Who hath my hart trewly,   15
   Be suere, and ever shall.

94

Lincoln's Inn. MS. Hale 135.   XIV *cent.*
f. 135 v.

   [Nou] spri[nke]s the sprai,
  Al for love icche am so seek
    That slepen I ne mai.

Als I me rode this endre dai
   O mi [pleyinge,]
S[ei]h I hwar a litel mai
   Bigan to singge:
   'The clot him clingge!   5
   Wai es him i lovve-l[on]gi[n]ge
   Sal libben ai.'

The repetition of the burden is indicated as follows: stza. 1: Nou sprinkes &c.
stza. 2: Nou sprinkes the sprai &c. stza. 3: Now s[p]ri[n]k . . . (*The line is partly
concealed by the binding.*)
l. 1. MS. this endre dai als i me rode.   l. 5. clingge] MS. clingges.

Son icche herde that mirie note,
  Thider I drogh;
I fonde hire [in] an herber swot   10
  Under a bogh
  With joie inogh.
Son I asked, 'Thou mirie mai,
  Hwi sinkes tou ai?'

Than answerde that maiden swote   15
  Midde wordes fewe:
'Mi lemman me haves bihot
  Of lovve trewe.
  He chaunges anewe;
Yiif I mai, it shal him rewe   20
  Bi this dai.'

95

Gonville & Caius College, Cambridge. MS. 383.   XV *cent.*
p. 41

    Rybbe ne rele ne spynne yc ne may
    For joyghe that it ys holyday.

Al this day ic han sou[ght;]
Spyndul ne werve ne vond Y nought;
  To myche blisse ic am brout
    Ayen this hyghe [ho]lyda[y].

Al unswope ys owre vlech,   5
And owre fyre ys unbech;
  Oure ruschen ben unrepe yech
    Ayen this hy halyday.

Yc moste feschun worton in;
Predele my kerchef undur my khyn;   10
  Leve Jakke, lend me a pyn
    To predele me this holiday.

94. l. 20 Yiif] MS. thiif.
95. The repetition of the burden is indicated as follows: stza. 1: Rybbe &c.
stzas. 2–10: R.

Now yt draweth to the none,
And al my cherrus ben undone;
Y moste a lyte solas mye schone   15
   To make hem dowge this holiday.

Y moste mylkyn in this payl;
Outh me bred al this schayl;
Yut is the dow undur my nayl
   As ic knad this holyday.   20

Jakke wol brynge me onward in my wey,
Wyth me desyre for te pleyghe;
Of my dame stant me non eyghe
   An never a god haliday.

Jacke wol pay for my scoth   25
A Sonday atte the ale-schoch;
Jacke wol sowse wel my wroch
   Every god halida[y.]

Sone he wolle take me be the hond,
And he wolle legge me on the lond,   30
That al my buttockus ben of son[d,]
   Opon this hye holyday.

In he pult, and out he drow,
And ever yc lay on hym y-low:
'By Godus deth, thou dest me wow   35
   Upon this hey holyday!'

Sone my wombe began te swelle
A[s] greth as a belle;
Durst Y nat my dame telle
   Wat me betydde this holiday.   40

l. 30. me] MS. me*n*.   l. 39. Durst] MS. drurst.

96

Gonville & Caius College, Cambridge. MS. 383.   XV *cen* .
p. 41

Alas, ales, the wyle!
Thout Y on no gyle,
  So have Y god chaunce.
Ala[s,] ales, the wyle
  That ever Y cowde daunce!

Ladd Y the daunce a Myssomur Day;
Y made smale trippus, soth for to say.
Jak, oure haly-watur cle[r]k com be the way,
And he lokede me upon; he thout that he was gay.
  Thout yc on ne gyle.   5

Jak, oure haly-watur clerk, the yonge strippelyng,
For the chesoun of me he com to the ryng,
And he trippede on my to and made a twynkelyng;
Ever he cam ner; he sparet for no thynge.
  Thout Y on [no gyle.]   10

Jak, ic wot, preyede in my fayre face;
He thout me ful werly, so have Y god grace;
As we turndun owre daunc[e] in a narw place,
Jak bed me the mouth; a cussynge ther was.
  Thout Y on no g[yle.]   15

Jak tho began to rowne in myn ere:
'Loke that thou be privey, and graunte that thou the bere;
A peyre wyth glovus ic ha to thyn were.'
'Gramercy, Jacke!' that was myn answere.
  Thoute yc [on no gyle.]   20

Only the last two lines of the burden are written at the head of the piece in the
MS.: Allas alas the wyle that euer y coude daunce. The entire burden is written
after stza. 1.

Sone aftur evensong Jak me mette:
'Com hom aftur thy glovus that yc the byhette.'
Wan ic to his chambre com, doun he me sette;
From hym mytte Y nat go wan [we] were mette.
    Thout Y [on no gyle.]   25

Schetus and chalonus, ic wot, a were yspredde;
Forsothe tho Jak and yc wenten to bedde;
He prikede, and he pransede; nolde he never lynne;
Yt was the murgust nyt that ever Y cam ynne.
    Thout Y [on no gyle.]   30

Wan Jak had donn, tho he rong the bell;
Al nyght ther he made me to dwelle;
Y trewe we haddun yserved the reaggeth devel of helle;
Of othur smale burdus kep Y nout to telle.
    Thout Y [on no gyle.]   35

The other day at prime Y com hom, as ic wene;
Meth Y my dame, coppud and kene:
'Sey, thou stronge strumpeth, ware hastu bene?
Thy trippyng and thy dauncyng, wel it wol be sene.'
    Thout Y [on no gyle.]   40

Ever bi on and by on my damme reched me clot;
Ever Y ber it privey wyle that Y mouth,
Tyl my gurdul aros, my wombe wax out:
Evel yspunne yern ever it wole out.
    Thout Y on no gyle.   45

l. 33. Y] MS. of y.

97

Gonville & Caius College, Cambridge. MS. 383.   XV *cent.*
p. 210

Were it undo that is ydo,
    I wold be war.

Y lovede a child of this cuntre,
And so Y wende he had do me;
Now myself the sothe Y see,
    That he is far.

He seyde to me he wolde be trewe   5
And chaunge me for none othur newe;
Now Y sykke and am pale of hewe,
    For he is far.

He seide his sawus he wold fulfulle;
Therfore Y lat him have al his wille;   10
Now Y sykke and mourne stille,
    For he is fare.

98

British Museum. MS. Sloane 2593.   XV *cent.*
f. 34 r.

'Kyrie, so kyrie,'
Jankyn syngyt merie,
    With 'aleyson.'

As I went on Yol Day in owre prosessyon,
Knew I joly Jankyn be his mery ton.
[Kyrieleyson.]

97. The repetition of the burden is indicated as follows: stza. 1: were it undo
that is ido &c. stzas. 2, 3: were it undo &c.
   The air is indicated by the following line written before the burden: bryd on brere y tell
yt to none oth*u*r y ne dar. *After stza. 1 is written and deleted*: brid on the brere &c.

Jankyn began the Offys on the Yol Day,   f. 34 v.
And yyt me thynkyt it dos me good, so merie gan he say,
   'Kyrieleyson.'   6

Jankyn red the Pystyl ful fayre and ful wel,
And yyt me thinkyt it dos me good, as evere have I sel.
   [Kyrieleyson.]

Jankyn at the Sanctus crakit a merie note,   10
And yyt me thinkyt it dos me good: I payid for his cote.
   [Kyrieleyson.]

Jankyn crakit notes, an hunderid on a knot,
And yyt he hakkyt hem smallere than wortes to the pot.
   K[yrieleyson.]   15

Jankyn at the Angnus beryt the pax-brede;
He twynkelid, but sayd nowt, and on myn fot he trede.
   [Kyrieleyson.]

Benedicamus Domino: Cryst fro schame me schylde;
Deo gracias therto: alas, I go with chylde!   20
   K[yrieleyson.]

99

Gonville & Caius College, Cambridge. MS. 383.   XV *cent.*
p. 68.

      Care away, away, away,
        Murnynge away!
      Y am forsake, another ys take;
        No more murne yc may.

    I am sory for her sake;
      Yc may wel ete and drynke;
    Wanne yc sclepe yc may not wake,
      So muche on here yc thenke.

I am brout in suche a bale   5
  And brout in suche a pyne,
Wanne yc ryse up of my bed,
  Me liste wel to dyne.

I am brout in suche a pyne,
  Ybrout in suche a bale,   10
Wanne yc have rythe god wyne,
  Me liste drynke non ale.

100

Huntington Library. Christmas carolles newely Inprynted (Richard Kele).   *c.* 1550.
p. [20]

My harte of golde as true as stele,
  As I me lened to a bough,
In fayth, but yf ye love me well,
  Lorde, so Robyn lough!

My lady went to Caunterbury,
  The Saynt to be her bothe;
She met with Cate of Malmesbery;   p. [21]
  Why wepyst thou in an apple rote?

Nyne myle to Mychelmas,   5
  Our dame began to brew;
Mychell set his mare to gras;
  Lorde, so fast it snew!

For you, love, I brake my glasse;
  Your gowne is furred with blew;   10
The devyll is dede, for there I was;
  Iwys, it is full trew.

And yf ye slepe, the cocke wyll crow;
  True hart, thynke what I say;
Jacke Napes wyll make a mow,   15
  Loke who dare say hym nay.

The repetition of the burden is indicated as follows: stzas. 1, 3–8: My hart. &c.
stza. 2: My harte. &c.   burden, l. 3. me] Orig. my.
  l. 4. wepyst] Orig. shepyst.

I pray you, have me now in mynde;
   I tell you of the mater:
He blew his horne agaynst the wynde;
   The crow gothe to the water.   20

Yet I tell you mekyll more: p. [22]
   The cat lyeth in the cradell;
I pray you, kepe true hart in store,
   A peny for a ladell.

I swere by Saynt Katheryn of Kent,   25
   The gose gothe to the grene;
All our dogges tayle is brent;
   It is not as I wene.

'Tyrlery lorpyn,' the laverocke songe;
   So meryly pypes the sparow;   30
The cow brake lose; the rope ran home;
   Syr, God gyve yow good morow.

NOTES ON MANUSCRIPTS AND PRINTED SOURCES CONTAINING CAROLS IN THIS SELECTION

A. MANUSCRIPTS

LONDON: BRITISH MUSEUM

Cotton Titus A. xxvi. XVI, XVII cents., A miscellany.

No. 86 (variant) in the same hand as religious poetry, including Lydgate's *Fifteen Joys of Our Lady*, preceding, and *Ypotis*, following.

The MS. is apparently from Chester or its neighbourhood (see Notes on No. 86). A draft of a letter from a schoolboy to his parents on ff. 179 r., 180 r. gives the names of John and James stryttell [Strethull] of Mobberly, near Knutsford, Cheshire. There was a manor called Strethull, and a family of the name is recorded from Mobberly in the seventeenth and eighteenth centuries (George Ormerod, *The History of the County Palatine and City of Chester*, 2nd ed., rev. Thomas Helsly, London, 1882, i. 418, 468). On f. 144 is a note of ownership in the name of Richard Redhood, and on f. 266 r. another in the names of Sir Christopher Septvans alias Harflete, Thomas Septvans alias Harflete, and their father, rector of Wingham and Ash in Kent, and there are statutes of ordination of the secular college of Wingham.

Egerton 3307. *c.* 1450. Portions of the Mass and processional music, chiefly for Holy Week; the processional hymn *Salve festa dies* with a strophe to St. George, a motet in honour of St. Dunstan; a Goliardic drinking song found also in *Carmina Burana*, English carols and Latin *cantilenae*, all with polyphonic musical settings by anonymous composers. The liturgical part of the MS. is completely divided from the carols and *cantilenae*. This very important MS. has a close relationship to Bodl. Library MS. Arch. Selden B. 26, with which it has six correspondences too close for much intermediate transmission; there are also correspondences with several other carol MSS.

Nos. 9, 15, 20, 23, 30, 31, 36, 49, 50, 59, 62, 69, all in one hand which has also written the Latin *cantilenae* and which differs from the other three hands which have written the liturgical pieces.

The provenance of the MS. has been much discussed. The immediate provenance was not revealed by the dealer who sold it to the British Museum. Schofield's attribution to the college of St. George's, Windsor (not the Chapel Royal of the King's household, but both were languishing under Henry VI) is open to many serious objections. The present editor has presented at some length the case for Meaux Abbey (Cistercian), near Beverley, Yorks., a house of luxury and culture. This was accepted by Bukofzer. Stevens expresses doubt, but offers no alternative beyond Windsor. Frank Ll. Harrison rejects the suggestion of Meaux 'for liturgical reasons', holding that the service-pieces of the Sarum rite would not have been permitted in a Cistercian monastery where 'the uniformity of its texts and music was rigorously imposed'. But Meaux cheerfully ignored other Cistercian regulations against luxury, the presence of women, and church decoration. (For the practice of Fountains and other Cistercian houses see H. K. Andrews and Thurston Dart, 'Fourteenth-Century Polyphony in a Fountains Abbey MS Book', *Music and Letters*, xxxix (1958), 2–3, and Denis Stevens, 'The Second Fountains Fragment: A Postscript', ibid., p. 153.) Harrison's statement that 'the presence of carols suggests that the collection was written for a collegiate church or household chapel' is surprising in view of the definitely monastic origin of many MSS. containing carols.

The English carols show a predominantly East Midland dialect with a few definitely northern forms, corresponding closely to the language of preserved contemporary documents from Beverley and vicinity. Two crosses patonce and the 'words' 'Mieulx en de cy' and 'En de cy mieulx' must be regarded as marks of ownership. Though the motto has not been located elsewhere, puns in such use were ubiquitous, and 'Meaux' was pronounced, then as now, like 'mieulx'. The coat of arms of Meaux included a cross patonce, and a cross of this form was rarely used in marginal notations for performance or other directions. Correspondences with Bodl. MS. Eng. poet. e. 1, probably from Beverley, and with Nat. Lib. Scot. MS. Advocates 19. 3. 1 from Bardney Abbey, Lincolnshire, are of possible significance.

For full descriptions of the MS. and discussions of provenance see Bertram Schofield, 'A Newly Discovered 15th-Century Manuscript of the Chapel Royal—Part I', *Musical Quarterly*, xxxii (1946), 509–36; Manfred F. '[idem]—Part II', ibid. xxxiii (1947), 38–51, and *Studies in Medieval and Renaissance Music* (N.Y. 1950), pp. 113–75; Richard L. Greene, 'Two Medieval Musical Manuscripts: Egerton 3307 and Some University of Chicago Fragments', *J.A.M.S.*, vii (1954), 1–34; Stevens, p. 125; Frank Ll. Harrison, *Music in Medieval Britain* (London, 1958), p. 275 and *passim*.

Harley 275. XV cent. A religious miscellany.
No. 9 (variant) in a hand different from all others in the MS.

Apparently the volume is from Essex. A letter on f. 148 v., dated 1451, from Thomas Kemp, Bishop of London, to Sir Thomas Davell (Davall) concerns the marriage of William Stratton and Johanna Clerk in the parish church of Dunmow.

Harley 2253. XIV cent. (first half). A highly important collection of English and French prose and poetry.
No. 92 in the same hand as all the other English poetry.
From Herefordshire, probably written at Leominster Priory, cell of St. Mary's Abbey, Reading (Benedictine). For fuller description see G. L. Brook, *The Harley Lyrics* (Manchester, 1948).

Harley 4294. XV (second half), XVI (first half) cents. An English translation of the *Dialogues of Sydrac and Boctus*, didactic verses signed Ricardus Spery, two medical recipes, and two carols.
Nos. 21 (variant), 81, in the one of the two hands in the MS. (XVI cent., early) which has written the other verses.
Accounts on f. 82 r. connect the MS. with Bromley, apparently Bromley in Kent, as going to London is casually recorded.

Harley 5396. XII, XV cents. Three MSS. bound in one. Latin sermons collected by J. Felton, vicar of Oxford, and a miscellany of English poetry.
No. 34A in the same hand as all the other English poetry and the accounts. *E.E.C.* No. 36 b is signed in another hand: 'Wylyam northe of yorke'.
The volume is from the Midlands. A merchant's accounts name, among other places, Woolaston, Weston, and Henbury (Glos.), Coventry, London, Northampton, Barton (county not indicated), Kingsthorp (Northants.), and Uppingham (Rutl.). On f. 285 r. in a different hand is a statement of ownership by Richard Taylour.

Harley 7358. XV cent. (first half). A theological miscellany.
Nos. 43 (variant), in the hand of the whole MS.
From East Lulworth, Dorset (not East Walworth as given in *E.E.C.*, p. 328), a small village on the coast six miles west of Corfe Castle. The MS. contains the form of a will dated from there in 1374. The colophon gives the name of the scribe as 'Sperhauckus de est lolleworth', i.e. John Sperhauck, rector of 'Chaluedonharyng', i.e. Chaldon Herring or East Chaldon, near East Lulworth (*Papal Letters*, ix, 5, under date of 1438). The MS. may have been derived from material in Bindon Abbey (Cistercian), from the ruins of which Lulworth Castle was later built by the Howards, Earls of Suffolk. On f. 10 v. is 'Edwardus Willem willem'.

Latin liturgical notes relating to the Virgin and St. Thomas of Canterbury have been defaced.

Royal 17. B. XLIII. XV cent. Mandeville's *Travels,* the romance *Sir Gowghter, St. Patrick's Purgatory, The Vision of Tundale.*
No. 58 in a hand of about 1500, different from the three other hands in the MS., which has also written some scribbles, among them the unhelpful name 'Johan'.
There is no evidence of provenance.

Royal Appendix 58. XVI cent. (first quarter). English part-songs with musical settings by Cornysh, Parker, Cooper, Drake, and anonymous composers.
No. 42 (variant) in one of several hands which has written some other songs as well.
The MS. may be assumed to have been produced in London.

Sloane 2593. XV cent. (first half). English and Latin carols and songs and two English ballads. One of the best-known and most important of all carol MSS. It is defective at the beginning, at least 47 leaves having been lost. There is no music.
Nos. 2 (variant), 3 (variant), 10, 24, 29, 40, 44 (variant), 47 (variant), 48 (variant), 54, 63, 70, 73, 76, 77, 79, 80 (variant), 82, 98, all in the same hand, which has written the entire MS. except for a note, medical recipes, and scribbles in three other hands on ff. 35 v.–37 v.
From Bury St. Edmunds, almost certainly from the great Benedictine monastery there. It contains the only preserved English carol in honour of St. Edmund (No. 63, on which see Notes). It also offers the only two known English carols in honour of St. Nicholas (No. 64 and *E.E.C.,* No. 315), and the boy-bishop who was rewarded at Bury, e.g. in 1418, 1429, and 1537, was there known as 'the bishop of St. Nicholas' (*Reports of the Historical Manuscripts Commission,* XIV, appendix, part viii, pp. 124–5, 'Seven Sacrist rolls of the abbey'). The whole MS. is written in a specifically East Anglian form of language. The memorandum on f. 36 v. reads: 'Johannes bardel debet istum librum the qweche bardel is of . . . dwellyd . . . In In'. The omissions are tantalizing, but Bardel (Bradel, Bardwell) is a Suffolk name found in and near Bury and infrequent elsewhere. Bardwell is a parish near Ixworth. The name is borne by one of the 'knights of St. Edmund' mentioned in the *Chronicle* of Jocelin de Brakelond (ed. H. E. Butler, London, 1949, p. 121). The owner of this MS. may be the same monk of Bury who is one of two named in inscriptions in Bodl. MS. Holkham Misc. 37: f. 197 v. 'Liber dompni Johannis Berdwell [the surname incompletely erased] monachi sancti E.';

f. 198 r. 'Eadmundo sancto pertinet iste liber'. The other monk whose name is in the book is John Wulfspett.

The three Latin songs are the famous 'Meum est propositum in taberna mori', a rondeau, 'Procedenti puero', also found in a manuscript from Tours of about 1148 (Victor Luzarche, ed., *Office de Pâques ou de la Résurrection* [&c.], Tours, 1856, pp. 64–66, and in *Anal. Hym.* xx. 90, No. 93), and a *cantilena*, 'Non pudescit corpore', in praise of St. Thomas of Canterbury, which is undefaced and therefore shows that the MS. did not continue in use in a secular house.

Addit. 31042. XV cent. (middle). A miscellany.

No. 91, in the hand of Robert Thornton, written in two sittings and at a different time from the pieces before and after it. The carol is defective at the end, where two leaves have been torn out, but remains of initials on the stubs show that the carol can have had at most four more stanzas.

Most of the MS. is also in the hand of the famous scribe Robert Thornton, who wrote the 'Thornton MS.', Lincoln Cathedral A. 5. 2. [91]. He was of Ryedale, near Helmsley, Yorks., and the language of the MS. is accordingly northern. See the New Paleographical Society, *Facsimiles of Ancient Manuscripts* (London, 1913–30), 2nd ser. ii, plate 45. A note on f. 49 r. (XV cent. late) reads: 'John Nettleton's boke'. The name is also on f. 139 v. According to M. Y. Offord, 'This is presumably the John Nettleton of Hutton Cranswick in the East Riding of Yorkshire, whose name occurs in a list, thought to have been compiled in about 1565, of owners of medieval manuscripts' *The Parlement of the Thre Ages*, E.E.T.S., Or. Ser., No. 243, 1959, p. xii). Sir Israel Gollancz and Magdalene M. Weale (*The Quatrefoil of Love*, E.E.T.S., Or. Ser., No. 195, 1935, viii) date the hand as XVI cent. (middle). See also Karl Brunner, *Archiv*, cxxxii (1914), 316–27.

Addit. 31922. XVI cent. (first half). Secular part-songs in English and French, and forty-nine instrumental pieces, by various composers.

No. 93, written by the one of the three hands which has written most of the manuscript.

The volume must have been written in or near the royal court. It has apparently been in Kent as well, for a scribble on f. 129 v. reads: 'ser John leed in the parishe of Benynden (Benenden)', probably a priest. Other names are 'vynsent Wydderden', 'Syr John Berde', Davey Jones, and Jane Reve. The Reverend Lambert Larking suggested that the book might have been left on a royal visit to Hempsted, then the seat of Sir Henry Guilford, K.G., Comptroller of the King's Household (William Chappell, 'Some account [&c.]', *Archaeologia*, xli, part ii, 370–86).

A complete musical edition has been prepared by Dr. John Stevens, *Music at the Court of Henry VIII*, Musica Britannica, xviii (London, 1961). See also Stevens, *Music and Poetry at the Early Tudor Court* (London, 1961), pp. 386–7.

Addit. 5665. *c.* 1500. The 'Ritson MS.' English carols, sacred and secular one; French song; Latin masses and motets. Though some of the latter derive from the Sarum Processional, the MS. as a whole is not made up of processional music. All the carols have musical settings in two and three parts. The composers include Sir Thomas Pakke, otherwise unknown, Turges, John Cornysh, Henry Petyre, John Wythe, Richard Smert, and John Trouluffe.

Nos. 7 (variant), 11 (variant), 12 (variant), 21 (variants), 33, 55, 69 (variant), all, like the other English carols, in one hand of the eight represented in the volume.

The MS. appears to be from Devonshire, as several deeds (one dated 17 October 1510) relate to the West Country, and Smert, as pointed out by Stevens, was rector of Plymtree, near Exeter, from 1435 to 1477 (p. 125).

Addit. 14997. XV, XVI (first half) cents. Poems in Welsh by many different bards; charms and medical recipes in Latin and English, a poem in English asking drink, a schoolboy's macaronic end of term song (see Notes on No. 4).

No. 4 in the same hand as the schoolboy's song, the charms and recipes, and some of the Welsh poems. There are several other hands.

The MS. is obviously of Welsh origin and was in Welsh ownership until its presentation to the British Museum in 1844 by the Cymmrodorion Society.

Addit. 40166 (C3). XV cent. A fragment of two leaves, one much decayed, containing an English poem on signs of the Judgement (six days only, instead of the usual fifteen), rules of Latin syntax with English marginalia, and two carols.

No. 27 in the same hand as the other carol (*E.E.C.*, No. 26).

From Hailes Abbey, Gloucestershire (Cistercian); see Notes on No. 27.

LONDON: PUBLIC RECORD OFFICE

Chancery Miscellanea, Bundle 34, File 1, No. 12. *c.* 1400. A fragment of two leaves, stained and faded and partly illegible, containing a Latin poem on the Epiphany, and three English poems, two of them carols.

No. 24 (variant) in the same hand as *E.E.C.*, No. 36c, and a macaronic poem on pride. This hand differs from that of the Latin poem.

There is no indication of provenance. Conceivably the two leaves were removed from a volume because of their containing the carol on St. Thomas of Canterbury.

LONDON: LINCOLN'S INN

Hale 135. XIII (late), XIV (early) cents. The *De Legibus Angliae* of Henry de Bracton.

No. 94 in a hand, different from that of the body of the book, which has written at other times several memoranda dated 1302–5 concerning the swans of Sir Alan de Thorneton, owner of the volume. He was apparently a resident of Lincolnshire. On the verso of the first fly-leaf is a note with the name of Thomas de Verdun, rector of the church of 'Farnlham' [? Farnham, Suffolk]. The carol may be regarded as from Lincolnshire. The volume was later owned by Selden, whose motto is on f. 5 r.

LONDON: WESTMINSTER ABBEY

20. XIV, XV cents. The *Tractatus de Sphaera* of Johannes de Sacro Bosco, an astronomical diagram, a treatise and verses on grammar.

No. 39 (variant) in a hand different from the several hands of the other items.

On f. 38 v. are written the name John Foster, the date 1489, and on a scroll the 'word' or motto 'audaces fortuna iuvat'. On an endpaper is the name Thomas Moyle. There are many John Fosters, and this one has not been identified, nor has the 'word', though popular with many later armigerous families, been found associated with any individual or institution in the fifteenth century. The provenance of the MS. remains unknown.

OXFORD: BODLEIAN LIBRARY

Arch. Selden B. 26 (Summary Catalogue No. 3340). VIII, XV, XVII cents. All the carols are contained in the first of five unrelated MSS. bound together, of XV cent. (middle). A collection of English and Latin songs and carols, all with musical settings in two and three parts.

Nos. 7 (variant), 11, 12, 25 (variant), 50 (variant), 52, 69 (variant), 85, 90. There are ten different hands in the MS. To the list given by F. M. Padelford in *Anglia* xxxvi (1912), 81, should be added a hand [J] which attached an additional stanza to No. 62 on f. 23 r. All the carols in this selection except Nos. 52, 69 (variant), and 85 are in the same hand, Padelford's 'F'; No. 69 (variant) is in hand 'C' and Nos. 52, 85 in hand 'D'.

This very important MS. must be from Worcester. The stanza added to No. 52 is accompanied by a crude drawing of a cock from the same pen. A cock, in the later fifteenth century, was the very widely known and frequently depicted rebus or badge of John Alcock, successively Bishop of Rochester, Worcester, and Ely, joint Lord Chancellor of England, Master of the Rolls, founder of Jesus College, Cambridge, and of the grammar school at Hull. Alcock was notoriously fond of applying his rebus wherever possible, and it is, of course, the principal charge and crest of the arms of Jesus College. It could hardly indicate anyone else. The carelessly written stanza has the Northern spelling to be expected of Alcock, a native of Beverley and educated there. No document in Alcock's own hand, surprisingly, appears to be extant, but there is a specimen of his signature as Bishop of Worcester on a bond dated 22 June 1483 (Public Record Office, Ancient Deeds A 9322). This could be from the same hand as the stanza, but cannot be judged certainly so. The whole MS. of carols is earlier than Alcock's episcopate (1476–86); we may conjecture that it came into his possession and that he added to the carol, probably from memory, another stanza known to him.

The MS. has a very high proportion of carols and Latin songs to the Virgin, and it may well have been connected with the boys' choir of the Chapel of the Blessed Mary in the nave. In 1478 Alcock endowed this chapel with £100 for masses and antiphons and responds for his own soul and those of his parents and benefactors. (Ivor Atkins, *The Early Occupants of the Office of Organist and Master of the Choristers of . . . Worcester*, Worcestershire Historical Society, 1918, pp. 2–8).

The language of the texts is appropriate to Worcester, as is the speed-the-plough carol No. 85, on which see the Notes. Worcester was an abbey where there was much carolling; see Introduction, p. 29.

A specially interesting entry in the Journal of Prior More may indicate that MSS. like this were added to when new and desirable carols were sung by visitors. Among the Christmas expenses for 1518 are 16*d.* 'rewarded to syngars of carralls at cristmas day at ny3th', and, according to two successive entries, 6*s.* 8*d.* 'payd to Richard skryvenar for wrytyng' and 4*d.*, 4*d.*, 2*d.*, 1*d.*, 4*d.*, 2*d.*, 2*d.*, 'rewarded for carralls'. This is a large payment, possibly at overtime rates, to a scribe, who would not usually be working on Christmas Day. We know from other entries that this Richard was capable of writing not only the Journal itself but 'ij queres of a masseboke' for which he was paid 4*s.* He must have written a good deal on this Christmas (ed. Ethel S. Fegan, Worcestershire Historical Society, 1914, pp. 76, 80, 82).

The word 'Childe' written at the top of f. 28 v. in a hand different from that of the carol below (*E.E.C.*, No. 34) has been taken to be that of the composer, and Frank Ll. Harrison has suggested that it may refer to William Child, assistant master at Eton in 1446 to 1449, later a Fellow of New College, Oxford, and rector of West Lydford, Somerset, who died in 1487 (*Music in Medieval Britain*, pp. 420, 456). Since composers' names in general are not given by this MS., it is more probably a note of ownership. The Childe family were important tenants of Worcester Abbey, and in the early sixteenth century Prior William More entrusted much business to Richard Childe and gave him many rewards (Fegan, op. cit., *passim*).

The MS. has a special connexion with BM. MS. Egerton 3307, having six pieces in common with it. The music in some of these is so similar as to rule out the possibility of oral transmission or even many intervening MSS. If Egerton 3307 is correctly assigned to Meaux Abbey or its neighbourhood, Alcock, revisiting Hull and his native Beverley, may have been an agent of the transmission. One carol found in both MSS. (No. 69) is marked in the Selden MS. with the initials J. D. These may refer to the great composer John Dunstable, as the music is in a style used by him, but there is no further evidence. As a canon and prebendary of Hereford Dunstable could easily have had contact with Worcester Abbey.

Ashmole 1379 (Summary Catalogue No. 4666). *c.* 1500. A prose treatise and a poem, in English, on the medicinal properties of rosemary.

No. 45 in a hand later than that of the rest of the MS.

The provenance is not apparent. The hand of the carol has written on p. 3: 'Robertus Hyckys hujus libri possessor. Robert Hyckys ys the ower of thys boke.' A bit of account-roll pasted on the last leaf and dated 1519–20 has the names of John Colcootte and Roger Deyer.

Bodley 26 (Summary Catalogue No. 1871). XIII, XIV cents. Latin religious treatises and sermons, astrological and physiognomical material, the arithmetical treatise of Johannes de Sacro Bosco, in parts of two different MSS. bound together.

No. 6, in Franciscan sermon notes on the locks in the heart of a sinner and their keys, in the same hand.

The provenance is not known, but stanza 3 of the carol is also found in Helmingham Hall MS. LJ. I. 7 from Norfolk.

Douce 302 (Summary Catalogue No. 21876). XV cent. (first half). The poems of John Audelay, imperfect at the beginning and with two later gaps in the text; a religious treatise in prose and the Latin poem *Cur Mundus Militat sub Vana Gloria*.

Nos. 2, 22, 25, 61, all in one of the three hands found in the MS. with corrections by a second.

Audelay was a chaplain resident in the Augustinian monastery of Haghmond, Shropshire.

On f. 35 r. is the following erased note (transcribed by N. R. Ker): 'The owner of thys boke who lyst to demawnd/ Ihon Barkre hyt ys a chanon of Launde [Augustinian priory of St. John Baptist, Launde, Leicestershire]/ gyvyn to hym hyt was, with a gud mynd/ Be on Wyatt a mynstral both curtess and [kynd]'. A second erased note on the same page records ownership by 'Wm Vyott a mynstrall yn Coventre'. This is the only note of ownership by a minstrel in all the carol MSS.—and the minstrel gives the volume to a religious.

For a full description of the MS. see Ella Keats Whiting, ed., *The Poems of John Audelay*, E.E.T.S., Or. Ser., No. 184, 1931, pp. vii–xi.

Eng. poet. e. 1 (Summary Catalogue No. 29734). XV cent. (second half). English and Latin carols and songs, religious and secular, with musical settings for one Latin piece and the burden of one carol. An important carol MS., similar in scope to B.M. Sloane 2593, with which it has eight pieces in common. It also has thirteen pieces in common with Balliol MS. 354, as well as correspondences with several other MSS. and Richard Kele's printed books.

Nos. 3, 8 (variant), 12, (variant), 17, 19, 21, 35, 37, 41 (variant), 44, 47, 48, 51, 53 (and variant), 56, 69 (variant), 75, 78, 81 (variant), 86 (variant), 88, 89, in two different hands.

It is highly probable that this excellent and varied collection of carols comes from Beverley Minster, Yorkshire. A special devotion to St. John the Evangelist is indicated by its being the only MS. to offer two distinct English carols to this saint (No. 21 and *E.E.C.*, No. 104) and by its including the Latin processional hymn, not elsewhere found complete, in honour of St John, 'Psallimus cantantes', marked 'Cantus' and provided with the only full musical setting in the MS. The first strophe of this hymn, followed by English strophes in the same form, is found in Richard Kele's *Christmas carolles newely Inprynted* of about 1550. In the region of the dialect of the MS., East Midland with some northern forms, there was no other religious house of importance dedicated to St. John the Evangelist. The generous selection of convivial poetry, and especially the satire on abbots and monks in the Goliardic 'Bonum vinum cum sapore" accords well with the life of the prosperous and by no means ascetic secular canons of the college at Beverley. No other MS. except Balliol 354 has correspondences with so many of the known carol manuscripts. This indicates a place of much intercourse with other houses, and Beverley in the fifteenth century was a place of great importance, high in the favour of Henry V, on a main route to the north, and eleventh in size among all English cities.

The fact that the carol to St. Thomas of Canterbury in this MS. (*E.E.C.*,

No. 115) and the St. Thomas stanza of No. 3 are defaced indicates that the book was in an institution continuing through the Reformation, such as Beverley Minster, rather than in a monastery. It is worth noting that the carol to St. Thomas in Egerton 3307 (No. 23) is not defaced.

Laud misc. 683 (Summary Catalogue No. 798). XV, XVII cent. Poems by John Lydgate; a seventeenth-century treatise on military musters; a discourse on a national bank by John Yonge, gentleman.

No. 42 (variant) in the hand (XV cent.) that has written the poems by Lydgate.

The only indication of provenance is that in 1633 the book was in Braintree, Essex. On f. 105 r. a fifteenth-century note marks it as 'mastres Coles boke'. Seventeenth-century owners were John Coker, John Yonge, John Stevens, and Archbishop Laud.

OXFORD: BALLIOL COLLEGE

354. XVI cent. (1503–36). The commonplace book of Richard Hill, grocer of London, containing religious and secular English prose and poetry, collectanea of useful information, puzzles, riddles, records of Hill's own family, and a chronicle of past and contemporary public events.

Nos. 5, 8, 13, 16, 17 (variant), 21 (variant), 26, 28, 32, 34B, 38, 41 (variant), 42, 47 (variant), 51 (variant), 53 (variant), 66, 67A, 71, 78 (variant), 81, 83, 86, 87, all in one hand but written at varying times.

For a full description of the MS. see Dyboski, pp. xiii–lix, and E. Flügel, 'Liedersammlungen des XVI. Jahrhunderts', *Anglia*, xxvi (1903), 94–105.

CAMBRIDGE: UNIVERSITY LIBRARY

Ee. 1. 12. XV cent. (1490–1500). English songs and carols and translations of Latin hymns by James Ryman, Franciscan of Canterbury.

Nos. 1, 8 (variant), 14, 18, 60, 65 in two of the three hands in the MS., one possibly Ryman's own.

Ryman's authorship is established by a colophon on f. 80 r.: 'Explicit liber ympnorum et canticorum quem composuit Frater Iacobus Ryman ordinis Minorum ad laudem omnipotentis dei et sanctissime matris eius marie omniumque sanctorum anno domini millesimo ccccmo LXXXXIIo.' The first C and the L in the date have been erased.

The contents of the entire MS. except for ff. 1, 2, 110 are printed by Zupitza, pp. 167–338.

Addit. 5943. XV cent. (first quarter). A miscellany including Latin sermons, Richard Rolle of Hampole's *Emendatio Vitae* and *Melum Contemplativorum*, English, French, and Latin songs, accounts, and memoranda.

No. 72 in one of the several hands which has written nothing else in the MS.

The volume is from Somerset. A Latin note on f. penult. v. records that the book is the property of John — (the surname is thoroughly erased), now (10 December 1418) a Carthusian monk at Henton Priory, Somerset, to whom it has been given by Thomas Turke, formerly perpetual vicar of 'Biere [Beer, Somerset]'. Some of the accounts record receipt, apparently by an archdeacon, of sums from various Somerset vicars, including those of Horton, Staunton, Sheepwick, and Hungerford. Other names written in the MS. are 'hennyngis haroer' and 'wymundus permissione divina'. The MS. was formerly owned by Lord Howard de Walden.

CAMBRIDGE: GONVILLE & CAIUS COLLEGE

383. XV cent. (middle). A trilingual student's exercise and commonplace book containing grammatical, theological, and legal material, with forms of letters in French and Latin. There are many memoranda and much penmanship practice. The carols are written in odd blank spaces in the MS. in the same fashion as other notes and memoranda. Two English carols appear with a carol in French between them (see *E.E.C.*, pp. xxvi–xxvii).

Nos. 24 (variant), 84, 95, 96, 97, 99 in one of the two hands in the MS., probably that of the owner, Wymundus London.

The MS. is from Oxfordshire and very probably the notebook of an Oxford student. Among the places mentioned in memoranda of various kinds are 'Tadmerton a la ostel de Joh. Tayrel' [Tadmarton, Oxon, four miles south-west of Banbury, a manor of Abingdon Abbey]; 'couentre'; 'Lydȝerd Tregoȝ' [Lydiard Tregoze, Wilts.]; 'Hanlee' [Henley]; 'Beckley in com. oxonn.'; 'Wyttely' [Wheatley, Oxon, cited as domicile of Robert 'Walteper', i.e. of Waterperry, Oxon]; 'Myddynhall est bonus puer' [i.e. surname from Mildenhall, near Marlborough, Wilts.]; 'Wynchecomb' [Glos., near Cheltenham]; 'Ooxsenfoord' as domicile of John Ware. It is quite possible that this Wymundus London was the 'London' and 'w London' whose name occurs regularly in the bursary books of Magdalen College, Oxford, in 1484–5. This London was a chorister, promoted demy in 1485, and would be an appropriate person to have noted down secular and quite unacademic songs which obviously refer to the countryside of Oxfordshire (A. B. Emden, *A Bibliographical Register of the University of Oxford to A.D. 1500*, Oxford, 1958, ii. 1158).

A copy of a letter in French on f. 45 reads: 'le porteur de cestes est seneschel de nostre hostiel et est appellee Sir Walter trimenel'.

CAMBRIDGE: ST. JOHN'S COLLEGE

S. 54 (259). XV cent. (second half). A pocket-book of carols in a contemporary wallet-like wrapper; defective at beginning and end, the two outer leaves of the quire having been lost.

Nos. 29 (variant), 39, 57, 74 in the two principal hands of the four in the MS.

The MS. is certainly from East Anglia, but cannot yet be placed more exactly. It has obvious similarities and some correspondences with B.M. Sloane 2593 and Bodl. Eng. poet. e. 1.

On the inside of the wrapper is written: 'puer natus hodie syt we down on owr kne' (a scrap of a carol, cf. *E.E.C.*, No. 35, stanza 5); 'Fuit homo miserens et deus'.

CAMBRIDGE: TRINITY COLLEGE

O. 3. 58. XV cent. (first half). A unique roll of English carols, of vellum, 6 feet 8 inches in length, made of three sections laced together. On the dorse of the roll are faded and barely legible Masses of the use of Sarum: 'Sancta Trenitate', 'De Angelis', 'Corporis Christi', and 'De Sancta Cruce'.

Nos. 8 (variant), 21 (variant), 25 (variant), 46, 52 (variant), 90 (variant), all in one hand.

The MS. by its language is from East Anglia, but there is no external evidence of location.

BRIDGWATER, SOMERSET: TOWN HALL

Bridgwater Corporation Muniments, 123. XV cent. A Latin indenture, dated 8 August 1471, between one Master Maurice, prebendary of the prebendal church of Llangoullo, in the diocese of St. Davids, and Sir Hugh, perpetual vicar of that church , and one Thomas ap Rees ap Davyd of that parish, conveying to the latter two parties the said church for five years at a rent of twenty shillings per annum. Scribbles: 'hay hay w . . .' / 'and a . . .'.

On the dorse are two English carols.

No. 7 in the same hand, different from that of the indenture but of about the same date, as the other carol (*E.E.C.*, No. 362).

EDINBURGH: NATIONAL LIBRARY OF SCOTLAND

Advocates 18. 7. 21. XIV cent. (second half). The alphabetically arranged commonplace book of sermon materials of Johan de Grimestone, a Franciscan friar. Much English verse is interspersed, especially in the section 'De Passione'.

Nos. 43, 44 (variant) in one hand, that of Grimestone himself, who has written the whole volume.

Grimestone's home friary is not known, but the language is that of the northern part of the East Midland region. Grimestone was undoubtedly from this part of the country, but Dr. A. G. Little has pointed out that he was given a licence to preach in the diocese of Bath and Wells, at Dorchester, by Bishop Ralph of Shrewsbury (1329–63). As befitted a friar, he was thus both an active preacher and a traveller (Homer G. Pfander, *The Popular Sermon of the Medieval Friar in England*, N.Y., 1937, p. 5).

On f. 9 v. is: 'Orate pro anima fratris Johannis de Grimistone qui scripsit istum librum cum magna solicitudine Anno domini 1372. Aue maria pro anima sua pro amore dei.'

On f. 67 v. in a hand of XV cent. is a memorandum with the names of Sir Thomas Helder, Cornell, and Sir Wa[l]ter Haukke.

On f. 108 v. is: 'Iste liber constat Wililmo Broin quem deus amat et deabolus odit.'

Advocates 19. 3. 1. XV cent. (second half). A miscellany of religious and secular prose and poetry, including Lydgate's *Life of Our Lady* and *Stans Puer ad Mensam*, *The Trental of St. Gregory*, a prose life of St. Katherine, and the romances *Sir Gowther* and *Sir Ysumbras*.

Nos. 9 (variant), 41, the first in the hand of John Hawghton, who has written most of the volume, including *E.E.C.*, No. 378, the second in another hand which has also written some prognostics of thunder.

The MS. is from Bardney Abbey, Lincolnshire (Benedictine), a slack and rather worldly house, where John Hawghton (Hawton, Howton, Howtone) was noted as dilatory in making his profession. The conviviality of the monks of Bardney and their fondness for female society gave great concern to the bishop's chancellor in 1437, and seven years later Brother John Howtone was still 'abiding in apostasy' (A. Hamilton Thompson, ed., *Visitations of Religious Houses in the Diocese of Lincoln*, ii, part i, Canterbury and York Society, Canterbury and York Series, xxiv, London, 1919, pp. 10, 11, 14, 15, 25, 32).

An account of expenses on f. 173 v. begins: 'M[emorandum] þat þes bene þe parcell þat I hawfe spend þe ferst when I went to gybbysmere' [Gibsmere, near Southwell, the country seat of the bishops of Lincoln ('my lord harsbechope' in the account)]. Other places mentioned in the MS. are 'Stapylforthe' [Stapleford, Lincs.] and Somerton Castle at Boothby, Lincs. Other names in the MS. are 'gorgye Hopkyns', 'gorge sawton', 'Rychard harysun', 'Roger restun', 'Mychaell shrybroke' (owner of the book). Other scribes' names occurring are 'John Allwod', 'heeg', 'hyheg'.

BROGYNTYN, OSWESTRY: LORD HARLECH; ON DEPOSIT IN
ABERYSTWYTH: NATIONAL LIBRARY OF WALES

Porkington 10. XV cent. (third quarter). A miscellany of English religious and secular prose and poetry, containing some 55 items.

Nos. 42 (variant), 68, the first in hand 'S', the second in hand 'O' of the nineteen that Kurvinen distinguishes in the MS. Hand 'O' has written much of the miscellaneous English verse in the MS.

The volume is written in the language of the West Midlands and has apparently been in Wales for part of its existence, a number of Welsh names appearing in scribbles. On f. 52 v. the name 'H. Hattun' written on a scroll may be that of the compiler. The provenance has not been more closely determined. A very full description of the MS. is given by Auvo Kurvinen in *Neuphilologische Mitteilungen*, liv (1953), 33–67.

SHERBORNE ST. JOHN, NEAR BASINGSTOKE: MR. DENIS HILL-
WOOD, ON DEPOSIT IN IPSWICH, IPSWICH AND EAST SUFFOLK
RECORD OFFICE, COUNTY HALL

The Brome MS. XV cent. (second half). A commonplace book containing short miscellaneous items and the 'Brome' play of *Abraham and Isaac, The Fifteen Signs of Doomsday*, and *Owain Miles*.

No. 53 (variant) in the same hand as other poems in the volume.

The MS. was probably the property of the Cornwallis family of Brome Manor, Suffolk. The Robert Melton who wrote some accounts in the volume appears to have been their steward. The MS. was discovered in the 1880's, when Brome had passed from the family of Cornwallis to that of Kerrison. On the death of Sir Edward Kerrison it became the property of the late Mrs. R. Douglas Hamilton, from whom it was inherited by the present owner. It is clearly of Suffolk origin.

B. PRINTED SOURCES

OXFORD: BODLEIAN LIBRARY

Rawlinson 4to. 598(10).

A single leaf, paper, 5 × 4 in., damaged and mended at both edges and with a mended tear in the middle. Printed by Wynkyn de Worde in 1521.

This fragment is obviously the last leaf of a carol-book printed for sale. It is the earliest printed item in the bibliography of English carols. See T. F. Dibdin, ed., *Ames's Typographical Antiquities* (London, 1810–19), ii. 250–2, 394.

Contents: recto. *E.E.C.*, No 424 B.

verso. No. 32 (variant) and the following colophon: Thus endeth the Christmasse carol=|les / newely enprinted at London / in the |

fletestrete at the sygne of the sonne by | wynkyn de worde. The yere of our lor=|de. M. D. xxi.

The verso of the fragment is reproduced in facsimile by Edward Bliss Reed, *Christmas Carols Printed in the Sixteenth Century*, p. 3.

SAN MARINO, CALIFORNIA: HENRY E. HUNTINGTON LIBRARY AND ART GALLERY

Christmas carolles newely Inprynted.

A collection of one complete volume and parts of four others, printed by Richard Kele, *c.* 1550. $3\frac{7}{16} \times 5\frac{1}{2}$ in., pp. 48.

The title-page of the complete book reads as follows: ¶Christmas ca=|rolles newely Inprynted. | [Woodcut of the Crucifixion with two woodcut floral side-ornaments.] ¶Inprynted at London in the Powl=|try by Rychard Kele, dwellyng at the | longe shop vnder saynt Myldre=|des chyrche.

Contents: Nos. 20 (variants), 44 (variant), 75 (variant), 100. *E.E.C.*, Nos. 42b, 81B, 106, 107, 119, 163b, 164, 213, 256, 265, 278, 364, 376, 460, 461, 474. Pieces not in carol form: 'Psallemus cantantes'; *A caroll of the Innocentes.*

The entire collection is reproduced in facsimile by Edward Bliss Reed, *Christmas Carols Printed in the Sixteenth Century*. For detailed bibliographical information and history see Reed's Introduction, pp. xl-lxiv.

NOTES ON TEXTS

Separate mention is made here of only those publications
of texts which are not recorded in *E.E.C.*

1. *Farewell to Advent*

E.E.C., No. 3; A. G. Little, *Archaeologia Cantiana*, liv (1942), 2: B.–R. 4197.

One is inclined to doubt that this carol is of Ryman's own composition, in view of the more patient piety of the rest of his work, but perhaps it is unjust to deny him the possibility of some lighter moments. The single stanza on the same theme on f. 74 v. of the MS. is more characteristic of him and was undoubtedly suggested by ll. 45–48 of this carol (*pr.* Zupitza, p. 272):

> Prince, duke, and erle, lord, knyght, and squier,
> With alle other in youre degree,
> Caste oute Advent into the myere,
> For he with us to long hath be,
> And welcome we that King so fre
> That now was borne for love of us
> Of mayde Mary, named Jhesus.

The personification of Advent as a periodic visitor is parallel to that of Christmas in No. 38 and *E.E.C.*, Nos. 5 and 6, and of the New Year in No. 4. A similar personification of Lent is indicated by l. 47, with which compare *E.E.C.*, No. 4, stza. 2, l. 1, and No. 38, l. 11. It is probable that Advent was sometimes actually impersonated as we know Christmas and Lent to have been. In a procession in Norwich in January 1448 appeared 'Lenten cladde in white with redde herrings skinnes and his hors trapped with oyster shelles after him in token yᵗ sadnesse and abstinence of merth shulde followe and an holy tyme' (E. L. Guilford, *Select Extracts Illustrating Sports and Pastimes in the Middle Ages*, London, 1920, p. 52).

l. 17. Compare a line in the song of complaint against Lent, 'Wo worthe the, Lenttone, that ever thowe wast wrought' (Thomas Wright, ed., *Songs and Ballads*, London, 1860, No. X, p. 14):

> Muskyls, ly gapyng agenste the newe mone.

l. 35. The mention of Boughton Blean, the hamlet best known through Chaucer's *Canon's Yeoman's Prologue*, l. 3, is a sign that the carol comes from Canterbury, whether of Ryman's original authorship or not. In 1384 there was a good-sized chapel and hospital for lepers and infirm persons at Boughton-under-Blean which would have been an appropriate haven for such a meagre figure as Advent (*V.C.H. Kent*, London, 1926, ii. 208). With l. 37 compare the proverbial phrase of emphasis 'neither in Kent nor Christendom' which Grose (*A Provincial Glossary*, London, 1787) lists as local to Kent. It appears, however, in Spenser's *Shepherd's Calendar* (Sept., l. 153) and elsewhere. See V. S. Lean, *Collectanea* (Bristol, 1902), i. 107.

2. *A Welcome to Yule*

E.E.C., No. 7A; W. Sandys, *Christmastide* (London, 1852), p. 218; B.-R. 3877.

(Other text: B.M. MS. Sloane 2593, f. 32 r., *E.E.C.*, No. 7B; *O.B.C.*, p. 213.)

It is to be doubted that Audelay was the original author of this carol. Probably he is following a prototype of which the text in MS. Sloane 2593 is another derivative.

Audelay regards the Christmas season as consisting of the twelve days to Epiphany, while the Sloane version follows the alternative custom of extending it to Candlemas. A stanza of that text not found in Audelay's reads:

> Wolcum be ye, Candylmesse,
> Wolcum be ye, Qwyn of Blys,
> Wolcum bothe to more and lesse;
> Wolcum, Yol.

Both traditions flourish in popular custom, some communities of England removing Christmas greenery after Twelfth Night, others leaving it in place until Candlemas. Compare No. 3.

The conception of Christmas as a visitor to whom a formal welcome is given survives in such a speech as that of Father Christmas as presenter of a mummers' play:

> Here comes I, Father Christmas, welcome or welcome not,
> I hope old Father Christmas will never be forgot.

(Chambers, *M.S.* i. 216.)

Erik Routley (*The English Carol*, London, 1958, p. 74) errs by associating this carol with 'John Awdelay (*fl.* 1559–1577), stationer and printer'.

3. *The Christmas Feasts*

E.E.C., No. 8a; Rickert, p. 223; &c.; B.-R. 3343.

(Other text: B.M. MS. Sloane 2583, f. 33 v., *E.E.C.*, No. 8b.)

The device of devoting one stanza each to the important days of the Christmas season, as used here and in *E.E.C.*, No. 9 and App., No. ii, is probably educational as well as rhetorical in intention. Compare the last stanza of a late fifteenth-century *noël* by Jehan Tisserant (Bibliothèque Nationale, MS. français 2368, f. 14 r.):

> Par douze jours fut nouel acomply,
> Par douze vers sera mon chant finy,
> Par chascun jour j'en ay fait vng coupplet.

A similar device survives in traditional English folk-song, but without the ecclesiastical application, in the well-known cumulative piece, 'The first day of Christmas' (W. H. Husk, *Songs of the Nativity*, London, [1868], p. 182). In their comment on the modern song, first found in a children's book of about 1780, *Mirth without Mischief*, Iona and Peter Opie (*The Oxford Dictionary of Nursery Rhymes*, Oxford, 1952, pp.122-3) suggest that it may be 'an irreligious travesty' of a carol like this one. But the carol is not cumulative; its stanzas are too long for cumulative use, and it does not notice some of the twelve days.

4. *Christmas Mirth*

E.E.C., No. 10; K. Hammerle, *Archiv*, clxvi. 204; Robbins, *Secular Lyrics*, p. 3; B.-R. 2343.

On the implied context of this carol see Introduction, p. 30, and the 'messenger' burden of No. 25. The macaronic complaint of a school-boy, 'On days when I am callit to þe scole' (*pr.* K. Hammerle, *Archiv*, clxvi. 203), immediately precedes this carol in the manuscript and is in the same hand, a circumstance which strengthens the probability that the carol relates to a scholastic celebration and is not the utterance of a professional 'minstrel' as suggested in the notes in *E.E.C.*, p. 355. See Notes on No. 83.

'A Plea for Another Drink' (*pr.* Robbins, *Secular Lyrics*, p. 5, notes pp. 228-9) is in a different hand and is probably not directly related to this carol. Its very interesting use in English of a Welsh lyric form is well explained by Robbins, but it seems to be more suitable to the visitation of a known neighbour by an amateur singer than to use by a 'minstrel'.

It is unusual to find the same rhymes used in all stanzas of a carol, as here. Compare *E.E.C.*, Nos. 22, 234.

burden. This was still in circulation in 1553. It is sung in the interlude *Respublica,* Act. V, Scene 8:

> haye, haie, haie, haie,
> I wilbe merie while I maie.

([Sir] W. W. Greg, ed.: E.E.T.S. Or. Ser., No. 226, 1952, p. 57.)

l. 20. The last words of the carol, 'care away', are of frequent occurrence in the refrains or burdens of popular song. See notes on No. 99. The phrase also appears in an old jingle from Nottinghamshire on Care Sunday or Passion Sunday, the second before Easter:

> Care Sunday, care away,
> Palm Sunday and Easter Day.

(P. H. Ditchfield, *Old English Customs Extant at the Present Time*, London, 1901, pp. 69–70). The meaning of 'Care' as applied to the Sunday is uncertain.

5. *Christmas Sports*

E.E.C., No. 11; Robbins, *Secular Lyrics*, p. 3; C. & S., p. 234; Rickert, p. 220; *O.B.C.*, p. 211; &c.; B.–R. 1866.

This carol is written as if to be led by a master of festivities or 'Lord of Misrule' who has the power to 'punish'. The appointment of a Lord or Abbot of Misrule as governor of Christmas feasts was a regular custom of the English and Scottish courts, colleges of the universities, Inns of Court, and private establishments. See the excellent account in Chambers, *M.S.* i. 403–19. Stocks were specifically part of the equipment of the Lord of Misrule at the English court in 1551, when George Ferrers held the dignity and had 'holds, prisons, and places of execuc[i]on, his cannypie, throne, seate, pillory, gibbet, hedding block, stocks, little ease [probably a pillory] and other necessary incydents to his person' (A. J. Kempe, ed., *Manuscripts and other rare Documents from the Reign of Henry VIII to that of James I, preserved in the Muniment Room at Loseley House*, London, 1836, p. 87, quoted by Chambers, *M.S.* i. 406).

The obligation of each person present, under pain of some kind of forfeit, to contribute to the general entertainment is characteristic of many English holiday customs; l. 5 implies that a song is the preferred performance, as in No. 4.

l. 2. The marshal of a medieval hall had the duty, among others, of seating the guests at a feast in the correct order of precedence. A groom served under a marshal, building the fires and performing other practical tasks in the hall. See *The Babees Book*, pp. 310–11, for 'The Boke of Curtasye', bk. iii, ll. 379–422, which deal with the marshal.

6. *Of the Nativity*

E.E.C., No. 12a; B.–R. 29.

(Other partial text: Helmingham Hall, Suffolk, MS. LJ I. 7, f. 140 r., collation *E.E.C.*, No. 12b.)

This piece, which occurs in some Franciscan sermon notes, is the earliest Nativity carol yet discovered. See Brown's notes, *R.L. 14 C.*, pp. xii, 272.

The discrepancy in the metre between the first stanza and the other two might be accounted for by regarding the piece as made up of two originally different sets of verses. The third stanza, at least, must have circulated without a burden, as it so appears in the Helmingham Hall MS., where it is also quoted in a Latin homily, without any indication that it is there regarded as part of a carol or song.

It is equally possible that the short third and sixth lines were omitted in error from the first stanza, perhaps through confusion with the four-line form of the burden. For the first stanza to be sung to the same melody as the other two, such lines would, of course, be indispensable.

Margit Sahlin (*Étude sur la carole mediévale*, p. 58) says of this carol that it is 'certainement un de ces *noëls* ou *lullaby carols* (*kindelwiegenlieder*) que l'on chantait en dansant autour d'un berceau arrangé sur l'autel ou autre part dans l'église, comme il était d'usage en bien des endroits'. There is no evidence for so positive a statement. But even if the piece were used for a dance around such a Christmas crib the derivation of the burden from secular dance-song is still probable. R. H. Robbins (*Stud. Phil.* lvi. 576) oddly attempts to make Dr. Sahlin's suggestion inconsistent with such a dance-song origin. As a matter of fact, the text in MS. Bodley 26 imme-diately follows a reference to the wedding feast of the Lamb in Revelation xix. 9: '. . . et hic est cena de qua in apocalipsi "beati qui ad cena[m] agni vocati sunt", ad quam cenam specialiter vocat deus 3ª hominum genera sicut alibi etc.' Quotation of the carol seems to have been suggested to the preaching friar by the mention, not of any church service, but of the revelry at a feast, the known setting of many later carols. Note l. 6, 'For your marriage', which is hardly intelligible in the carol without the sermon-context. The subject of rejoicing rather than of the Nativity scene itself is further emphasized by the note written beside and below the third stanza: 'Secundum primus thema tristicia vestra convertetur in gaudium Joh. 16. Verba ista sunt Christi ad discipulos. . .' (John xvi. 20). See Homer G. Pfander, *The Popular Sermon of the Medieval Friar in England* (N.Y., 1937), pp. 45–46.

7. Of the Nativity

E.E.C., No. 14a, B.–R. 2377.

(Other texts: Bodl. MS. Arch. Selden B. 26, f. 10 r., with music; *pr.* with music: Stevens, p. 14; B.M. MS. Addit. 5665, f. 36 v., with music; *pr.* with music: Stevens, p. 94.)

The burden of this carol is taken from the famous 'Laetabundus' Nativity prose. See Introduction, pp. 37–38. In the other versions the burden is reduced to 'Alleluia.' The 'holly and ivy' phrase attached to the carol in the MS. is probably an indication of the tune of a popular carol intended for use with the religious piece. It need not have been a 'holly-

and-ivy' carol in its full content, for preserved folk-song gives us examples of the words used in other contexts. For instance, a nineteenth-century Irish version of the 'Hunting of the Wren' sung on St. Stephen's Day by young men *en quête* contains the lines:

> Sing holly, sing ivy—sing ivy, sing holly,
> A drop just to drink, it would drown melancholy.

The singers carried a holly-bush decorated with ribbons and wrens (T. Crofton Croker, *Researches in the South of Ireland*, London, 1824, p. 232). More than a hundred years later the song was recorded in Vermont with a stanza recalling the association of birds with the two trees:

> Between the holly and ivy tree
> Were all the birds come singing to me,
> Sing holly, sing ivy,
> To keep next Christmas, it will be holly [*sic*].

(Helen Hartness Flanders and Marguerite Olney, *Ballads Migrant in New England*, N.Y., 1953, p. 58.)

The sophisticated settings of the other two versions probably replaced simpler and more popular tunes in the case of this carol as of others.

8. *Of the Nativity*

E.E.C., No. 21A; *pr.* Rickert, p. 183; B.–R. 1471.

(Other texts: Bodl. MS. Eng. poet. e. 1, f. 35 v., *E.E.C.*, No. 21B; *pr.* Rickert, p. 50; T.C.C., MS. O. 3. 58, with music; *E.E.C.*, No. 21C; *pr.* with music: Stevens, p. 5; C.U. Lib., MS. Ee. 1. 12, f. 1 r., with music; *E.E.C.*, No. 21D; *pr.* with music: Stevens, p. 111 (in part).)

ll. 13, 14. Compare *E.E.C.*, No. 234C, stza. 4, from B.M. MS. Sloane 2593. Of all the figures of speech which the Middle Ages applied to the Virgin Mary none is more prominent in the carols than the simile which likens the action of the Holy Spirit in causing her to conceive to the sun's shining on a glass, which it penetrates without injuring. It is, of course, echoed and re-echoed in theological writings, so that it is idle to point to a particular passage as a 'source' for any particular carol. The most authoritative use of the figure and the one which probably reached the most readers is that of St. Augustine, which is incorporated in the sixth Lectio for Matins on the Third Sunday in Advent (*Br. Sar.* i, col. cvi): 'Solis radius specular penetrat, et soliditatem ejus insensibili subtilitate pertransit...ad ingressum et egressum ejus specular integrum perseverat. Specular ergo non rumpit radius solis: integritatem virginis ingressus aut egressus numquid vitiare poterat deitatis?'

The figure also appears in No. 19 and in *E.E.C.*, Nos. 56, 63, 67, 73, 84, 174, 194, 200, 207. 208, 246, 281.

9. *Of the Nativity*

With music; *pr.* with music: Stevens, p. 52.

(Other texts: Nat. Lib. Scot., MS. Advocates 19. 3. 1, f. 59 r.; *E.E.C.*, No. 23A; Brown, *R. L. 15 C.*, p. 123; B.M., MS. Harley 275, f. 146 v.; *E.E.C.*, No. 23B; B.-R. 340.)

The burden proper to this carol is probably only the first two of the four lines found in the MS. and here printed, as the music calls for only two lines and the chorus-repeats of the burden do not include more. M. F. Bukofzer has established the rule for the texts of polyphonic carols that no new words not in the initial burden are introduced into the chorus-repeats. The scribe of the Egerton MS. probably had in mind or in hand a version with different music or with none which did include the second pair of lines. There may well be influence from No. 12, which is the only other carol to use the line 'Consors paterni luminis' from a hymn for Matins on the Tuesday after the Octave of Epiphany (*Hym. S.*, p. 47) and which has as the first line of its burden a line very much like the first line of the burden of the Harley 275 text of this piece: 'Joy we all now yn this feste'. For a fuller discussion of the relations of the three texts see R. L. Greene, review of Stevens, *J.A.M.S.* vii (1954), 80–82.

The text here printed, though inferior to the other two, probably represents the earliest form of the carol. The recovery of this text invalidates Brown's statement that 'the arrangement in Harley seems to be correct' (p. 320). Harley's burden is a commonplace, apparently substituted when the earlier burden was made into, or mistaken for, a first stanza. The finding of the Egerton text confirms the note in *E.E.C.*, that the Advocates text represents the original arrangement (p. 357). The Advocates text has four stanzas (2, 5, 7, 8), the Harley text three (1, 5, 7) which are not in the Egerton version.

Except for the hymn-line already mentioned and the phrase 'Ecce ancilla Domini', the Latin lines appear not to be borrowed but to have been composed with the English lines to make a true macaronic poem.

l. 21. *He was namyd the thyrd kyng*. This odd line undoubtedly results from a misreading of the 'For he was man' that appears in stza. 9, l. 1 of the Harley text. Note also 'For he was man' in stza. 4, l. 1 of Rymans' *E.E.C.*, No. 127. The following Latin line has been adjusted here by the insertion of 'qui'. The 'incensum' of both texts should, of course, be 'myrrham'.

10. *Of the Nativity*

E.E.C., No. 28; *pr.* Rickert, p. 48; B.-R. 3643.

ll. 15, 16. This wholly unhistorical reference to the presence of the prophets at the Circumcision is probably the result of the writer's acquaintance with some form of dramatic service or procession of the prophets in which they appeared in appropriate costumes. See Karl Young, *The Drama of the Medieval Church* (Oxford, 1933), chap. xxi. As Professor Young points out (ii. 153, 154), this observance took place in some churches, notably Tours and Rouen, on the Feast of the Circumcision. The author of the carol has apparently taken somewhat literally the symbolic marshalling of the prophets which is based ultimately on the famous pseudo-Augustinian sermon *Contra Judaeos, Paganos, et Arianos.*

11. *Of the Nativity*

E.E.C., No. 30; with music; *pr.* Rickert, p. 165; with music: Stevens, p. 18; B.–R. 2733.

(Other text: C.U. Lib., MS. L. 1. 11, f. 32 r., with music; *pr.* with music: Stevens, p. 114.)

The text in the Cambridge MS. was first reported by M. F. Bukofzer, *Renaissance News*, ii (1949), 66. It consists of the burden and stanzas 1, 4, 2, in that order.

ll. 1, 2 occur with slight variation as the first two lines of *E.E.C.*, No. 74, by James Ryman.

l. 4. *bereth the belle.* This common phrase denoting excellence is still the subject of much discussion. Francis Grose (*A Classical Dictionary of the Vulgar Tongue*, ed. Eric Partridge, London, 1931, p. 32) calls it an allusion to the custom of putting a bell on the harness of the lead-horse of a team. *O.E.D.* suggests that it may be from 'bell-wether'. Gomme (*The Gentleman's Magazine Library*, London, 1886, ii. 90) and others think it refers to the giving of a bell as the prize for country races. The idea of a prize, such as the famous bell awarded at Chester races, is more plausible than that of animal bells, as the context in which it appears often refers to a quality or activity in which the pre-eminence is shown. See the citations in *The Middle English Dictionary* and the correspondence in *The Times Literary Supplement*, 4 July 1952, p. 437, 18 July 1952, p. 469.

12. *Of the Nativity*

E.E.C., No. 31a; with music; *pr.* with music: Stevens, p. 19; B.–R. 18.

(Other texts: Bodl., MS. Eng. poet. e. 1, f. 32 v.; *pr.* Rickert, p. 53; B.M., MS. Addit. 5665, f. 28 v., with music; *pr.* with music: Stevens, p. 85.)

The arrangement of the Latin as first and fourth lines of couplet-rhymed stanzas is unique in the carols.

The Latin lines are from hymns, mostly of the Christmas season, as follows:

l. 1	Epiphany, Lauds	*Br. Sar.*, i, col. cccxxix
l. 4	Vigil of Christmas, I Vespers	*Br. Sar.*, i, col. clxvi
l. 5	York, Christmas, Prime	*Hym. S.*, p. 13
l. 8	Advent, First Sunday, Matins	*Br. Sar.*, i, col. xviii
l. 9	Christmas, Lauds	*Br. Sar.*, i, col. clxxxix
l. 12	York, Christmas, Nones (Adam vetus quod polluit)	*Hym. S.*, p. 14
l. 13	York, Christmas, Terce	*Hym. S.*, p. 13
l. 16	Tuesday after Octave of Epiphany, Matins	*Hym. S.*, p. 47
l. 17	First Sunday after Trinity, I Vespers	*Br. Sar.*, i, col. mclxvii
l. 20	The 'Gloria', first said Christmas, Matins	*Br. Sar.*, i. col. clxxi

13. *Of the Nativity*

E.E.C., No. 51; E. Flügel, *Anglia*, xxvi. 265; Rickert, p. 243; B.–R. 2346.

The use of 'wassail' in religious carols is so rare in comparison with its occurrence in traditional folk-song for Christmas that one suspects that its pagan associations were still felt strongly enough to cause disapproval. But 'Yule', on the other hand, is freely used.

The threefold 'wassail' which begins the burden of this piece strongly suggests its performance in a setting like that prescribed for the Twelfth Night wassail of Henry VII:

'Item the [singers of the household] chapelle may stond at the on side of the halle: and when the steward comythe in at yᵉ halle dore wᵗ the waissaille, he muste cry thris, "Wassaile," &cᵃ: and then shall the chapelle answere it anon wᵗ a good songe: and thus in like wyse, and it plese the Kinge to kep the gret chambre.'

(Francis Grose, 'Ceremonies and Services at Court, In the Time of King Henry the Seventh', *The Antiquarian Repertory*, London, 1807, i. 330.)

14. *Of the Nativity*

E.E.C., No. 66; B.–R. 488.

The Latin burden of this carol is also used by Ryman as the burden of another carol which follows it in his MS. (*E.E.C.*, No. 65). It is also the burden of a Latin *cantilena* on the Nativity found with music in Bodl. MSS. Ashmole 1393 and Arch. Selden B. 26 and in B.M., MS. Egerton 3307 (*pr.* Stevens, pp. 32, 26, 51). In each carol the first stanza paraphrases the Latin burden, but the later stanzas diverge. Bukofzer discusses the music of the Latin pieces and points out its derivation from that associated with vernacular *ballata* or *virelai*. Stevens (p. 119) suggests that the music preserved for the Latin texts would have served equally well for the English carols. The relationship is an interesting link between the work of Ryman and the important Selden and Egerton MSS.

ll. 9–12. Isaiah vii. 14.

ll. 15–20. Matthew i. 23.

ll. 33–36. Ryman here attributes the sun-glass commonplace to a Father who seems not to have used it. He may be quoting from a wrongly attributed source, or, more probably, is simply seeking to give the impression of learning. See Zupitza's notes, *Archiv*, xciii. 383–90.

15. *Of the Nativity*

With music; *pr.* with music: Stevens, p. 36.

This carol is unique in being trilingually macaronic throughout and in having less than a quarter of its words in English. With the exception of the single word 'Noël', which had become thoroughly naturalized, French words and phrases are extremely rare in the carols. Less than a dozen carols contain any French at all, and such expressions as are used are of the simplest kind. Nos. 53, 62, *E.E.C.*, No. 314, 'pur charite'; No. 87, 'Bevis a towt'; *E.E.C.*, No. 6, two lines; *E.E.C.*, No. 417, 'prenegard', *E.E.C.*, No. 420, 'bon jowre a vous' and 'par la pompe', B.-R. 795 (not in *E.E.C.*), 'Fetes belle chere . . . Verse le bavere'. The French lines in this piece seem not to be quoted but to have been composed for their places. It is possible, of course, that they remain from a French original which has been partially translated into English. If this is so, the carol is unique in this respect as well.

The sources of the borrowed Latin lines are as follows:

l. 1	Psalm xlvii. 1, used as beginning of prose for Christmas	*Anal. Hym.* ix. 13
l. 5	Hymn for Christmas, Lauds	*Br. Sar.* i, col. clxxxix
ll. 8, 9	From 'A solis ortus cardine', above	*Br. Sar.*, i, col. cxc
l. 12	From a York prayer of the Five Joys, 'Gaude virgo, mater Christi'	*Horae Eboracenses*, Surtees Society, No. cxxxii, 63

l. 13.   From 'Christe, redemptor omnium',   *Br. Sar.*, i, col. clxxi
         hymn for Christmas, Matins
l. 17   The 'Gloria', first said Christmas,   *Br. Sar.*, i, col. clxxi
         Matins

l. 1. *Omnes gentes plaudite*. This psalm-line begins a set of macaronic couplets calling for drink in the carol manuscript B.M., Sloane 2593, ff. 10 v., 11 r.:

> Omnes gentes plaudite;
> I saw myny bryddis setyn on a tre. (&c.)

l. 6. *le*: wide.

l. 18. *Fortime*: Most strong or very strong (*très fort*). Stevens (p. 145) reads *fortune* and unnecessarily emends to *fontaine*.

16. *Jolly Wat the Shepherd*

E.E.C., No. 78; *pr.* A. W. Pollard, *Fifteenth Century Prose and Verse* (Westminster, 1903), p. 87; B.–R. 3460.

The carol of Wat is justly famous for its gaiety and realism. Its similarity in conception and tone to the shepherd scenes in the mystery plays is striking. The occurrence of the Northern word 'warroke' and the payment of twopence to actors playing 'Joly Wat and Malkyn' at York in 1447 suggest that the original home of the carol may have been Yorkshire (Lucy Toulmin Smith, ed., *York Plays*, Oxford, 1885, p. xxxviii). The offering of homely gifts to the infant Jesus is paralleled as well in various French *noëls*, e.g. J. R. H. de Smidt, *Les Noëls et la tradition populaire* (Amsterdam, 1932), Nos. 9A, 10, 19A. Acquaintance with mystery plays is probably responsible for the introduction of the incident in this carol and in a well-known *noël* by Jehan Tisserant in Bibliothèque Nationale MS. français 2368, f. 67 r. (stza. 7):

> Je luy donnay vng vray don,
> Nau, nau,
> Mon billart *et* ma pellote,
> Et Guillot mon compagnon,
> Nau, nau,
> Sa trude et sa marote.

The wish to provide an analogy to the gifts of the Magi is doubtless the ultimate reason for the use of the incident.

l. 20. Mall appears to be a favourite ewe (compare Chaucer, *Nun's Priest's Tale*, l. 11), Will, the bell-wether.

l. 29. *warroke*: warroch (Sc.), a stunted or puny child, here apparently applied by Wat to his helper. See John Jamieson, *An Etymological Diction-ary of the Scottish Language* (Paisley, 1879–82), *s.v.* 'Warroch'.

l. 45. The rhyme demands the transposition of 'scrype' and 'skyrte' in-stead of the MS. reading.

l. 53. *cape*: cope, cloak. This line has attracted some attention because of its bit of visual detail. It may be a reminiscence of the costume given Joseph in a mystery play, as suggested by W. J. Phillips (*Carols*, p. 108), hardly, as Esmé Wingfield-Stratford thinks, a reference to his 'round hat' or halo in a church window (*The History of British Civilization*, London, 1930, pp. 350–1).

The first stanza appears to have one line too many, l. 5. The form of the stanza is really more satisfactory with this 'extra' line, and it may be wondered whether in singing it may have been inserted in all the stanzas.

17. *Of the Shepherds*

E.E.C., No. 79A; *pr.* Flügel, *Anglia*, xxvi. 237; B.–R. 112.

(Other texts: Balliol MS. 354, f. 222 r.; *E.E.C.*, No. 79Ab; *O.B.C.*, p. 208; &c.; MS. formerly owned by Thomas Sharp, destroyed 1879; with music; *E.E.C.*, No. 79B; *pr.* with music: John P. Cutts, *Renaissance News*, x (1957), 5–7; Edmondstoune Duncan, *The Story of the Carol* (London, [1911]), p. 76.

The two stanzas used in the Coventry 'Taylors and Shearemens Pagant' are marked as different songs because of their use in different parts of the play. As there sung, with the burden once after the stanza, their character as parts of a carol is somewhat obscured. The date of B is given by the following note (Hardin Craig, *Two Coventry Corpus Christi Plays*, E.E.T.S., Ex. Ser. No. lxxxvii, 1931, p. 31): 'Tys matter / nevly correcte be Robart Croo / the xiiijth dey of marche / fenysschid in the yere of owre Lorde God / M CCCC & xxxiiijte. / then beyng mayre mastur Palmar / also mastris of the seyd fellyschipp Hev Corbett / Randull Pynkard and / John Baggely.'

The shepherds in mystery plays seem regularly to have been counted on for a song. In the Chester play of the adoration of the shepherds Gartius exclaims:

> Nowe sing on! let us see!
> some songe I will assaie,
> All men singes after me,
> for musique of me learne you may.

(Tunc omnes pastores cum aliis adiuvantibus cantabunt hilare carmen.)

The stage direction suggests a carol. Three MSS. indicate a burden or refrain: 'sing tooly holy holy loo' and 'Singe troly loly [troly] loe' (Her-mann Deimling ed., E.E.T.S., Ex. Ser., No. lxii, 1926, p. 151, ll. 455–8).

18. *Of the Shepherds*

E.E.C., No. 81A; B.-R. 2332.

(Other text: Hunt. Lib. *Christmas carolles newely Inprynted* (Richard Kele), p. [25]; *E.E.C.*, No. 81B; Rickert, p. 104; &c.)

This carol is of special interest as the only one of Friar James Ryman's composition to appear elsewhere than in his MS. A shortened version (with five stanzas instead of nine) which is yet fairly close to Ryman's text in its wording is among the pieces printed for general sale by Richard Kele of London about 1550. This one instance is enough to show that Ryman's work was known outside of his own friary and to keep us from dismissing it as 'closet' verse or as 'mediocre productions' for use only in church or cloister, as R. H. Robbins seems to do (*Stud. Phil.* lvi. 575).

19. *Of the Life of Christ*

E.E.C., No. 93; B.-R. 3235.

The heading of the piece in the MS. indicates that this is a carol written to the tune of a secular song, possibly the one referred to in the interlude *Thersites* (1537): '*And I were a maid again* now may be here song' (W. Carew Hazlitt, ed., *A Select Collection of Old English Plays*, 4th ed., London, 1874, i. 405). The song 'And I war a maydn' in B.M. M.S. Addit. 31922 is in a different metre. See John Stevens, *Music and Poetry in the Early Tudor Court* (London, 1961), pp. 418–19 and Index of Selected Songs. It is followed in the MS. by No. 67, which has a similar indication of tune and is in the same stanza-form.

ll. 13–30. All the nine orders of angelic beings are specifically named, although not in traditional order of rank.

l. 24. *Kery*: Kyrie eleison.

l. 53. *herte rote*: a term of endearment.

l. 69. *corpolence*. *O.E.D.* records this use in the sense of 'bodily substance' only from 1625.

l. 72. *thyrty golden pence*. The substitution of gold coins for the silver of the Biblical account is a feature of the legend which identifies the money taken by Judas with the coins for which Joseph was sold, which were later held by the Queen of Sheba, and which were given to Jesus by Melchior. Mary lost the coins, according to the legend, and they were found by a shepherd, who placed them in the Temple. See C. Horstmann, ed., *The Three Kings of Cologne* (E.E.T.S., Or Ser., No. 85, 1886), pp. 94–100, 248–51.

l. 96. *Crucifige*: Mark xv. 13, 14; Luke xxiii. 21; John xix. 15.

l. 100. *Lunges*. Longinus, the legendary name of the Roman soldier who pierced the side of Christ with his spear (John xix. 34). According to the legend Longinus was cured of a disease of the eyes by a drop of the holy blood and was converted.

l. 120. *hys membres*: 'by' is to be understood.

20. *Of St. Stephen*

With music; *pr.* with music: Stevens, p. 39.

(Other texts: Hunt. Lib. *Christmas carolles newely Inprynted* (Richard Kele), p. [33]; *E.E.C.*, No. 101A; *E.E.C.*, No. 101B; ibid., p. [42].)

The occurrence of this carol in two differing texts in the carol-books of Richard Kele is a highly interesting sign of the popularity with a later secular public of fifteenth-century carols of monastic circulation. One of the texts (*E.E.C.*, No. 101A) is longer than this one (9 stanzas, with nearly identical burden), the other shorter (4 stanzas, with different burden). Three of the stanzas of this shorter version are verbally very close to the Egerton text, probably too close to be the result of completely oral transmission. It even has 'ylke' in l. 1 for the 'ilk' of Egerton, for which, as Stevens remarks, the music seems to require a final *e*.

21. *Of St. John the Evangelist*

(*a*). *E.E.C.*, No. 103Aa; with music; *pr.* with music: Stevens, p. 10; B.-R. 3776.

(*b*). *E.E.C.*, No. 103Ab.

(Other texts: Balliol MS. 354, f. 222 r.; *E.E.C.*, No. 103Ac; Rickert, p. 126; B.M. MS. Addit. 5665, f. 37 v.; with music; *pr.* with music: Stevens, p. 95; ibid., f. 48 v.; with music; with music: Stevens, p. 105; B.M. MS. Harley 4294, f. 81 v.; *E.E.C.*, No. 103B.)

This carol is found in more different texts (as a carol) than any other. Stevens (p. 117) points out that it is 'the only polyphonic carol found in three different musical settings'. The *b*-text here printed differs from the others in being written in the third person as a narrative and not addressed directly to St. John. The change from the more usual version has been thoroughly made, in the burden as well as in the stanzas.

The second line of the burden, used also in *E.E.C.*, No. 104, properly refers to St. John the Baptist and comes from the prose for his day (*Sar. Mis.*, p. 477).

l. 15. This is a commonplace found in most accounts of the life of St. John. Compare, for example, that in *The South-English Legendary*, ed. Charlotte D'Evelyn and Anna J. Mill, ii, E.E.T.S., Or. Ser., No. 236, 1956, p. 595, ll. 34–36:

> And for þer nas noþur of ham · þat clene maide nas
> Clene maide to wardi oþer · riȝt it was to do
> Þeruore inis swete warde · oure Louerd hure tok two.

22. *Of the Innocents*

E.E.C., No. 108; B.-R. 601.

ll. 1, 2. In these rhyming lines Audelay is apparently using a carol commonplace. Compare No. 29, ll. 76, 77 (not found in the other texts) and the incomplete and damaged carol on the succession of Christmas feasts in G. & C. C. C. MS. 383 (*E.E.C.*, Appendix, No. ii), ll. 9–12:

> The children [of Israel] cried, 'Wa, wa!'
> Her wondus smertus sore;
> Crist in cradul seide, 'Ba, ba!'
> Man synne . . .' [MS. damaged]

l. 4. *cowth hem fray*: did kill them.

l. 5. The tradition was that Herod was called to Rome directly after his interview with the Magi and was a year on the road each way. Hence, when he returned, he ordered the killing of all male children of two years and under. Compare Mirk's *Festial*, ed. T. Erbe, E.E.T.S., Ex. Ser., No. lxxi, 1897, part i, p. 36.

l. 9. Audelay's figure of 140,000 as the number slain is not quite the customary one. The number was generally put in the Middle Ages at 144,000, in defiance of all historical possibility, by identifying the Innocents with the white-clad host of Revelation xiv. 3. Compare the Townely Play of 'Herod the Great', ed. G. England, E.E.T.S., Ex. Ser., No. lxxi, 1897, p. 180, ll. 487–9.

> A hundreth thowsand, I watt / and fourty ar slayn,
> And four thowsand; ther-at / me aght to be fayn;
> Sich a morder on a flat / shall neuer be agayn.

l. 13. *crisum*: in their chrisom-cloths or baptismal robes, innocent children (usually applied to those a month old or less).

l. 24. Revelation xiv. 3.

23. *Of St. Thomas of Canterbury*

With music; *pr.* R. L. Greene, *J.A.M.S.* vii. 7; with music: Stevens, p. 48.

This carol on St. Thomas, like No. 24 in all its four MSS. and Audelay's *E.E.C.*, No. 113, has been spared the defacement prescribed by Henry VIII in 1538 for all memorials of the saint. But *E.E.C.*, No. 115, in Bodl. MS. Engl. poet. e. 1 has been cancelled, and in *E.E.C.*, No. 116 in B.M. MS. Addit. 5665 the name 'Thoma' has been erased.

The narrative in this carol follows the accepted accounts, but it is more explicitly biased against the king than any of the other carols.

ll. 6–15. Compare Lectio ii at First Nocturn of Matins on St. Thomas's Day (*Br. Sar.* i, col. ccxlix):

Confiscantur interim in Anglia omnes archiepiscopi redditus, vastantur praedia, possessiones diripitunur: et excogitato novo supplicii genere, tota simul proscribitur Thomae cognatio. Omnes etiam amici ejus, vel familiares, vel quicunque eum quocumque titulo contingebant, sine delectu conditionis aut fortunae, dignitatis aut ordinis, aetatis aut sexus, pariter relegantur. Nam et senes et decrepiti, vagientes in cunis, et mulieres in puerperio decubantes, in exilium acti sunt.

ll. 19–20. Compare Lectio iiii at Second Nocturn (*Br. Sar.* i, col. ccli):

Suscipitur itaque a clero et populo cum gaudio inaestimabili illachrimantibus omnibus et dicentibus, Benedictus qui venit in nomine Domini. Sed post dies paucos iterum damnis et injuriis supra modum et numerum affectus est. . . .

ll. 18, 23–25. Compare Lectio iii at First Nocturn (*Br. Sar.* i, col. ccl):

Sex igitur annis exulans, continuis variis et innumeris afflictus injuriis, et quasi lapis vivus in structuram caelestis edificii multimodis tunsionibus atque pressuris conquadratus: quo magis impulsus est ut caderet, eo firmius et immobilius stare probatus est.

l. 26. Compare Response at Vespers on the eve of St. Thomas (*Br. Sar.* i, col. ccxlv):

Jacet granum oppressum palea,

and the lines from the following Versicle and Prose:

Cadit custos vitis in vinea:
dux in castris, cultor in area.

Fit pastoris caede sanguinea.
Pavimenta Christi marmorea
Sacro madent cruore rubea,

as well as Lectio v at Second Nocturn (col. ccliii):

Sic itaque granum frumenti oppressit palea, sic vineae custos in vinea, dux in castris, in caulis pastor, cultor in area caesus est. . . .

ll. 29, 30. These lines suggest an acquaintance with the twelfth-century Anglo-Norman poem *La Vie de Thomas Becket par Beneit* (or a derivative of it), ll. 967, 971–2 (ed. Börje Schlyter, Études Romanes de Lund, iv, Lund, 1941):

La voiz [of Christ] dist. . . .
'Kar en tun sanc est glorifiee
Tute seynte Iglise e honuree
Sanz longe atente.'

ll. 31–35. Compare stza. 1 of Audelay's carol, *E.E.C.*, No. 113:

> For on a Tewsday Thomes was borne,
> And on a Tuysday he was prest schorne,
> And on a Tuysday his lyve was lorne,
> And sofyrd martyrdam with myld chere.

The importance of Tuesdays in the life of St. Thomas is dwelt on in both prose and poetical treatments of his life, e.g. Herbert de Boseham's *Vita Sancti Thomae* (ed. J. C. Robertson, Rolls Series, London, 1877), lib. iv. cap. 3, the 'Translation' in the *South-English Legendary*, pp. 691–2, ll. 53–72, and most strikingly in a fifteenth-century English hymn beginning 'Gaude, lux Londoniarum' (*Anal. Hym.* xxix. 89). Each of the seven stanzas of the hymn describes an important Tuesday in Thomas's life, his birth, his summons by the King, his exile, the revelation of his future martyrdom, his official recognition as a martyr. Audelay seems to be alone in ascribing his being 'shorn priest' to a Tuesday as well. He was actually ordained priest on Saturday, 2 June 1162.

The 'seven' of the carol shows acquaintance with the tradition, though the stanza mentions only six.

24. Of St. Thomas of Canterbury

E.E.C., No. 114a; Wright, *Songs and Carols* (London, 1836), No. xi; Rickert, p. 129; &c.; B.–R. 1892.
(Other texts: G. & C. C. MS. 383, p. 68; *pr.* K. Brunner, *Anglia*, lxi. 151; Brown, *R. L. 15 C.*, p. 189; P.R.O. Chancery Misc. Bundle 34, File 1, No. 12, f. 1 r.; collation *E.E.C.*, No. 114c; Balliol MS. 354, f. 227 v.)

The account of Becket's murder given in this carol follows fairly closely the historical facts as recorded in the early prose lives of the saint, e.g. Herbert de Boseham's *Vita Sancti Thomae* (ed. J. C. Robertson, Rolls Series, London, 1877), lib. vi.

l. 14. *paleys*: the Archbishop's Palace at Canterbury whence Becket fled to the Cathedral. Compare Herbert de Boseham, lib. vi, cap. 1.

ll. 19, 20. The calling of the Archbishop 'traitor' by the knights is recorded in various lives, together with his denial of its justice.

ll. 21–24. This characteristically unselfish thought of Becket's for his household and servants is noted in several lives, e.g. Herbert de Boseham, lib. vi, cap. 4.

l. 25. *aunter*. The altar in the NW. transept of Canterbury Cathedral. See Paul A. Brown, *The Development of the Legend of Thomas Becket* (Philadelphia, 1930), pp. 117–20.

ll. 26, 27. These gruesome details are authentic. As Carleton Brown points out (p. 331), this stanza, as also in the P.R.O. text, is out of strict chronological order. The G. & C. C. text lacks this stanza and the Balliol text the following stanza. Brown makes unnecessary difficulty over 'Optans celi gaudia' which obviously modifies the 'he' of l. 25, not the plural pronoun referring to the murderers.

l. 35. *poyntes*. The references to 'points' in this and other carols of St. Thomas (*E.E.C.*, Nos. 113, 115) have puzzled previous editors (e.g. Wright and Whiting). In this text and No. 115 their number is fifty-two; in the P.R.O. text and No. 113 it is fifty; the G. & C. C. text has 'fyftene tokenus'.

The correct explanation is provided by an exposition in Middle English in T.C.D. MS. E. 5. 10, f. 122 r. and v. (XV cent.), headed 'Articuli sancti Thome Cantuariensis episcopi', and beginning:

> Ye schulle vnderstond how that kynge harre þe secunde at his peralament at Northehampton made a blanke charter and commandyd all the lordes of the lande to pute to theyre Seales. The glorious ma[r]ter saynt Th[omas] was bode to put to his seale and he sayde nay telle that he harde þe pointes that schulde be wrytyn in the sayde Charter. The fyrst ponyt was this that þer schulde no prest ne clerke monke chanon ne frere no more reuerence then another seculer mon schulde haue.

The paragraph marks and the 'also's' that follow indicate a list of fourteen points which may very briefly be summarized as follows:

2. No abbot, prior, 'person vicary', or parish priest should ask duties or tithes.
3. A fee of 20s. to the king from any commoner putting his child to school.
4. Fees to the king from those taking minor and priests' orders.
5. Fees for burial in consecrated ground.
6. Duties to the King and lord when a husband predeceases his wife.
7. Fee to the king from any couple married in church.
8. Fee to the king for a child's christening.
9. Fee to the king for a mother's purification.
10. Fee to the king for confirmation by a bishop.
11. Death by hanging for a father and burning for a mother in the case of murder or negligence in the death of a child under the age of seven.
12. Offenders against temporal law taking sanctuary in a church to be sought out, a man hanged, and a woman burnt, and the church to require reconsecration.

13. Commoners to eat white bread, pullet, capon, pig, goose, veal, or mutton only on four days in the year.
14. No commoner spending less than ten pounds a year to wear any coloured cloth.

The list concludes:

'thise poyntys with other mo were the poyntes that saynt Thomas of Caunterbury suffred martyrdom for.'

A curious survival of the tradition of fifty-two points as late as 1532 is found in the petition to Cromwell of William Umpton, one of the grooms of the King's Hall, who has been a prisoner in the Tower for fourteen months, 'loaded with irons'. According to poor Umpton, 'a pardoner of St. Thomas's hospital at Woodstock said that St. Thomas of Canterbury died for 52 points concerning the commonwealth; "which 52 your said orator denied, one excepted for the clergy, and that the said 52 points were a dance called Robin Hood [apparently equivalent to frivolous nonsense]." Then the pardoner asked him if he would compare Robin Hood with St. Thomas before my lord of Lincoln; on which he fortuned to ask the same pardoner why St. Thomas was a saint rather than Robin Hood? For this he was accused of heresy. . .' (James Gairdner, ed., *Letters and Papers . . . of the Reign of Henry VIII*, London, 1880, v. 551). Umpton was ahead of his time, and his petition was fruitless.

25. *Of the Nativity and New Year*

E.E.C., No. 117a; B.–R. 21.

(Other texts: T.C.C. MS. O. 3. 58; with music; *pr.* Rickert, p. 167; with music: Stevens, p. 8; Bodl. MS. Arch. Selden B. 26, f. 15 v.; with music; *pr.* with music: Stevens, p. 20.)

The possibilities of an effective dramatic use of this carol have been several times pointed out, e.g. in *O.B.C.*, p. 51. It would seem that the original conception of the author was that the entire stanza should be sung by a soloist, representing the messenger, and the burden with its query by a chorus in regular carol-fashion. The two settings preserved, however, are for two parts throughout, and in *c* the last four lines of the stanza are marked as a chorus.

The spirited rhythm is so much superior to Audelay's usual metres that his original authorship must be regarded as doubtful.

The version in the T.C.C. MS. roll has 'yoles' in l. 2 of the burden in place of Audelay's 'New Eris' and the 'yeres' of the Selden MS. The New Year's burden (prefixed in spite of the Nativity content of the stanzas) is particularly interesting in the light of the probability of the manuscript's Worcester provenance, as it appears from Prior William More's journal that carols were sung in hall there on New Year's Day as well as on Christmas and other days of the Nativity season. Both carols and some kind of observance involving 'messengers' at the annual feast for civic officials appear together in the journal's entry for Epiphany 1519 (Ethel S. Fegan, ed., *Journal of Prior William More*, Worcestershire Historical Society, 1914, p. 77):

> Item in rewards for the bryngyng of yere giffs 4*s*. 8*d*. 8*d*.
> Item in rewards to pleyers children when ye balys with ther company dyned with me . . . 12*d*.
> Item to syngers of carralls 20*d*. Item rewarded to iiij pleyers a pon ye Epiphani Day belonging to sir Edward beltenop 3*s*. 4*d*. Item in rewards to serten persons beyng messyngers 5*s*. 8*d*.

26. *Of the New Year*

E.E.C., No. 120; *pr.* E. Flügel, *Anglia*, xxvi. 242: B.-R. 1873.

The last stanza suggests that the carol was designed for use by a master of revels or other singer welcoming a company on behalf of their host. The 'What cher?' refrain is admirably effective when conceived as sung by the soloist of the stanzas. It is at once the cue to the assembly in the hall to join in the burden and a challenge which is pointedly repeated and answered by them in the words of the hearty burden.

The failure of the rhyme in the last stanza is not unparalleled in the carols. Holthausen's suggestion of 'lere' (*Anglia*, xvii. 444) is possible.

27. *Of the New Year*

E.E.C., No. 121; *pr.* Robbins, *Historical Poems*, p. 62; B.-R. 320.

This carol is obviously designed to be sung at a social gathering, probably a dinner, but it contrasts sharply in tone with the other New Year carols. It is more similar in theme and tone to the anonymous Christmas song of 1555–60 with refrain but no burden in the Maitland Folio Manuscript (No. lxxiv, pp. 211–12, *pr.* [Sir] W. A. Craigie, S.T.S., New Ser., No. 7, i (1919), 238–9):

> In honour of this christinmes
> Now everie man suld him address
> To sing and dance and mak gud cheir
> wait nane how lang he levis heir

(Five stanzas in all; the fourth line is the refrain.)

Robbins (*Historical Poems*, p. 278) suggests for it an approximate date of 1445, at the end of the Hundred Years' War, saying, 'The return of

soldiers and the formation of private armies, the continued famine con-
ditions (e.g. 1438, 1439, 1445), and the economic turbulence of servants
seeking better jobs all point to such a date.' He gives it the title 'The Day
Will Dawn'.

The theme of mutability is common enough in carols, e.g. No. 76 and
E.E.C., Nos. 382, 386, 388, and the hope of reunion expressed in No. 38,
ll. 17–19, is somewhat wistful. But it may be that Robbins's title and comment and the note in *E.E.C.*, '. . . the democratic spirit of the last stanza
is something different from the ordinary pious depreciation of worldly
greatness', imply a wider political significance than the carol actually has.
The fragment of MS. in which its only copy is preserved is shown by the
presence (on the same page as the carol) of a carefully, if crudely, drawn
coat of arms (Argent, a lion rampant gules with a cross above it within
a bordure sable bezantée) to have come from the Cistercian abbey of
Hailes in Gloucestershire, which bore these arms of its founder and great
benefactor, Richard, Earl of Cornwall (the crozier for difference is not
laid across the lion here). Since the carol appears to come from a period
when Hailes was undergoing hardship and impoverishment, from which
it was to be rescued by the restoration of pilgrimages to its treasured relic
of the Holy Blood, it should perhaps be regarded as a reflection of the
discontent of a particular abbey, which in the preceding century had
had to summon the King's aid 'against persons who threatened and
assaulted their men and servants and carried away their goods' (William
Page, *V.C.H.*, *Gloucester*, London, 1907, ii. 97), rather than a general
proletarian protest.

28. *Of the Epiphany*

E.E.C., No. 123A; *pr.* E. Flügel, *Anglia*, xxvi. 239; Rickert, p. 117; B.–R.
3527.

(Other text: *E.E.C.*, No. 123B; *pr.* Brown, *R.L. 15 C.*, p. 126; Rickert,
p. 117; B.–R. 2730.)

In the other version, from MS. B.M. Sloane 2593, no burden is written,
but before stanza 1 appears: dic ✠. This is perhaps the scribe's indication
of the 'Alleluia' burden.

l. 1. The figure of the blossom from the thorn is a slight variation of
the 'Rod of Jesse' and 'Root of Jesse' symbolism. Compare *Cursor Mundi*
(Fairfax text), ll. 9269–72:

> Iesse he [Isaiah] saide of his roting
> certanly a wande sulde spring
> out of þat wande a flour suld brest
> atte sulde bringe vs alle to rest.

E.E.C., No. 35B, also from this MS., begins:

> This nyght ther is a child born
> That sprange owt of Jessis thorn.

ll. 5, 6. The use of a well as a figure of Christ is related to a legend told of the Nativity in Mirk's *Festial* (part i, p. 26):

> 'Yn tokenyng of þys þyng, þat same day Cryst was borne yn Bede-leem, a well yn Rome of watyr turned ynto oyle and ran soo all þat day, schewyng þat þe well of grace and of mercy was borne þat day þat schuld ȝeue grace and mercy to all þat wold come to hym þerfor.'

The well of mercy as a figure applied to Christ appears in a hymn from the Thornton MS. (*pr.* Patterson, p. 131), but it is more often associated with the Virgin, as in Chaucer's *Prioress's Tale*, l. 204, and *E.E.C.*, Nos. 199, 207. A well as the type of the Divine mercy appears in *E.E.C.*, No. 306 and in B.M. MS. Sloane 2593, f. 32 v., where 'lauacra puri gurgitis selestis angnus attigit peccata' is translated (Wright, *Wart. Club*, p. 96):

> The welle haght waschyn vs fro wo,
> The lomb of heuene is comyn vs to.

ll. 9, 10. The symbolism connects the birth of Christ with the previous long captivity of Israel in Egypt.

ll. 17–20. This stanza appears as stza. 4 of *E.E.C.*, No. 35 and as stza. 6 of *E.E.C.*, No. 124A. The sequence referred to is probably that for the Mass on Epiphany, of which ll. 9, 10 run (*Sar. Miss.*, p. 465):

> Huic magi munera deferunt preclara aurum simul thus et myrram.
> Thure deum predicant. auro regem magnum. hominem mortalem myrra.

It appears to have been something of a *passe-partout* stanza. It has a recognizable survival in various versions of the favourite traditional carol 'The First Nowell', e.g. *O.B.C.*, No. 27, stza. 6:

> Then entered in those Wise Men three,
> Fell reverently upon their knee,
> And offered there in his presénce
> Both gold and myrrh and frankincense.

29. *Of the Epiphany*

E.E.C., No. 125A; *pr.* Rickert, p. 112; B.–R. 2339.

(Other texts: St. J. C. MS. S. 54, f. 7 v.; *E.E.C.*, No. 125Ba; Bodl. MS. Eng. poet. e. 1, f. 31 v.; B.M. MS. Harley 541, f. 214 r.; *E.E.C.*, No. 125C; *pr.* Rickert, p. 110; &c.; B.–R. 2333.)

Only in the text here printed does this long narrative of the Epiphany appear as a true carol with a burden. This burden is taken from a hymn for Christmas not in the Sarum Use (H. A. Daniel, ed., *Thesaurus Hymnologicus*, Leipzig, 1855–6, i. 344) and is not very well adapted metrically to the form of the stanzas. The probability is that the original form of the piece was that of a song without a burden, as the 'bob-and-wheel' type of stanza is not frequently used with a burden.

l. 38. The comparison of sun and glass here is probably an echo of the familiar figure for Christ's conception.

ll. 76, 77. Compare No. 22, ll. 1, 2, and note thereon, and *E.E.C.*, Appendix, No. ii, ll. 13–16.

30. *Of the Epiphany*

With music; *pr.* with music: Stevens, p. 40.

This carol of only one stanza is obviously the beginning of a longer one, not preserved, on the Epiphany with at least two more stanzas for the other magi and their gifts. The burden may have been suggested by the

> Ave, regina celorum,
> Mater Regis angelorum

of the Antiphon of the Virgin which so begins (*Horae Eboracenses*, Publications of the Surtees Society, cxxxii, 1920, p. 29).

31. *Of the Epiphany*

With music; *pr.* with music: Stevens, p. 43.

This carol follows the tradition that the baptism of Christ took place on the anniversary of the Epiphany.

burden, l. 1. The first line of a hymn by St. Augustine of Hippo (H. A. Daniel, ed., *Thesaurus Hymnologicus*, Leipzig, 1855–6, ii. 192). ll. 9–12. Matthew iii. 17; Mark i. 10–11; Luke iii. 22.

32. *A Carol Bringing In the Boar's Head*

E.E.C., No. 132A; *pr.* E. Flügel, *Anglia*, xxvi. 257; B.–R. 3313.

(Other texts: Bodl. Rawlinson 4to 598 (10), printed by Wynkyn de Worde; *E.E.C.*, No. 132B; W. Sandys, *Christmastide* (London, 1852), p. 231; Rickert, p. 91; Robbins, *Secular Lyrics*, p. 48; &c.; Traditional version, Queen's College, Oxford; *E.E.C.*, No. 132C.)

The version here printed of this best known of the boar's head carols is probably earlier in the form of its text than the version printed by Wynkyn de Worde in 1521, even though it may have been written later in Richard Hill's MS. The last stanza marks the ceremonial serving of the boar's head as a custom confined to the Christmas season. The 'byrdes syngynge' of l. 2 may mean an actual garnishing of the charger with captive live birds, a procedure not too elaborate for a Tudor feast.

The note in *O.B.C.* p. 25, is erroneous. Wynkyn de Worde prints no music with the carol.

On the Queen's College, Oxford, version see Introduction, p. 32. It is more likely that the college adopted a well-known carol from general circulation than that a carol originating in the college gained currency of the kind indicated by Hill's and Wynkyn de Worde's recordings.

33. *A Boar's Head Carol*

E.E.C., No. 133; with music; *pr.* with music: Stevens, p. 66; J. Stafford Smith, *Musica Antiqua* (London, 1812), p. 22; B.–R. 3315.

The boar's head as a symbol of Christ occurs only in this carol, as far as I am aware. In the better known No. 32 it is said to be served in Christ's honour, but it is not explained symbolically, as here. The fragment (apparently the final stanza) of a boar's head carol in St. J. C. MS. S. 54, f. 1 r. (*E.E.C.*, Appendix, No. iii) concludes with a pious exclamation:

> The borys hed have we in broght;
> Lok ye be mery in hert and thoght!
> And he that all this world has wrowt
> Save yow and eke me!

34. *Holly Against Ivy*

A. *E.E.C.*, No. 136A; Rickert, p. 265; B.–R. 1226.

B. *E.E.C.*, No. 136B; *pr.* E. Flügel, *Anglia*, xxvi. 279; Rickert, p. 264. See Introduction, pp. 32–34.

Both preserved texts of this carol are given in this selection because of the unusually wide difference in form as compared with most carol-variants and because of the interesting lines found only in B. Version A, from a Midland MS. of the mid-fifteenth century, unquestionably derives from an older text than does Richard Hill's Version B, and it gives the clearer suggestion of a carol which was used in some sort of game between men and women. Version B, with its four-line stanzas which use some of A's couplets in a different order, is definitely more self-conscious and literary. Its 'chairs of gold', its long simile of a herd of bullocks used to characterize the clumsiness of any dancing done by the women, and its long treatment of the wood-pigeon, still among the most despised of English birds, and its insult to ivy all impress the hearer as belonging to a sophisticated and on the whole less successful reworking of a simple original. Nevertheless it is Version B that gives the only suggestion of a direct connexion with the very popular traditional song 'The Holly and the Ivy', most texts of which begin one or more stanzas with 'The holly bears a berry'. Apparently this one phrase at least has survived from the Middle Ages to appear in a piece of which Margaret Dean-Smith insists on the modernity (*Guide*, p. 74): 'Although now so well-known, the text of "The Holly and the Ivy", with the possible exception of the Cornish version given in [*J.F.S.S.* viii (1931), 113–15], (cp. "Cherry, holly and ivy" in the same number [pp. 111–12], appears to derive from a single source, a Birmingham broadside published by Wadsworth, according to Husk "about one-and-a-half centuries since", i.e. c. 1710.' But it was probably not written in a Birmingham printing-office.

A, l. 12. *poppynguy*. Rather than to the parrot, as usual, the word must refer here to an English bird, probably the disliked green woodpecker, although *O.E.D.* first records such use from 1612.

A, l. 14; B, l. 4. The association of the owl with ivy is traditional over many centuries, and the expression 'like an owl in an ivy-bush' is proverbial. See, for example, William George Smith, *The Oxford Dictionary of English Proverbs* (Oxford, 1935), p. 44. The expression sometimes refers to the enmity of the smaller birds towards the owl and their concerted attacks on it. In *The Owl and the Nightingale* human attack is also described (ll. 65–68, 1115–20). Compare a simile from the seventeenth century, 'With that they all fell upon him, as an Oule in an ivie bush' (*Notes and Queries*, 9th ser. ix, 157).

J. Payne Collier's ballad, 'Full mournfully hootes Madge Howlet, Under the ivy bushe', is apparently one of his fabrications made to fit entries in the Stationers' Register and has no evidential value (*Twenty-five Old Ballads and Songs*, London, 1869, p. 32).

35. *In Praise of Ivy*

E.E.C., No. 138; *pr.* Robbins, *Secular Lyrics*, p. 46; Rickert, p. 263; &c.; B.–R. 3438.

Compare other carols on the virtues of letters, *E.E.C.*, Nos. 83, 180.

l. 13. *V*: pronounced, of course, as 'U'.

l. 22. Is the comely lady meant to be the Virgin herself? At any rate she conforms to the tradition of the female sponsorship of Ivy, and the stanza makes of the carol a *chanson d'aventure*.

36. *In Praise of Ivy*

With music; *pr.* with music: Stevens, p. 44.

The connexion of ivy with Christmas is not made explicit in this interesting carol, but from its inclusion in the series of carols in this MS. we can safely assume that it was meant for use in the Nativity season. It differs from the other holly-ivy carols in that it sings the praise of the plant itself, making no symbolic application.

l. 9. Here the reference seems to be to ground ivy (*Nepeta hederacea*); in the next stanza it shifts to climbing ivy (*Hedera helix*).

l. 11. There are many medieval prescriptions for the use of ivy in medicine, e.g. *Liber de Diversis Medicinis* in the Thornton MS. (Lincoln Cathedral A. 5. 2), mid-fifteenth century, from the North Riding of Yorkshire and written by the scribe of No. 91 (ed. Margaret Sinclair Ogden, E.E.T.S., Or. Ser., No. 107, 1938, p. 17): 'An oþer [for toothache]. Tak yven and salte & stampe to-gedir & mak a playster & laye to þe cheke, for þat hales wale'; and *An Herbal* [1525, printed by Richard Banckes of London] (ed. Sanford V. Larkey and Thomas Pyles, N.Y., 1941, p. 27): 'The virtue thereof is, if it be sodden in wine till it be thick, and then lay it all hot to a botch, it shall break it.' An infusion of ivy is often recommended for sore eyes. A long list of its medical uses is given by Hermann Fischer,*Mittelalterliche Pflanzenkunde* (Munich, 1929), p. 211.

ll. 13, 14. The phrase 'In bok' suggests that the author of the carol may have known the widely circulated *Blason des Couleurs*, written between 1435 and 1458 by Sicille, Herald of King Alphonse V of Aragon, (ed. Hippolyte Cocheris, Paris, 1860). Compare 'De la Couleur Verde et de ses Livrees' (p. 83): 'La couleur verde est délectable à la veue et luy donne grant plaisir, et traict les yeulx à la regarder et les reconforte, et pare quant ils sont grevez.'

l. 17. The reference to 'gret stormys of snaw and hail' pretty certainly indicates a North-of-England origin for the carol.

ll. 22–25. The fairest bird, otherwise unspecified, cannot be the owl traditionally associated with ivy. This is another mark of originality in this carol; it may even be a reply to the taunt directed toward Ivy in No. 34.

l. 31. Widely differing opinions have long been held as to the effect of a growth of ivy on masonry. The *Encyclopaedia Britannica* (14th ed., *s.v.* Ivy) holds with the author of the carol: '. . . a fair growth of ivy on sound walls that afford no entrance beyond the superficial attachment of the claspers is, without any exception whatever, beneficial. It promotes dryness and warmth, reduces to a minimum the corrosive action of the atmosphere, and is altogether as conservative as it is beautiful.' But many caretakers believe the opposite.

l. 34. *at hye*: Stevens glosses 'at eye', i.e. at first sight or plainly. This makes good sense, of course, but for the possibility of a reference to the lost hamlet of Hythe in Holderness see R. L. Greene, *J.A.M.S.* vii (1954), 24–25. 'Eye' and 'Hythe' as place-names were more or less interchangeable, and a famous confusion of Eye in Suffolk and Hythe in Kent once resulted. The hamlet of Hythe was still well enough remembered in the eighteenth century to be given a special note on a map of Holderness.

37. *Of the Purification*

E.E.C., No. 140; B.–R. 503

This is a farewell to the Christmas season which emphasizes, not the festal aspect of Candlemas like No. 38, but its religious meaning, in which the Virgin is, of course, the central figure. It is unusual in praying for 'purification' of the individual soul, through Mary's help, and in not confining itself to the historic incident of her own ritual appearance in the Temple (Luke ii. 22–24).

The 'revertere' of the burden is probably from Canticles vi. 12: 'Revertere, revertere, Sulamitis; revertere, revertere, ut intueamur te,' rather than Isaiah xliv. 22: '. . . revertere ad me, quoniam redemi te.' Compare the burden of *Carmina Burana* (ed. Johann A. Schmeller, Breslau, 1894), No. 142:

> Revertere, revertere
> iam, ut 'intuear' te.

38. *Farewell to Christmas*

E.E.C., No. 141; *pr.* E. Flügel, *Anglia*, xxvi. 245; A. W. Pollard, *Fifteenth Century Prose and Verse* (Westminster, 1903), p. 89; Rickert, p. 225; B.–R. 1198.

Like No. 37 this carol puts 'the end of Christmas' at Candlemas rather than at Twelfth Day. See note on No 2. Less usual in popular tradition is the notion of l. 2 that Christmas begins as early as 'Hallowtide', i.e. the first of November, though it was the medieval custom for the King to announce at All Hallows his election of the place at which he would spend his Christmas.

The dramatic personification of Christmas in this piece is parallel to that in No. 2 and *E.E.C.*, No. 5, to which it forms an interesting complement. The refrain and burden are like an echo of the latter. The whole carol implies the impersonation of Christmas by a singer. An aristocratic or at least a well-to-do gathering is the audience to which it is expressly directed.

A closely similar conception of a farewell to Christmas is the basis of the delightful seventeenth-century song for Candlemas beginning:

> Christmas hath made an end,
> Welladay, welladay.

(Norman Ault, ed., *Seventeenth Century Lyrics*, London, 1928, p. 324.) In this song Lent is also personified as in No. 1.

l. 14. *Merchall*. See note on No. 5, l. 2.

ll. 21-23. Compare Gower, *Confessio Amantis*, bk. iv, ll. 2814-15:

> Bot he seith often, 'Have good day,'
> That loth is forto take his leve.

39. *Sweet Jesus*

E.E.C., No. 142a; B.-R. 30.

(Other MS. versions: Westminster Abbey 20, f. 20 r.; *pr.* R. L. Greene, *ELH*, vii. 225.)

(Other traditional versions: *pr. A Good Christmas Box, Containing a Choice Collection of Christmas Carols* (Dudley, 1847), pp. 96–98; Frank Sidgwick, ed., *Popular Carols* (London, 1908), pp. 29–31.)

On the survival of this carol and of *E.E.C.*, No. 152 in modern oral tradition see Introduction, p. 24.

The 'lollay' burden of this carol is written in a hand different from that of the stanzas in a space presumably left for it at the top of the page. The piece is not a regular lullaby carol, but is related to the type through its presenting a narrative of the life of Christ such as is given at much greater length in *E.E.C.*, No. 149a, a carol which has as its burden the first two lines of this burden. It seems likely that the Westminster Abbey text represents the earlier form, using as burden what is here the first stanza. Significantly these four lines are not bracketed in the manuscript as the following stanzas are. The change is of the same type as that found in No. 44.

The nineteenth-century version from the broadside includes a stanza on Holy Thursday which has no counterpart in the St. J. C. MS. but which is matched by the last stanza of the Westminster Abbey text (following the stanza on Easter and hence out of chronological order like the Good Friday stanza in this text):

> On the Holy Thursday
> To hevene he toke his way,
> Ther to abyde forever and day,
>   And Jhesus [is hys name.]

For a fuller discussion and collation of texts see Greene, op. cit., pp. 225–31.

Another traditional piece with an obvious relation to 'Sweet Jesus' is 'All in the Morning', which Margaret Dean-Smith (*Guide*, p. 47) treats as a version of this carol. It is found in Sandys, pp. 117–18, with title 'Upon Christmas Day', and in R. Vaughan Williams, *Eight Traditional English Carols* (London, 1919), p. 4, as derived from W. H. Shawcross, *A Garland of the Old Castleton Christmas Carols* (Castleton, 1904), pp. 10–12. Shawcross's text begins as follows:

> It was on Christmas Day,
>   And all in the morning,
>   [repeated as l. 2 of all stanzas]
> Our Saviour was Born,
>   And our Heavenly King;
>
>   And was not this a joyful thing,
>   And sweet JESUS they call'd Him by Name.
>   [repeated as refrain after each of next four stanzas]
>
> It was on New Year's Day,
> They Circumcised our Saviour
>   And our Heavenly King; (&c.)

40. *Of the Virgin and Child*

E.E.C., No. 143; *pr.* Rickert, p. 66; *O.B.C.*, p. 220; &c.; B.–R. 1351.
The metre of this, the masterpiece of the lullaby carols, makes the same effective use of the 'rest' as does 'I sing of a maiden', which is in the same MS. One is inclined to attribute it to the same unknown author.

41. *Of the Virgin and Child*

E.E.C., No. 150A; *pr.* A. Brandl and O. Zippel, *Middle English Literature*, 2nd ed. (N.Y., 1949), p. 114; Rickert (composite text), p. 59; B.–R. 3627.
(Other texts: Bodl. MS. Eng. poet. e. 1, f. 17 v.; *E.E.C.*, No. 150B; *pr.* F. E. Budd, *A Book of Lullabies 1300–1900* (London, 1930), p. 34; Balliol MS. 354, f. 226 r.; B.M. MS. Royal Appendix 58, f. 52 v., with music.)
The burden of this lullaby dialogue has four lines in common with the first stanza of another of the same type, *E.E.C.*, No. 151, found in three texts. In Bodl. MS. Eng. poet. e. 1 the stanza reads:

> Thys endrys nyght
> I saw a syghth,

> A mayd a cradyll kepe,
> And ever she song
> And seyd among,
>   'Lullay, my chyld, and slepe.'

It is apparently from this or a similar carol that the opening *chanson d'aventure* formula has been borrowed and made into a burden.

With only the omission of one 'lulley' the burden also appears prefixed to a lullaby dialogue in Bodl. MS. Ashmole 189, ff. 106 v., 107 r. in the same hand that has written *E.E.C.*, Nos. 86b and 333 (*pr.* Brown, *R.L. 15 C.*, pp. 7–8). This piece varies the carol form by prefixing a four-measure couplet to each six-line stanza. The whole poem is closely related to the group of lullaby carols.

42. *A Dialogue of the Virgin and Child*

E.E.C., No. 152a; *pr.* Rickert, p. 72; R. L. Greene, *ELH*, vii, 232; B.–R. 22.

(Other MS. texts: Bodl. MS. Laud misc. 683, f. 105 v.; Nat. Lib. W. Porkington 10, f. 201 r.; *pr.* Joshua Sylvester [pseud.], *A Garland of Christmas Carols, Ancient and Modern* (London, 1861), p. 41; Brown, *R.L. 15 C.*, p. 1.)

(Other traditional texts: Harvard College Library, MS. HCL 25258. 27.5*, 'Carol Book A', p.8; ibid., 'Carol Book B', pp. 58–59; Sandys, pp. 122–3.)

ll. 25–27 of this lullaby dialogue which predicts the sufferings of Christ in his Passion are found as stza. 7, ll. 1–3 of *E.E.C.*, No. 153, a similar dialogue also from the Balliol MS.

The version of this piece in MS. Porkington 10 has no burden and presents the stanzas (omitting the second and tenth) in alternation with stanzas of the Latin hymn 'Christe qui lux es et dies.' There is no relation between the texts and no indication of how, if at all, the resulting piece is to be sung. This is the only instance in the carols of such an arrangement.

Two of the traditional texts of the carol come from 1767 and 1777. They are written in two carefully prepared manuscript books of carols then in use in Cornwall which were written for one John Webb in the neighbourhood of Boskenna. For fuller description see Richard L. Greene, *ELH*, vii (1940), 234–6. In these there is no initial burden but a chorus after the stanzas only. The text from 'Carol Book A' begins:

> There is a child born to our blessing shall bring:
> I heard a maid 'lullo by lollo' to sing:

'Peace, my dear child, of thy weeping,
    For thou shall be our heavenly King.'

Now sing we, and now sing we,
'To the gloria O tibi, Domini.'
    [Repeated after each stanza]

'O mother, O mother, your wishes are naught—
It is not for me such carrols are wrought—
Such were never and nor no woman thought—
    To the gloria O tibi, Domini,'
            (&c.)

According to Sandys, the version in his book is also from Cornwall.

That carols of the Passion were used in the fifteenth century, as in modern folk-singing, to celebrate the Nativity season is shown by the heading of the Laud misc. version: 'here begynneth a cristemasse song'. The device of having the infant Jesus recount in the future tense the details of his crucifixion has survived into modern times in French folk song, e.g. 'Complainte de la Passion' in Lucien Decombe, ed., *Chansons populaires recueillies dans le Département d'Ille-et-Vilaine* (Paris, 1884), pp. 242–3. Two stanzas of this piece, which was used as a *quête* song, somewhat resemble stanzas of the carol:

Avant qu'il soit vendredi nuit,
    Vous voirez mon corps pendre;
Et vous voirez mes bras tendus,
    Tant qu'ils pourront s'étendre.

Vous voirez mon chef couronné
    D'un couronn' d'épin' blanche;
Vous voirez mon côté percé
    De trois grands coups de lance.

43. *A Lullaby for the Christ Child*

E.E.C., No. 155a; B.–R. 2024.
    (Other text: B.M. MS. Harley 7358, f. 12 v.)
    This carol is unique among the lullabies in being addressed to the infant Christ by the author as spokesman for sinful mankind. Its burden is taken from the melancholy lullaby found among the Kildare poems of the earlier part of the fourteenth century (B.M. MS. Harley 913, f. 32, *pr.* Brown, *R.L. 14 C.*, pp. 35–36), or from a common source. It also appears as stza. 9, l. 1 of *E.E.C.*, No. 148A. See F. E. Budd, *A Book of Lullabies:*

1300–1900 (London, 1930), pp. 2, 3. The carol, although in a shorter line and tail-rhyme stanza, shares with the earlier Franciscan lullaby the same fine austerity of spirit mingled with real tenderness.

44. *Of the Passion*

E.E.C., No. 157B; B.–R. 1219.

(Other texts: B.M. MS. Sloane 2593, f. 23 r.; *E.E.C.*, No. 157C; B.–R. 2111; Nat. Lib. Scot., MS. Advocates 18. 17. 21, f. 121 r.; *E.E.C.*, No. 157D; B.–R. 2036; Hunt. Lib. *Christmas carolles newely Inprynted* (Richard Kele), p. [31]; *E.E.C.*, No. 157A; *repr.* Bliss, p. 49.)

The three later texts of this carol have been made out of some version of the dialogue of Mary and Jesus written in couplets and without a burden in Friar Johan de Grimestone's commonplace book of 1372. The three have different burdens. The text here printed uses as a burden the first two lines of what is the first stanza of the versions in Kele's print and B.M. MS. Sloane 2593. The latter contents itself with a burden of 'Nowel, el, el, el, el, el, el, el, el, el, el, el, el, el, el, el!' The Kele text prefixes as a burden:

> Gaudeamus synge we
> In hoc sacro tempore;
> Puer nobis natus est
> Ex Maria virgine.

The burden of the text here printed is also used as the burden of *E.E.C.*, No. 158, a dialogue of the Passion between Mary and St. John the Evangelist from the Balliol MS. This is one of the best instances of the rather free interchangeability of burdens in the carols.

l. 1. Compare ll. 310–11 of the Digby Play 'The Burial of Christ' (ed. F. J. Furnivall, E.E.T.S., Ex. Ser., No. lxx, 1930, pp. 181–2):

> From the Crowne of the hede vnto the too,
> This blessit body was wrappit all in woo.

45. *The Cold Wind*

E.E.C., No. 170; B.–R. 3525 (indexed by first line of burden).

Even if no parallel were preserved, the burden of this carol would suggest that it is a sacred parody of a secular song in general circulation. That it should be so regarded is made practically certain by the presence in *A Compendious Book of Godly and Spiritual Songs* (1567), among other

'moralized' pieces, of one which is obviously based on the same prototype:

> The wind blawis cauld, furius & bauld,
>   This lang and mony day:
> But Christis mercy, we man all die,
>   Or keip the cauld wind away.

> This wind sa keine, that I of meine,
> It is the ryte of auld,
> Our Faith is inclusit, and plainlie abusit,
> This wind hes blawin tó cauld.

(Burden and stanza 1, ed. A. F. Mitchell, S.T.S., No. 39, 1897, pp. 189–92.)
The same image, again associated with the Passion, appears in the burden
of *E.E.C.*, No. 171 in the printed Douce fragments f. 48 of about 1550:

> Blowe the winde styl, and blow nat so shyl;
> My blode, man, I shed for the al at wyl.
> Blowe the winde styl, and blowe nat so shyll;
> This paine to suffre is my Fathers wil.

Professor Bertrand H. Bronson has pointed out to the editor the likeness of this image to that which begins the ballad *The Unquiet Grave*
(Child, No. 78); see also *Guide*, p. 113.

46. Mary, the Rose

E.E.C., No. 173; with music; *pr.* C. & S., p. 105; Rickert, p. 8; M. G.
Segar, *A Mediaeval Anthology* (London, 1915), p. 65; &c.; with music:
Stevens, p. 10; B.–R. 3536.
   The last lines of the stanzas of this carol are taken from the last lines of
the demi-strophes of the 'Laetabundus' prose. See Introduction, pp. 37–38.
It is unusual in its employment of the same words for burden and first
stanza.
   In its frequent use of the rose as a symbol of the Virgin the Church
applied to her the words of Ecclesiasticus xxiv. 18: 'Quasi palma exaltata
sum in Cades, et quasi plantatio rosae in Jericho.'

47. Mary, the Rose-Bush

E.E.C., No. 175A; B.–R. 1914.
   (Other texts: Balliol MS. 354, f. 220 v.; *E.E.C.*, No. 175 B; Rickert,
p. 9; &c.; B.M. MS. Sloane 2593, f.6 v.; *E.E.C.*, No. 175C; B.–R. 1893.)

The five 'branches' represent the traditional Five Joys of the Virgin. The version in the Balliol MS. adds a sixth 'branch' as the sign of all the Joys collectively, and the version in the Sloane MS. reduces the number of Joys to three, probably for the sake of brevity rather than because of any differently reasoned conception of the figure.

The curious reader may consult the 'explication', ponderous to the point of hilarity, of the Sloane and Balliol versions of this carol by Leo Spitzer, '*Explication de Texte* Applied to Three Great Middle English Poems', *Archivum Linguisticum*, iii (1951), 137–52. Spitzer did not know of the existence of the text of Eng. poet. e. 1, printed in 1935 with the other two in *E.E.C.* (and many decades before by Wright), and hence 'postulated' the existence of a text 'X' and another 'Y'. In spite of the ubiquity of the rose-symbol, he suggested a common Latin original for this carol and the well-known German nativity song, 'Es ist ein' Ros' entsprungen' of 1599, though there are no verbal resemblances. On his comment that the Joys of Mary 'according to the traditional theme' are always given in an odd number, see Notes on No. 51. He found it obvious 'That the author of [Sloane] was inspired by the single line of [Balliol], "Of her bosum a blossum spronge"', not knowing that the line in the text here given is closer, in fact, identical. A note invites us to 'imagine our poem [the Sloane version] as it may have been presented in the original MS.: the letters of the text embedded in a luxuriant foliage so that the whole page would have the appearance of a flowering thicket'. But the Sloane MS. is entirely without illumination, and no preserved carol MS. remotely resembles his vision.

48. *Of Mary and the Letters of Her Name*

E.E.C., No. 180A; 31; B.–R. 1650.

(Other texts: B.M. MS. Sloane 2593, f. 24 v.; *E.E.C.*, No. 180B; Rickert, p. 7.)

For the use of initial letters in other carols see *E.E.C.*, Nos. 83, 139. The rhetorical device of using the letters of Mary's name in an acrostic survives at least into seventeenth-century verse in her honour. In 'The Garland of the Blessed Virgin Marie' it includes ivy among the symbols of the Virgin:

> Here are five letters in this blessed name,
> Which, changed, a five-fold mystery design,
> The M the Myrtle, A the Almonds claim,
> R Rose, I Ivy, E sweet Eglantine.

Stanza 5 reads:

> The fourth is humble Ivy, interserst,
> But lowly laid, as on the earth asleep,
> Preservëd in her antique bed of vert,
> No faith's more firm or flat than where't doth creep.

(Signed 'B. I.', in A. Stafford, *The Female Glory*, 1653, *repr.* Norman Ault, *Seventeenth Century Lyrics*, 2nd ed., N.Y., 1950, pp. 118–19.) A good medieval example occurs in the speech of the angel in the Play of Mary in the Temple in *Ludus Coventriae*, ed. K. S. Block, E.E.T.S., Ex. Ser., No. cxx, 1922, p. 80, ll. 244–51. In the Play of the Parliament of Heaven in the same cycle an acrostic seems to be intended by the four capital letters in l. 196 (ibid., p. 103):

> The name of þe mayde ffre
> Is Mary þat xal Al Restore.

Compare the acrostic on ivy in *E.E.C.*, No. 139.

l. 16. *terys of blod*. Mary's weeping of blood is a detail which frequently occurs in ME. accounts of the Passion, e.g. in *E.E.C.*, Nos. 159, 160, and in *The Northern Passion*, Additional text, ll. 1747–50:

> Oure lady herde thies wordis swete
> and teris of blode scho gane downe lete
> all was hir face by rowne with blode
> whene scho by helde Ihesu one the rode.

(ed. Frances A. Foster, E.E.T.S., Or. Ser., No. 145, 1913, i. 204.) The Harleian text has (l. 1750); 'þat water and blude both scho gret.' The tradition is probably due to a wish to provide a parallel to the water and blood which flowed from the side of Christ (John xix. 34).

49. *To the Virgin*

With music; pr. with music: Stevens, p. 54.

l. 6. *stynter of our stryff*: Compare *E.E.C.*, No. 227, a carol to the Virgin by James Ryman, stza. 1, l. 2: 'Graunter of peace, seaser of stryffe'.

ll. 9, 10. Compare the thirteenth-century poem, 'Of on that is so fair and bright', *E.E.C.*, No. 191B, stza. 2, ll. 5, 6:

> Of alle thou berst the pris,
> Levedi, quene of parays,

and the carol derived from it, *E.E.C.*, No. 191A, stza. 7, l. 1.

50. *To the Virgin*

With music; *pr.* with music: Stevens, p. 36.

(Other text: Bodl. MS. Arch. Selden B. 26, f. 25 v.; with music; *E.E.C.*, No. 190; *pr.* Rickert, p. 17; B.-R. 3674.)

The first seven stanzas of this carol are in the Selden MS. and are so close verbally to this text as to make it virtually certain that there has been written transmission without many intermediate copies. But the 'aboue echone' of the Selden text appears here in the northern form 'abown ilkon'. There is an equally close correspondence between the musical settings of the two texts.

The carol is little more than a list of some of the most frequently cited scriptural 'types' of the Virgin, a theme favoured by James Ryman in some of his carols, e.g. *E.E.C.*, Nos. 192-4, 226.

ll. 5–8. Numbers xxiv. 17.

ll. 11, 12. Numbers xvii.

ll. 17, 18. Judges vi. 37–40.

ll. 23, 24. Ezekiel xliv. 1–3.

51. *Of the Five Joys of Mary*

E.E.C., No. 232B; B.-R. 2098.

(Other texts: St. J. C. MS. S. 54, f. 2 r.; *E.E.C.*, No. 232A; Balliol MS. 354, f. 223 v.; *E.E.C.*, No. 232C.

Brown (*R.L. 15 C.*, p. 303) notes that 'English tradition down to the end of the fourteenth century uniformly recognized Five Joys of the Virgin, viz.: the Annunciation, Nativity, Resurrection, Ascension, and Assumption, whereas on the Continent the number of Joys is regularly seven, through the addition of Epiphany and the Purification'. The other version of this carol gives the orthodox five, but this text replaces the Assumption by the Last Judgement and puts the Ascension on Holy Thursday. In traditional English folk-song the Joys number variously seven, eight, nine, ten, and twelve and deviate as widely from medieval custom as in the fourth stanza of the well-known piece 'The first good joy that Mary had' (*O.B.C.*, No. 70):

> The next good joy that Mary had,
> It was the joy of four;
> To see her own son, Jesus Christ
> To read the Bible o'er.

See also *Guide*, p. 82.

l. 12. From the Latin hymn, 'A solis ortus cardine', Christmas, Lauds, *B.S.* i, col. clxxxix.

52. *To the Virgin*

E.E.C., No. 235a; with music; *pr.* Brown, *R.L. 15 C.*, p. 110; B.-R. 3385.

(Other texts: T. C. C. MS. O. 3. 58; with music; *pr.* Rickert, p. 12; with music: Stevens, p. 2; Hunt. Lib. *Christmas carolles newely Inprynted* (Richard Kele), p. [43].)

l. 8. *dignite*: The Kele version has 'benygnyte', which is hardly more satisfactory. The original reading was probably 'Trinite'.

l. 9. John i. 14, x. 30.

ll. 13–15. There is nothing in the book of Jeremiah to justify such a definite statement. The author is relying on Jeremiah's general reputation as a prophet.

53. *Of the Annunciation*

E.E.C., No. 239a; with music; *pr.* with music: Stevens, p. 110; B.-R. 3736.

(Other texts: Mr. Denis Hill-Wood; on deposit at Ipswich, Ipswich and East Suffolk Record Office, Brome MS., f. 79 v.; Balliol MS. 354, f. 229 v. *pr.* A. W. Pollard, *Fifteenth Century Prose and Verse* (Westminster, 1903), p. 93; Bodl. MS. Eng. poet e. 1, f. 51 v.; with music.)

ll. 27, 28. Expanded and partially transposed from the words of Luke i. 38.

54. *Of the Annunciation and Other Joys of Mary*

E.E.C., No. 242; *pr.* Rickert, p. 13; B.-R. 2113.

The Latin lines are taken from a prayer of the Five Joys, 'Gaude virgo, Mater Christi' (*Horae Eboracenses*, Publications of the Surtees Society, cxxxii, 1920, pp. 63–64). The same lines are used in E.E.C., No. 230, of which John Audelay claims authorship.

55. *The Trouble of Joseph*

E.E.C., No. 259; with music; *pr.* Rickert, p. 24; with music: Stevens, p. 68; B.-R. 1322.

The carol is cast in the form of a dialogue between Joseph and the informing angel. ll. 13–17 allude to his previous resolution to desert Mary, presumably on the grounds of her guilt.

burden. A very similar burden is prefixed to E.E.C., No. 260, which is not, however, a carol of the trouble of Joseph, but a pedantic theological discussion of 'reason'.

ll. 1–7. Compare Mirk's *Festial*, 'De Anunciacione Dominica', p. 107: 'But when Ioseph se hur gret wyth chyld, he merueylt gretly how þat myght be.'

56. *Of the Virgin's Motherhood*

E.E.C., No. 261; *pr.* Rickert, p. 20; B.–R. 3822.

This interesting carol presents a clear case of religious imitation of secular lyric. The prototype is a song of the *genre* in which a betrayed maiden laments her pregnancy, a theme represented in *E.E.C.*, Nos. 452–7, and common in medieval French lyrics as well. The blessed state of the Virgin and her rejoicing would have the effect of a striking contrast to hearers familiar with the type of song parodied. The first stanza may have come from such a piece without much change.

The heading in the MS. names the air for which the carol is designed. It is not otherwise known.

57. *Christ and Sinful Man*

E.E.C., No. 266; *pr.* B.–R. 782.

The first stanza of this carol, modified, appears as the first stanza of a poem without a burden and with twenty-three six-line stanzas, each ending with the refrain-line 'Nolo mortem peccatoris'. It describes Christ's sufferings in an address to God the Father and turns at the end to an appeal to sinful man of the usual type. It is signed by John Redford, the author of the morality play *Wit and Science*, and is included among other poems at the end of that play in B.M. MS. 15233 (*pr.* J. O. Halliwell [-Phillips], *The Moral Play of Wit and Science*, Shakespeare Society Publications, xxxvii, London, 1848, pp. 68–73). It is written in two hands, one of which wrote the text of the play and the other of which wrote other poems including the songs for the play. It is interesting that of these songs one is in carol-form with the burden

> Gyve place gyve place to honest recreacion
> Gyve place, we say, now for thy consolacion

and one is in modified carol-form with the burden

> Welcum myne owne,
> Wellcum myne owne.

Redford was Master of the Choristers of St. Paul's Cathedral from 1531–4 to 1547.

Mr. James G. McManaway has recently discovered in the Folger Shakespeare Library, Washington, D.C., MS. Loseley 58 a transcript of Redford's poem, with slight verbal variations and the transposition of two stanzas, in the hand of Sir William More (1520–1600) and bearing the endorsement 'two dyttyes geven me by my .L. mountegou', i.e. Anthony Browne, first Viscount Montagu (1526–92). According to Mr. Mc-Manaway's dating by watermark the transcript must have been made between 1589 and 1592.

The first and second stanzas of this poem form the text of a six-part motet composed by Thomas Morley (1557–*c.* 1603), organist of St. Paul's and Gentleman of the Chapel Royal, in B.M. MSS. Addit. 29372–7, with the title *Tristitiae Remedium* and the date 1616. Prefixed to the text is the burden in the form in which it appears in Ryman's *E.E.C.*, No. 267 (text from Cantus part):

> Nolo mortem peccatoris [*bis*]
> Haec sunt verba Salvatoris,

but with the lines transposed.

burden, l. 2. From Ezekiel xxxiii. 11: 'Dic ad eos, vivo ego, dicit Dominus Deus. Nolo mortem impii, sed ut convertatur impius a via sua, et vivat'. The same phrase occurs in translation in the burden of *E.E.C.*, No. 268, by Ryman:

> Thus seith Jhesus of Nazareth:
> Of a synner I wille noo deth.

ll. 13, 14. These lines show that the carol was definitely intended for use at Christmas.

58. *Christ's Call to Mankind*

E.E.C., No. 270; B.–R. 2086.

This is a significant example of the use of a secular and amorous burden with stanzas written for a religious purpose. The carol was undoubtedly designed to be sung to a well-known secular tune. It is a parallel to the better-known cases of the religious imitation of the popular sixteenth-century song 'Come o'er the burn, Bessie' (*Madrigals by English Composers of the Close of the Fifteenth Century*, Plainsong and Mediaeval Music Society, London, 1890, No. 2) and of the likewise popular 'The hunt is up' (J. P. Collier, ed., *Extracts from the Registers of the Stationers' Company*, London, 1848, i. 129–30). Compare also the 'New Notborune Mayd vpon the Passion of Cryste' (E. F. Rimbault, ed., *P.S.* vi, 'Poetical Tracts', London, 1842, p. 33), and the examples in

Gude and Godlie Ballatis, 'With huntis vp', pp. 174–7, 'Iohne, cum kis me now', pp. 158–61, and others.

The burden seems to be definitely related to the lines which begin the address of Christ to man in Victoria and Albert Museum MS. Dyce 45 (c. 1560), ff. 21 v., 22 r. The lines of this song are bracketed as if in three-line stanzas, but the rhyme shows that there must earlier have been a six-line grouping: The song begins:

> Swete harte, be trwe,
> Chaunge for [no] newe,
> Come home to me agene;
> I shall full swetely
> Take the to mercye
> And delyver the owte of payne.

After the address of Christ these rather pedantic lines of explanation occur, supporting the probability that the piece is sacred parody of a secular love song:

> Thys lover trwe
> Whoo wolde renewe
> Mans soule to vertuouse lyfe
> Ys Chryste Jesu
> Wythe hys vertu,
> Mans soule to be hys wyfe.

If not the same secular song, then two which are closely similar in sentiment and verse-form must lie behind the carol and the song in the Dyce MS. The MS. also contains a text of the moralized 'Grievous is my sorrow', another version of which is in the *Gude and Godlie Ballatis*. The secular original is in B.M. MS. Sloane 1584, which contains *E.E.C.*, No. 446.

ll. 23, 24. The 'idols' are probably the images displayed at shrines where contributions are made. The use of the word here in such a sense is earlier than any instance recorded by *O.E.D.* The author of the carol evidently had Wycliffite or Lollard leanings.

59. *To the Trinity*

With music; *pr.* with music, Stevens, p. 40.

burden, l. 1. From the Gloria, first said Christmas, Matins (*Br. Sar.* i, col. clxxi): 'Qui natus es de virgine'; also used as burden, l. 2 of *E.E.C.*, No. 35A; in the third-person form as in this carol used as stza. 1, l. 4 of *E.E.C.*, No. 52.

burden, l. 2; ll. 4, 8, 12. From the Versicle following the 'Timor Mortis' Response in the *Officium Mortuorum* (*Br. Sar.* ii, col. 278): 'Deus in nomine tuo salvum me fac Domine, et in veritate tua libera me.' It is used as the last line of *E.E.C.*, No. 375. It also appears as the refrain of a prayer in quatrains in Bodl. MS. Ashmole 189, f. 105 r. (*pr.* Brown, *R.L. 15 C.*, p. 85).

ll. 1, 2. The formula of the Trinity is a ready-composed four-measure line and is naturally a commonplace, as in *E.E.C.*, No. 288 and others of Ryman's carols to the Trinity. 'Of myght(es) most' is almost inevitable as a rhyme, and Ryman so uses it in *E.E.C.*, Nos. 288, 290, 293, 304, 'As Lord and King of myghtes most', 305. There does not appear to be any question here of direct relationship to any of Ryman's compositions.

l. 6. This commonplace appears as l. 18 of No. 75 and as l. 1 of *E.E.C.*, No. 367.

60. *To the Trinity*

E.E.C., No. 284; *pr.* Frances M. Comper, ed., *Spiritual Songs from English MSS.* (London, [1936]), p. 178; B.–R. 2432.

This carol shows Ryman at his most characteristic as a mannered and repetitious versifier. l. 10 gives one clue to the mystic meaning of this carol, as does the refrain-line with its allusion to the infinity of God, of which the circle, O, is the symbol. The O's of the Advent Antiphons may have been in the author's mind as well.

61. *To St. Francis of Assisi*

E.E.C., No. 310; B.–R. 44.

ll. 2–4. St. Francis had a particular devotion to the Passion of Christ, as recorded in the *Vita Prima S. Francisci Confessoris, Auctore Thoma de Celano*, lib. i, cap. x (*Acta Sanctorum*, Oct., tom. ii, Paris, 1866, p. 706): 'Recordabatur assidua meditatione verborum eius [Christi] et sagacissima consideratione ipsius opera recolebat: praecipue incarnationis humilitas et caritas passionis ita eius memoriam occupabant, ut vix valeret aliud cogitare.'

ll. 9. 10. Actually St. Francis received the stigmata only two years before his death.

ll. 13–16. Apparently Audelay means that St. Francis divided his food in five parts in memory of Christ's five wounds. I have not seen this else-where recorded of the saint. The *Appendix Inedita ad Vitam Primam Auctoribus Tribus ipsius Sancti Sociis* (*Acta Sanctorum*, Oct., tom. ii, p. 727) says: 'non solum autem affligebat se in lacrymis, sed etiam abstinentia cibi et potus ob memoriam Dominicae passionis.'

ll. 21–24. St. Francis set out in 1212 on a mission to the heathen in Palestine, but his ship was wrecked, and he was forced to return. In 1219 he actually went to the Near East and attempted the conversion of some Mohammedans but soon returned to Italy.

l. 26. *talent*: purpose.   l. 27. *testament*: the Testament of St. Francis containing his last instructions to his brethren, dictated by him shortly before his death.

ll. 33–36. The first Rule was given out by St. Francis and orally approved by Pope Innocent III in 1210, not, as the carol implies, later than the Testament. The latter enjoins obedience to the Rule as it had been revised in the saint's lifetime.

62. *Of St. George*

With music; *pr.* B. Schofield, *Musical Quarterly*, xxxii. 513: with music: Stevens, p. 49.

The widespread national devotion to St. George prevents assigning of this carol on internal evidence to any particular locality. It is somewhat surprising that no other carol in honour of St. George has been preserved. There are references to him in No. 68, in *E.E.C.*, Nos. 308, 309a, and in a political carol of 1485 not in *E.E.C.*, 'Our ship is launched from the grounde', in T.C.D. MS. E. 5. 10, ff. 30 r.–31 r. (*pr.* Robbins, *Historical Poems*, pp. 191–3).

The carol appears to have been suggested by a non-liturgical rhyming prayer, the Commemoration of St. George widely circulated in the Prymer or Hours of the Blessed Virgin Mary (*Horae Eboracenses*, Publications of the Surtees Society, No. cxxxii, 1920, pp. 131–2; also in Sarum). It was well known on the Continent, and is edited from five MSS. (two of English origin) in *Anal. Hym.* xv. 206, and from another in xxxiii. 84. The York version begins:

> Georgie martyr inclite,
> te decet laus et gloria.

Of this l. 1 of the carol is pretty clearly a paraphrase. While l. 5 on the maid and the dragon can hardly be referred to any specific source, it may be noted that it corresponds to the lines at about the same point in the York prayer, ll. 4–8:

> per quem puella regia
> existens in tristicia,
> coram dracone pessimo
> te rogamus [rogans in *A.H.*] corde intimo
> saluata est . . .

ll. 9–12 of the carol seem to echo the Respond to the Versicle immediately following: '. . . ita eiusdem intercessione hostes nostros visibiles et invisibiles, ne nocere nobis valeant, precedere digneris'.

burden, l. 2. The most hackneyed epithet of St. George. It appears in No. 68 and in stza. 19 of the T.C.D. carol cited above, as well as in 'Speed Our King on His Journey [to France, 1430]', Brown, *R.L. 15 C.*, p. 196. It is the key line of a charm for a hag-ridden horse dated 1571 (George Lyman Kittredge, *Witchcraft in Old and New England*, Cambridge, Massachusetts, 1929, p. 220):

> *In nomine patris* &c.
> Saint George our Ladyes Knight,
> He walked day so did he night,
> Untill he hir found,
> He hir beate and he hir bounde
> Till truely hir trouth she him plyght
> That she would not come within the night,
> There as Saint George our Ladys Knight,
> Named was three tymes, Saint George.

ll. 6–8. The reference is to the famous apparition of St. George reported to have been seen above the field of Agincourt; 'the crownecle ye red' indicates that the carol must have been written at some interval of time after the battle and suggests that it is the product of a monastic house, the sort of place where a chronicle would be kept and read. Compare the expression of Lydgate in his poem to St. Edmund, l. 77 (MacCracken, part i, p. 126): 'Slain at Geynesboruh, þe cronycle who lyst se'. It is rather remarkable that no reference to St. George appears in the Agincourt Carol itself (No. 90).

63. *Of St. Edmund*

E.E.C., No. 312; *The Suffolk Garland* (Ipswich, 1818), p. 349; B.–R. 80.

This is the only extant English carol in honour of the patron saint of Bury St. Edmunds. It makes use of the most picturesque part of his legend. He was captured by the Danes at Hoxne in Suffolk in 870 and offered terms which his religious convictions would not allow him to accept. After his refusal the Danes beat him with cudgels and tied him to a tree for further scourging. He was then shot at until covered with arrows and finally beheaded. The head, thrown into the undergrowth of Heglesdune Forest, was discovered in the keeping of a wolf. I do not find the 'blind man' elsewhere recorded, some accounts giving the credit to a watchful native Christian, others to a miraculous pillar of light. The wolf, according to the legend, followed the head to the grave.

burden, l. 2. The first line of the antiphon for St. Edmund's Day (20 November), I Vespers (*Br. Sar.* iii, col. 1073). It was, of course, an antiphon specially valued at Bury. When Henry VI made his memorable visit to the abbey, on Christmas Eve of 1433, he dismounted at the abbey gate and was escorted by a solemn procession to the high altar, this antiphon being sung the while (Craven Ord, 'Account of the Entertainment of King Henry the Sixth at the Abbey of Bury St. Edmunds', *Archaeologia*, xv (1806), 67). Lydgate's poem 'To St. Edmund' implies constant use of the antiphon at Bury, saying of the town and monastery: (MacCracken, part i, p. 127, ll. 95–96):

> Aue rex gentis shal ech day be ther song
> Callyng to þe for helpe in ther most neede.

On two early fourteenth-century motets, based on this antiphon and thought to be from Bury, see Bukofzer, chap. i, and Frank Ll. Harrison, *Music in Medieval Britain*, p. 146.

64. *Of St. Nicholas*

E.E.C., No. 316; *pr.* B.-R. 1522.

l. 1. *Patras*: Patara in Lycia.

ll. 5–8. The legend of St. Nicholas and the three young clerks or children rescued from the brine-vat is familiar from medieval art. Cahier suggests (*Caractéristiques des saints dans l'art populaire*, Paris, 1867, i, 304) that it may be a popular corruption through misinterpretation of pictures or carvings of the more authentic story of the three officers condemned to death by Constantine and saved by Nicholas's intervention. The small tower in which these three were represented could easily be mistaken for a tub.

ll. 9–12. Nicholas was a patron saint not only of scholars but also of maidens. The story which follows, that of the three daughters of a decayed gentleman of Patara, is one of those most frequently told of the saint's life. The spirited speeches of the daughters were doubtless put into the carol for the sake of their moral effect on the hearers. The last two lines hastily summarize the solution of the difficulty. Nicholas filled three bags with gold on three successive nights and slipped them through the window of the maidens' house, thus providing them with the needed dowries.

ll. 13–16. The saving of a pig-stealer is plainly related to the character of St. Nicholas as the unofficial patron saint of thieves, but I have not met with the incident in any written life of the bishop.

65. *Of the Eucharist*

E.E.C., No. 318; *pr.* B.–R. 3583.

burden, l. 2. John vi. 50: 'Hic est panis de caelo descendens, ut si quis ex ipso manducaverit, non moriatur.' Compare John vi. 58.

66. *Christ, the Ear of Wheat*

E.E.C., No. 321; *pr.* Rickert, p. 186; Frances M. Comper, ed., *Spiritual Songs from English MSS.* (London, [1936]), p. 95; B.–R. 2681.

A longer treatment of the allegory of this carol is found in the Vernon *Proprium Sanctorum* as a homily on John xii. 24–26: '. . . nisi granum frumenti cadens in terram mortuum fuerit, ipsum solum manet', &c. (ed. C. Horstmann, *Archiv*, lxxxi. 83). The same symbolism is also applied to St. Thomas of Canterbury (ibid., p. 102); so also in *E.E.C.*, No. 116, l. 1: 'Oute of the chaffe was pured this corne.'

l. 12. *Mawndy*: the new commandment (mandatum novum) which Jesus gave his disciples at the Last Supper, John xiii. 14.

67. *The Corpus Christi Carol*

A. *E.E.C.*, No. 322A; *pr.* Annie G. Gilchrist, *J.F.S.S.*, iv. 53; Rickert, p. 193; B.–R. 1132.

B. *E.E.C.*, No. 322B; *pr.* Rickert, p. 194; Gilchrist, loc. cit.; *O.B.C.*, p. 222, music ed., p. 402.

C. *E.E.C.*, No. 322C; *pr.* with music: R. Vaughan Williams, *J.F.S.S.*, iv. 63; *O.B.C.*, p. 81, music ed., p. 126; &c.

D. *E.E.C.*, No. 322D.

This carol has been the subject of more discussion than any other in the whole canon. George Kane (*Middle English Literature*, London, 1951, pp. 174–5) points to it as the only surviving carol which 'can be called completely successful'. For summaries of the case for its being a poem of the Grail legend and of other comments see *E.E.C.*, pp. 411–12, and Richard L. Greene, 'The Meaning of the Corpus Christi Carol', *Medium Ævum*, xxix (1960), 10–21. This article suggests that it is a song on the displacement of Catherine of Aragon from the affections of Henry VIII by Anne Boleyn, whose much-exploited heraldic badge was a white falcon, and that the images of weeping and praying and contemplating the knight (Christ) refer to the strikingly similar picture of Catherine's incessant lamentation and devotions in her country exile, as reported by Nicholas Harpsfield. The carol would thus be a song of a political nature circulated by some of Catherine's many staunch partisans, and, in its use of a heraldic badge to indicate a prominent person, like other poems of the time and like some fifteenth-century carols, e.g. *E.E.C.*, No. 431, which exploits the device at some length.

The suggestion, originally made by Annie G. Gilchrist (*J.F.S.S.*, iv (1910), 52–62, that version **A** may have originated at Glastonbury (though it lacks the reference to the famous thorn found in C) is given some support by the fact that another of the carols in the Balliol MS., *E.E.C.*, No. 331, is found only there and in a very similar commonplace book, T.C.C., MS. O.9.38, which was written at Glastonbury Abbey in the later fifteenth century. A book opposing the divorce was said to have been found in the Abbey, and it would have been a suitable point of origin for a song partisan to Queen Catherine. Version B, in which the thorn does not blossom, has doubtless been influenced by the same verbal tradition that appears in the ballad *The Elfin Knight* (Child No. 2):

D, stanza 7

> And ye maun dry it upon a thorn
> That never budded sin Adam was born.

F, stanza 4

> Tell her to dry it on yon hawthorn,
> That neer sprang up sin Adam was born.

Variants appear in versions H, I, and J of the ballad and elsewhere.

burden. The MS. gives no warrant for regarding this external burden, as Miss Batho does (*Essays and Studies*, ix (1924), 93–94) as an internal refrain of the ballad type like the refrains of B and C.

68. *Of the Mass*

E.E.C., No. 323; *pr.* Brown, *R.L. 15 C.*, p. 183; B.-R. 298.

This *chanson d'aventure*, with its highly unorthodox religious imagery, its 'popular fantasy uncontrolled by the book' (*E.E.C.*, p. xcv), and its characteristic style, quite unlike that of the other religious carols, has a good claim to be considered as true folk-song, that is, a piece originating outside of learned clerical society and passed on by oral transmission. There is nothing in canonical or apocryphal scripture or in liturgy or hymnology to point to as a source. The burden is certainly a borrowing from a secular May song, possibly accompanied by the borrowing of a tune. The occurrence of l. 1 as the fourth line of the second and fourth stanzas tempts to the idea that perhaps it should be shifted to that position in the first stanza, but the result is unsatisfactory.

The only other occurrence in poetry known to me of the strange conception of Christ as officiating priest is in a version of the ballad *The Famous Flower of Serving-Men* (Child No. 106) collected as recently as 1942 from Mrs. Belle Richards of Colebrook, New Hampshire, by Marguerite Olney and published in Helen Hartness Flanders and Marguerite Olney, eds., *Ballads Migrant in New England*, p. 125:

> 'Twas all alone I dug his grave
> And all alone in it him I laid,
> *While Christ was priest and I was clerk*
> *I laid my love in the clay-cold earth.*

The collector remarks (p. 125): 'I have looked through many regional collections as well as the monumental work of Professor Francis James Child and of Cecil Sharp but have not discovered the especial grief of this passage.' The special magic of the passage is found in this carol and the likeness of the image confirms the collector's judgement that it comes from the reservoir of unlearned tradition.

A curious though slight similarity occurs in a folk charm for the grippe from Leinstrand, Trondheim, Norway, used by Lisbet Nypen in 1670 (R. H. Robbins, ed., *The Encyclopedia of Witchcraft and Demonology*, N.Y., 1959, pp. 363–4):

> Christ walked to the church with a book in his hand. Came the Virgin Mary herself walking. 'Why are you so pale, my blessed son?' 'I have caught a powerful grippe [?*greb*]'. 'I cure you of powerful grippe—cough grippe, intestinal grippe, back grippe, chest grippe—from flesh and bone, to beach and stone, in the name of the Father, Son, and Holy Ghost.'

l. 2. *wyhte*: wight, strong, mighty. Brown glosses as prep. 'with'. It might be for 'white'; compare 'pale' above.

l. 3. *Jhon*: the Evangelist.

l. 6. *Collas*. Sandison, following Madan, conjectures 'Nicholas', which seems probable.

l. 13. *knyghte*. Misread by Sandison as 'brighte'. See notes on No. 62.

69. *Amend Me and Pair Me not*

With music: *pr.* with music, Stevens, p. 53.

(Other texts: Bodl. MS. Arch. Selden B. 26, f. 5 r.; *E.E.C.*, No. 337a;

with music; *pr.* B.–R. 1234; Bodl. MS. Eng. poet. e. 1, f. 24 r.; *pr.* Brown, *R.L. 15 C.*, p. 278; B.M. MS. Addit. 5665, f. 66 v.; with music: *pr.* with music, Stevens, p. 88.)

ll. 5–7. Luke xvii. 3: '. . . Si peccaverit in te frater tuus, increpa illum; et si poenitentiam egerit, dimitte illi.'

70. *Against a Wicked Tongue*

E.E.C., No. 341; *pr.* B.–R. 3537.

l. 2. *Satenas*: The Satin-flower, also called Penny-flower. See *Leaves from Gerard's Herball*, ed. Marcus Woodward (Boston, 1931), p. 256. *peny-round*: the ground pennywort. Ibid., p. 120: 'Navelwoort, or Penniwoort of the Wall: There is a kinde of Navelwoort that groweth in watery places, which is called of the husbandman Sheeps bane, because it killeth sheepe that do eat thereof: it is not much unlike the precedent [the non-poisonous variety of the wall] but the round edges of the leaves are not so even as the other; and this creepeth upon the ground, and the other upon the stone walls.'

l. 11. Compare No. 91, l. 13.

ll. 13, 14. An ancient and widespread proverb of ultimately Biblical origin. (Proverbs xxv. 15, or Ecclesiasticus xxviii. 21. See Archer Taylor, *The Proverb*, Cambridge, Massachusetts, 1931, p. 58.) It occurs among the *Proverbs of Alfred*, ll. 460–1 (ed. Helen P. South, N.Y., 1931, p. 121) and among the proverbs in Balliol MS. 354 (*pr.* Dyboski, p. 132). For a long list of its occurrences see Max Förster, 'Kleinere mittelenglische Texte', in *Anglia*, xlii. 200, n. 7, and 'Frühmittelenglische Sprichwörter', in *Englische Studien*, xxxi. 6. It forms the refrain of Lydgate's 'Say the Best, and Never Repent' (MacCracken, part ii, p. 795).

l. 17. Note the suggestion of the varying degrees of the audience in the hall.

71. *Suffer and Be Merry*

E.E.C., No. 345; *pr.* M. G. Segar, *A Mediaeval Anthology* (London, 1915), p. 111; B.–R. 470.

There is an unpublished poem on this same theme in Nat. Lib. W. MS. Peniarth 395, f. 345 r. (B.–R. 4121), with the refrain 'thenke on this word: "suffren I mot." ' It begins: 'Whoso kon suffre and hald hym still.'

l. 1. Adapted from *The Proverbs of Wysdom* (ed. Zupitza, *Archiv*, xc. 243–8), l. 105: 'Be þou mery, þow þou be hard betid.'

l. 7. Compare *E.E.C.*, No. 344, stza. 3, l. 2: 'Her and se, and sey ryght novght.' The line is an adaptation of one of *The Proverbs of Wysdom*

(Zupitza, op. cit.), l. 99: 'Hyre and se, and be styll.' In the version from Bodl. MS. Bodley 9 it is 'Here, and se, and sey not.' As 'Hyre, and se, and sey not all!' it forms the refrain of a *chanson d'aventure* in T.C.C. MS. O. 9. 38, f. 26 v. (*pr.* Sandison, p. 121).

l. 14. *The Wise Man*: the author of *The Proverbs of Wysdom* or *The Wise Man's Proverbs*.

72. *Of Discreet Conduct*

E.E.C., No. 349; with music; *pr.* Brown, *R.L. 15 C.*, p. 285; B.–R. 1415.

The quandary forming the subject of this piece is also stated in *E.E.C.*, No. 340, ll. 9–16:

> Yyf a man go in clotes gay,
> Or elles in gud aray,
> Wekyd tongges yet wyl say,
>   'Wer cam the by therto?'
>
> Yyf a man go in cloys ill
> And have not the world at wyl,
> Wekyd tongges thei wyll hym spyll
>   And sey, 'He ys a stake; lat hym goo.'

A stake was a dull, slow fellow.

l. 13. There is a proverb: 'Take heed of an ox before, of a horse (or ass) behind, of a monk (or knave) on all sides' (G. L. Apperson, *English Proverbs and Proverbial Phrases*, London, 1929, p. 479), but it hardly seems applicable here. The stanza appears to be the advice of an older fowl or bird to a young one, but no fable or anecdote containing it has been identified.

ll. 18–20. A widely known proverb. Apperson records it from as early as 1300. It is among those in Balliol MS. 354, f. 200 v. (*pr.* Dyboski, p. 132): 'He that heweth to hye, þe chippis will fall in his eye'. *E.E.C.*, No. 348, on a similar theme, with the refrain: 'The mene ys best, as semeth me', phrases the saying thus (stza. 3, ll. 2, 3):

> To hew abow thy hedde, hit is but vanite,
> Lest in thy yee ther falle a chyppe.

73. *Of the Tokens of God's Displeasure*

E.E.C., No. 357; *pr.* B.–R. 3566.

The 'dear years', the 'two pestilences', and the 'wind's blast' referred to in this carol set the date of its original composition as not long after 1362, when these events would have been fresh enough in people's minds to make the allusions effective. The two plagues would be the great epidemics of 1348-9 and 1361-2, during the latter of which occurred the violent windstorm of 15 January 1362, mentioned by various chroniclers and in *Piers Plowman*. See Skeat's note on C. Passus VI, ll. 115, 117 (*The Vision of William concerning Piers the Plowman*, Oxford, 1886).

The special reference to damage by lightning at Lynn makes it fairly certain that the carol was written by someone in East Anglia and possibly in Lynn itself. I have been able to find no record of this particular destruction of the tolbooth and the Carmelite friary either in published histories of the town or by inquiry of local antiquarians. The later history of the Carmelite steeple implies that it had been built a hundred years before 1362. Its fall on a calm day, 9 April 1631, is well attested, and Charles Parkin (*An Essay towards a Topographical History of the County of Norfolk*, London, 1808, viii. 523) says that at that time it had 'continued upwards of 360 years'.

The tone of ll. 25-28 does not suggest that the author was himself one of the afflicted community. He might have belonged to one of the several rival orders with houses in Lynn, and one is tempted to suggest the Franciscans, whose steeple not only 'stood fast' in the tempest of 1362 but rises over King's Lynn to the present day.

The calamity would have been well known in Bury St. Edmunds, of course, and the carol may have originated there. It would have had considerable local application in the mid-fifteenth century, as the western tower of the abbey fell in 1430, and nine years later a violent storm did much damage.

With this carol compare the verses on the visitations of 1382 (*pr.* Brown, *R.L. 14 C.*, p. 186) especially ll. 57-62:

> Þe Rysing of þe comuynes in londe,
> Þe Pestilens and þe eorþe-quake—
> Þeose þreo þinges, I vnderstonde,
> Beo-tokenes þe grete vengaunce & wrake
> Þat schulde falle for synnes sake,
> As þis Clerkes conne de-clare.

ll. 1-4. Compare the first stanza of the fifteenth-century poem with 'O and I' refrain in C. U. Lib. MS. Gg. 1. 32, f. 3 r. (*pr.* Brown, *R. L. 15 C.*, p. 256; text from MS.):

Thynk, man, qwareoff thou art wrought, that art so wlonk *in* wede;
Thynk hou thou art hedyr brought, *and* of thyn end take hede;
Thynk hou dere God has the bought, *with* blysful blode to blede;
Thynk, for his gyle was it noght, bot, ma*n*, for thi mysdede.

The 'thynk, man' formula is also found in *E.E.C.*, No. 329 on Doomsday, also from MS. Sloane 2593.

74. *Of the Vanity of the World*

E.E.C., No. 366; *pr*. B.–R. 3654.

ll. 2, 3. James i. 10, 11.

l. 14. *wyth cuces owersette*: put off with excuses. Executors have a bad name in medieval literature: compare the burden and stanza 2 of *E.E.C.*, No. 382:

> Haue in mynd, in mynd, in mynd,
> Secuters be oft onekynd.
>
> Haue thi sowle in thi mynd;
> The secators be ryght onkynd;
> Mane, be thi own freynd;
> Lytyll joye ys son done.

l. 22. Compare the abuse of executors and the tales of their falsity in *Handlyng Synne* (ed. F. J. Furnivall, E.E.T.S., Or. Ser., No. 119, 1901, pp. 202, 203, ll. 6293–508 and 6257–62, especially ll. 6293–9):

> ȝe ryche men, before ȝow se,
> Þe whyles ȝe are yn ȝoure pouste;
> On ȝoure soules, y rede ȝow þenke;
> y warne ȝow of ȝoure eyres blenke;
> Ne haueþ no trust of ȝoure sokoure,
> Nat of ȝoure owne executoure;
> ȝyueþ ȝeself with ȝoure hondys.

In the same vein are the lines in one of the pieces not in carol-form in Bodl. MS. Eng. poet. e. 1 (Wright, *P.S.* xxiii. 34):

> What thou doest with thyn hond, that shalt thou fynd.
> Wyves be rekeles, chyldren be onkynd,
> Exceccuturs be covetys and hold that thei fynd.

There is a long disquisition, with *narraciones*, on executors good and bad in *Peter Idley's Instructions to His Son*, book ii, ll. 1618–2002 (ed. Charlotte D'Evelyn, Boston, 1935, pp. 185–91).

75. *Of the Fear of Death*

E.E.C., No. 370a; *pr*. B.–R. 375.

(Other texts: Balliol MS. 354, f. 177 v.; Hunt. Lib., *Christmas carolles newely Inprynted* (Richard Kele), p. [41].)

Other carols which make use of a talking bird in the *chanson d'aventure* are No. 78 and *E.E.C.*, No. 378. In the latter a turtle-dove sings the Latin for 'All flesh is grass'.

burden. The phrase which forms the text for this piece and for a number of other Middle English carols and poems on the theme of mortality is from the Response to the seventh Lectio in the third Nocturn of Matins in the Office of the Dead (*Br. Sar.*, ii, col. 278): 'Peccantem me quotidie et non poenitentem timor mortis conturbat me. Quia in inferno nulla est redemptio miserere mei Deus et salva me.' See Patterson, pp. 180–3 and R. L. Greene, *M.L.R.* xxviii. 234–8, and compare Lydgate's 'Timor Mortis Conturbat Me' (*pr.* MacCracken, part ii, p. 828). Finest of all is Dunbar's 'I that in heill wes and gladnes'.

A couplet like the burden appears to have been a commonplace at the time of the carol. At Witney the tomb of Richard Wayman and his wives, who died about 1500, bore the inscription:

> Man in what state that ever thou be
> Timor Mortis should trouble thee,
> For when thou least wenyst,
> Veniet te Mors superare.

(F. G. Brabant, *Oxfordshire*, London, 1919, p. 257.)

l. 6. Medieval hawking etiquette designated the musket, a small sparrow-hawk, as the bird appropriate to the use of a 'holy-water clerk'.

ll. 9–12. Compare the poem on the 'Timor mortis' theme in MS. Longleat 29, f. 145 v., stza. 7, ll. 1–4 (*pr.* R. L. Greene, *M.L.R.* xxvii. 236):

> Þer is no þyng þat ever God made
> More certeyn to us þan oure deþe is,
> But more uncerteyne þyng none is yhadd
> Þan þe ourre off deþe to us, ywysse.

ll. 15, 16. These words are not recorded in the canonical Scriptures as said by Jesus.

l. 18. This appears as l. 6 of No. 59 and l. 1 of *E.E.C.*, No. 367. It is, of course, a commonplace. It is still doing service in the burden of a mid-sixteenth-century carol in Bodl. MS. Rawlinson poet. 185, ff. 4 v.–5 v. (*pr.* Hyder E. Rollins, *Old English Ballads 1553–1625*, Cambridge, 1920, pp. 265–9):

> O mortall man, behold and see,
> This world is but a vanetie.

The carol is also found in B.M. MS. Addit. 15233, signed 'Mr. Thorne', and in *The Paradise of Dainty Devices* (1576) (ed. Rollins, Cambridge, Massachusetts, 1927, p. 54).

76. *Service Is No Heritage*

E.E.C., No. 381; *pr.* B.–R. 1433.

The second line of the burden of this carol is one of the commonest and longest-lived of medieval proverbs. On its origin see *Notes and Queries*, 1st ser. viii. 586–7, in connexion with its occurrence in Scott's novels. Swift quotes it in 'Mrs. Frances Harris's Petition', l. 44, and 'Directions to Servants', chap. x. It is the refrain of a *chanson d'aventure* in Bodl. MS. Rawlinson poet. 36, f. 2 r. (*pr.* Sandison, p. 119), and it is used by Hoccleve in *The Regiment of Princes*, l. 841. It appears reversed in the 'Consail and Teiching at the Vys Man Gaif his Sone', ll. 371–2 (*pr. Ratis Raving*, ed. J. R. Lumby, E.E.T.S., Or. Ser., No. 43, 1870, p. 100):

> Be weill wyllyt in thin office,
> For heritage is na seruice.

ll. 5, 6. Another proverb recorded by John Ray (*A Collection of English Proverbs*, Cambridge, 1678, p. 60): 'Winter-weather and women's thoughts change oft.'

77. *Of Truth's Banishment*

E.E.C., No. 385; *pr.* Robbins, *Historical Poems*, p. 146; B.–R. 72.
l. 8. *heye mene*: fine company.

78. *Try Your Friend Before You Need Him*

E.E.C., No. 389a; *pr.* B.–R. 3820.
(Other text: Balliol MS. 354, f. 230 r.)
For the convention of the talking bird in a *chanson d'aventure* compare No. 75 and *E.E.C.*, No. 378.
burden, l. 2. A widely current proverb. It is found in the *Wise Man's Proverbs* (l. 14, *pr.* F. J. Furnivall, *Englische Studien*, xxii. 442) and in Balliol MS. 354, f. 200 v. (*pr.* Dyboski, p. 132).
In Draxe's *Bibliotheca Scholastica* (London, 1633, p. 74) it appears as 'Trie thy friend before that thou hast need of him'.

79. *Gramercy Mine Own Purse*

E.E.C., No. 390; *pr.* T. Wright, *Songs and Carols* (London, 1836), No. iv; B.–R. 3959.

burden, l. 2. This proverbial phrase is also used in the burden of *E.E.C.*, No. 391 on the same theme:

> I may syng and sey, iwys,
> 'Gremercy my owne [purse.']

A poem with the refrain 'Ever, Gramercy, myn owne purse' is in Wynkyn de Worde's edition of *The Boke of St. Albans*, *repr.* Ritson, *Ancient Songs* (1790), p. 89, (1829), ii, 6, (1877), p. 151. Mayor John Shillingford of Exeter echoes the phrase in describing his merry mood in a letter to his 'Fellows' from London, 2 November 1447:

> ... therfor y take right noght by and sey sadly *si recte vivas*, &c. and am right mery and fare right well, ever thankyng God and myn awne purse. And y liyng on my bedde atte writyng of this right yerly, myryly syngyng a myry song, and that ys this, Come no more at oure house, come, come, come. Y woll not dye nor for sorowe ne for anger, but be myry and fare right well, while y have mony; ...

(Stuart A. Moore, ed., *Letters and Papers of John Shillingford, Mayor of Exeter 1447–50*, Camden Society, London, 1871, p. 16.)

Unfortunately he gives us no more of the song; what he quotes sounds like a carol-burden.

ll. 11 and 15 with their 'horn' and 'bow' more probably indicate that Jack has taken to hunting the deer than that he has become a 'vagabond musician' as suggested in *E.E.C.*, p. 429.

80. *In Praise of Women*

E.E.C., No. 395a; *pr.* Mary G. Segar, *A Mediaeval Anthology* (London, 1915), p. 108; B.–R. 4219.

(Other text: B.M. MS. Sloane 2593, f. 5 r.)

The excellence of the Virgin Mary is emphasized in this piece, as in *E.E.C.*, No. 394, as justification for an admiration for women in general. Unlike many of the carols to the Virgin, it praises her less as the recipient of a special supernatural sanctity than as the embodiment of all the good qualities to be found in her earthly sisters. The claim of l. 15 is unusual even in poems devoted to the praise of women, and here it is rested on the tradition of Mary's reticence. This was fostered by the fact that Scripture records her speaking on only four occasions, the Annunciation, the Visitation, the finding of Jesus in the Temple, and the Marriage at Cana.

Compare the long poem in similar strain printed from the Auchinleck

MS. by E. Kölbing, *Englische Studien*, vii (1884), 103 (see also F. Holt-hausen, *Archiv*, cviii. 290 and cx. 102), and the poem with refrain 'Of wimmen comeþ þis worldes welle', printed from the Vernon MS. by Brown, *R.L. 14 C.*, pp. 174–7 as well as Dunbar's 'In Prays of Woman', especially l. 2: 'Off erthly thingis nane may bettir be.'

81. *Women Are Excellent—or the Contrary*

E.E.C., No. 399a; *pr.* E. Flügel, *Anglia*, xxvi. 275; Robbins, *Secular Lyrics*, p. 35; Kaiser, p. 311; &c.; B.-R. 1485.
(Other text: Bodl. MS. Eng. poet. e. 1, f. 55 v.)

The regular return of the contradicting or 'destroying' burden makes the carol-form a good one for the employment of this particular type of humour. One can see the possibilities of mirth raised by its performance before women who might not at first understand the Latin of the burden. Chaucer's Chantecler and his translation of *Mulier est hominis confusio* come inevitably to mind. Among others Lydgate uses a similar device in his poem with the refrain 'So as þe crabbe goþ forwarde' (MacCracken, part ii, p. 465). For a long discussion of this piece see Utley, p. 165.

burden, l. 2. Utley (p. 256) points out the use of this phrase at the end of *The Scholehouse* by Edward Gosynhill [?].

Compare the use of the same Latin tag in the scribbled insult on f. 129 v. of the courtly song-book B.M. MS. Addit. 31922: 'vynsent Wydderden ys an onest man so sayeth Nycolas Benden Cuius est contrarium verum est.'

l. 2. A familiar and trite comparison.

ll. 8, 13–16. Compare *Peter Idley's Instructions to His Son*, bk. ii, ll. 1049–55:

> Jangelyng in churche among hem is not vsed,
> To telle of her housbandrye al the wooke before;
> And also hir housbandis shall not be accused,
> How croked and crabbed they be euermore.
> All suche thyngis, loo! they can kepe in store:
> They be as cloos and couert as the horn of Gabriell
> That will not be herde but from heuene to hell.

l. 19. *Gryzell*: a form with final *d* was doubtless used by the original author.

ll. 33–36. The love of women for the ale-house and the conversation there is one of the most frequent objects of derision among their satirical critics. Compare No. 86 for a more sympathetic view of this recreation.

82. *A Young and Hen-pecked Husband's Complaint*

E.E.C., No. 405; T. Wright, *Songs and Carols* (London, 1836), No. xii; C. &. S., p. 207; Robbins, *Secular Lyrics*, p. 38; Kaiser, p. 309; B.-R. 4279.

Similar realistic treatment of the theme of this carol survives in modern folk-song, e.g. 'Single Men's Warning', collected by Cecil Sharp from Tom Sprachlan at Hambridge in 1903 (James Reeves, *The Idiom of the People*, London, 1958, pp. 199–200, stanza 5):

> When dinner time come to home I repair
> And a hundred to one if I find my wife there
> She's gossipin' about with the child upon her knee
> And the turk of a sign of a dinner for me.

ll. 1, 2. The marriage of young men to older women was much commoner in the Middle Ages than in modern times. The frequency of early widowhood and the great importance of marriage in relation to matters of property were contributing causes. The classic instance is, of course, the matrimonial history of Chaucer's Wife of Bath.

l. 15. *not worght a reych*: a common expression for worthlessness.

l. 18. *al at ese*: a phrase of emphasis.

83. *The Schoolboy's Complaint*

E.E.C., No. 413; *pr.* E. Flügel, *Anglia*, xxvi. 283; H. S. Bennett, *England from Chaucer to Caxton* (London, 1928), p. 45; B.-R. 1399.

The contents of this carol, as well as the fairly frequent occurrence of carol-texts in MSS. containing school notes, e.g. G. & C. C. 383, Corpus Christi College, Cambridge, 233, and B.M. Cotton Titus A. xxvi, suggest that schoolboys as well as monks and friars were recorders and transmitters of carols.

Compare the even more rebellious monologue of a much-beaten schoolboy from Lincoln Cathedral MS. 132, f. 100 r., in which it is inserted between the school texts of the *Accentuarius* and the *Dictionarius* (*pr.* Robbins, *Secular Lyrics*, p. 105):

> Wenest þu, huscher, with þi coyntyse,
> Iche day beten us on þis wyse,
> As þu wer lord of toun?

and the reminiscence of a sad old man in 'The Day of Life—Night Comes Soon', ll. 33-36 (*pr.* Brown, *R.L. 15 C.*, pp. 230-3):

At vnder-day to skole I was I-sete,
   To lerne good as chyldern dothe,
But when my master woold me bete,
   I wold hym cowrs & wax full rowthe.

See also Sydney H. Nicholson, *Quires and Places Where They Sing* (London, 1942), p. 25.

Even better is the long lamentation of a boy at the choir school, presumably that of St. Paul's, as it is written by the choirmaster there, John Redford (see notes to No. 57):

(burden)   Of all the creatures, lesse or moe,
           We lytle poore boyes abyde much woe.

(stza. 3) Do wee never so well, he [the master] can never be content,
           But for our good wylles we ever more be shente,
           And oft tymes our lytle butokes he dooth all to-rent,
           That we, poore sylye boyes, abyde much woe!

(*pr.* J. O. Halliwell[-Phillips], *The Moral Play of Wit and Science*, Shakespeare Society Publications, xxxvii, London, 1848, pp. 62–65).

l. 7. *vi of the clok*. The usual time for children to rise. If our scholar had been at Eton at about this time, he would have kept even earlier hours. See G. G. Coulton, *Social Life in Britain from the Conquest to the Reformation*, p. 81.

l. 13. *Milked dukkes*. A saucy answer equivalent to 'None of your business'. Compare *The English Dialect Dictionary* (ed. Joseph Wright, Oxford, 1898–1905), *s.v.* Duck *sb*¹ 2. Phr. (3): '[West Yorkshire]. . . . This curious answer is made to an inquisitive person. "What is to' doin?" "Muckin ducks wi' an elsin [Cleansing ducks with a shoemaker's awl]".'

84. *Fare Far and Have Little*

E.E.C., No. 418; B.–R. 3971.

The note written before the burden of this carol to indicate the air of another piece to which it is to be sung is especially interesting, as we have two other songs which begin with the same words: 'alone y lyve alone'. Both are in later manuscripts. One, written about 1530, is in the carol-form and has the complete burden:

               Alone, I lyue alone
               & sore I syghe for on.

The first stanza reads:

> No wondre thow I murnyng make,
> for grevous syghys þat myne harte dothe take,
> and all is for my lady sake.
> [alone, I lyue alone.]

(P.R.O. MS. Exr. Misc. 22/1/1, *pr.* John Saltmarsh, *Two Mediaeval Lyrics,* Cambridge, 1933, and Robbins, *Secular Lyrics,* pp. 154–5).

There is music for three voices. The preservation of the second line of this burden confirms the indication that the burden of the carol should be accented thus:

> Hos ís to hóth at hóm,
> Ryd óut; it wól agón.

The other occurrence is in B.M. MS. Addit. 31922, f. 22 r. (*pr.* with music by 'Dr. Cooper', *A Collection of Songs and Madrigals by English Composers of the Close of the Fifteenth Century,* The Plainsong and Mediaeval Music Society, London, 1891, pp. 3, 4). The verbal text is the same.

All three of the preserved songs seem to have derived from a popular prototype: this carol with its good advice against vagabondage and its pious conclusion, and the two much more courtly love-songs, one with part-music and the other in a collection of part-songs.

The same burden appears with a short *chanson d'aventure* of the Passion in Richard Kele's print (*E.E.C.*, No. 164):

> [Alo]ne, alone, alone, alone,
> Sore I sygh, and all for one.

It is apparent that in England as well as in France and other countries sophisticated poets and composers of secular as well as sacred pieces drew freely on texts in more general circulation for the starting-points of their compositions. See John Stevens, *Music and Poetry in the Early Tudor Court* (London, 1961), pp. 40–48.

l. 12. *Myche yerne*: very swift, active: 'a fast rolling stone'.

l. 13. *groute*: root or dig up the earth, i. e. settle and work on the land.

85. *Speed the Plough*

With music; *pr.* Padelford, p. 104; C. & S., p. 241; Robbins, *Historical Poems*, p. 97; with music: Stevens, p. 112; *E.B.M.* ii. 132; B.–R. 3434 (indexed by first line of burden).

This delightful carol, omitted from *E.E.C.*, has been properly recognized as belonging to the genre by Stevens (p. 124) on the 'balance of the evidence', of which the stanza-marks prefixed to each group of three lines are the strongest (see Stevens, first ed., 1952, p. 124, and review by M. F. Bukofzer, *J.A.M.S.* vii (1954), 64). The pairing of successive three-line stanzas by the rhyme of their final lines shows that the lyric was not first written as a carol but was adapted to the form from a song in six-line stanzas, a common medieval metre. There is no way of telling whether this adaptation was made by the composer of the music in this manuscript or by some predecessor. The manner of its performance is unusual: the burden is sung in two parts, its last line repeated in three, and the stanza sung first in two parts and repeated in three.

As Stevens has pointed out, the carol is very probably intended for use on Plough Monday, the first Monday after the Epiphany. Plough Monday celebrations and feasts are recorded into modern times from many parts of England, frequent features being the drawing through the village streets of a decorated plough by the young men, with singing, dancing, and *quête*. This carol, of course, is intended for more sophisticated performance, probably by choir-boys. It would be highly appropriate to Worcester Abbey, which had a number of agricultural manors and much business with plough-land, ploughmen, and oxen. See, for example, Sidney Graves Hamilton, ed., *Compotus Rolls of the Priory of Worcester of the XIVth and XVth Centuries*, Worcestershire Historical Society, 1910, *passim*.

The ploughman figures, sometimes perfunctorily, in many songs from modern oral tradition, for example a version of *The Jolly Ploughboy* (Aldingbourne, Sussex, *c.* 1850–60) which was used as a Christmas carol and begins with Cain and Abel (Annie G. Gilchrist, *J.F.S.S.* viii (1931), 136). For other traditional songs see *Guide*: (The) Pretty/Simple Plough-Boy, p. 99; (The) Painful/Faithful Plough, p. 98; (The) Oxen Ploughing, loc. cit.; (The) Lark in The Morn, p. 83.

l. 6. *in the clay*. This would be appropriate to a carol from Worcestershire, where much of the soil in about half the county is a heavy clay (*V.C.H., Worcester*, London, 1906, ii. 310–12).

l. 9. '(God) speed the plough' is, of course, a widely used expression and toast through the centuries. It is on the wall of many an inn today as a decorated motto or combined with a pictorial figure in a print. Robbins (p. 301) refers to the Middle English poem in twelve stanzas in B.M. MS. Lansdowne 762, f. 5 r. (*pr.* W. W. Skeat, *Pierce the Ploughmans Crede*, E.E.T.S., Or. Ser., No. 30, 1867, pp. 69–72), to a play 'god spead the plowe', acted in 1593 and 1594, and to a book of the same title entered in the Stationers' Register in 1601.

l. 10. *Browne, Morel*, and *gore*. 'Browne' and 'Morel' (dark-coloured) seem to be the names of the plough-oxen. 'Gore' has presented difficulty to previous editors. Neither Stevens's 'dark-coloured' nor Robbins's suggestion of 'gray' meets the case. It is more likely that it is a dialect word for 'goad' and that the meaning is either 'Brown, Morel, and the goad' or alternatively, with 'Brown' as an adjective, 'Brown Morel and

Gore', the second ox being named for the goad. ('Gored stick' with the meaning 'cattle goad' is found in a recent version of an American folk-song (Alan Lomax, ed., *The Folk Songs of North America*, Garden City, N.Y., 1960, p. 111.) In any event there can be only two proper names:

> Thre oxen in plowgh may neuer wel drawe,
> Noþer be craft, ryȝt, ne lawe

('The Boke of Curtasye', bk. ii, ll. 287–8, *The Babees Book*, p. 307). 'Morel' appears more often as the name of a horse, e.g. in the sixteenth-century 'A merry Ieste of a Shrewde and curste Wyfe lapped in Morrelles skin' (*pr.* W. Carew Hazlitt, *Remains of the Early Popular Poetry of England*, London, 1866, iv. 180–226), where 'morel' means 'black'.

In the chorus of a ploughboy's song in modern oral tradition, 'known throughout Devon and Cornwall at the beginning of the 19th century', the names of oxen are introduced in much the same fashion as in the carol:

> With my Hump-a-long! Jump-a-long!
> Here drives my lad along!
> Pretty, Sparkle, Berry,
> Good-luck, Speedwell, Cherry!
> We are the lads that can follow the plough.

(S. Baring-Gould, H. Fleetwood Sheppard, and F. W. Bussell, eds., *Songs of the West*, [5th ed.] ed. Cecil J. Sharp, London, [1913], pp. 116–17). A parallel from French folk-song is quoted in the notes, p. 17.

ll. 13–15. The injunction to reward the oxen with sheaves is figurative and apparently equivalent to saying, 'Treat them like the human labourers', the men's bonus at harvest-time being reckoned in sheaves. This was the case as early as 1182 at Ripple, Worcs., where it was established that 'those who bind sheaves at reaping shall have a sheaf each, those who stack the corn likewise' (translated from Latin original, Marjory Hollings, ed., *The Red Book of Worcester*, Worcestershire Historical Society, 1934, p. 169).

There must have been many songs of the plough of true folk-origin in actual work, like spinning and milking songs, for the medieval plough-man would sing at his work for a practical reason, as would the milkmaid or the American cowboy. The thirteenth-century *Fleta* tells us:

> The Plough-driver's art consisteth herein, that he drive the yoked oxen evenly, neither smiting nor pricking nor grieving them. Such should not be melancholy or wrathful, but cheerful, jocund and full of song, that by their melody and song the oxen may in a manner rejoice in their labour.

(G. G. Coulton, *Social Life in Britain from the Conquest to the Reformation*, p. 166.)

86. *The Gossips' Meeting*

E.E.C., No. 419Aa; *pr.* Flügel, *Anglia*, xxvi. 208; A. S. Cook, *A Literary Middle English Reader* (Boston, 1915), p. 372; B.-R. 1362.

(Other texts: Bodl. MS. Eng. Poet. e. 1, f. 57 v.; *pr.* G. G. Coulton, *Life in the Middle Ages* (Cambridge, 1954), iii. 141; H. S. Bennett, *England from Chaucer to Caxton* (London, 1928), p. 134 (in part); B.M. MS. Cotton Titus A. xxvi, f. 161 r. (defective at beginning); *E.E.C.*, No. 419 b; Dyboski, p. 187; B.-R. *32.)

Some such piece as this was doubtless the model for 'The Good Gossippes songe' in the Chester Play of the Deluge (ed. H. Deimling, E.E.T.S., Ex. Ser., No. lxii, 1926, p. 57). This is the more probable as the MS. containing the widely variant version, B.M. MS. Cotton Titus A. xxvi, is connected with Mobberly, Cheshire, not far from Chester. Stanza 15 of this version contains a local allusion, not identified:

> Gadyr the scote, and lette us wend,
> And lette us goo home by Lurcas Ende.

One may conjecture a temporary place-name of 'Lucas End' from the dwelling in Watergate Street of Henry Lucas, 'hopper', who in 1542 was among the sixteen important tenants summoned to stand the special Christmas watch. Watergate Street was one of the places where disreputable ale-rooms were to be found in cellars. A hopper must have been a dealer in hops, introduced only in 1524, regarded as an adulterant by Noah's wife in the Chester play, and forbidden by statute later in the same reign. Chester was notorious as the only city permitting females between fourteen and forty to keep ale-houses, a practice eventually prohibited because of the resulting 'great slander and dishonest report' (Rupert H. Morris, *Chester in the Plantagenet and Tudor Reigns*, [Chester, 1895], pp. 236, 248, 431, 314, 425).

A song in Pepys's collection of ballads (Magdalene College, Cambridge, Pepysian Library, i. 436–7) tells of 'Fowre wittie Gossips' whose meeting to drink wine parallels much of the action of this carol. Utley (pp. 152–3, 241–3) calls the carol the closest parallel to Skelton's *The Tunning of Eleanor Rummyng*, which he says may have some verbal echoes. Other parallels cited by Utley are *The gospelles of dystaues* (prose) in the Huntington Library, not reprinted, 'Leve, lystynes to me' in Nat. Lib. W. MS. Porkington 10 (*pr.* F. J. Furnivall, *Jyl of Breyntford's Testament*, London, 1871, p. 27), the play of *Tom Tyler*, and Dunbar's *Kynd Kittok*.

In the Cotton MS. version 'Frankelyne the harper' comes in and plays for the gossips' dancing. Utley thinks that this suggests the use of the carol by minstrels, hardly a necessary inference. The last stanza solicits payment for the song, but it does not imply any instrumental accompaniment such as a minstrel would give; it could well be spoken by an amateur like one of the craftsmen-players:

> Off this proses I make an end
> Becawse I wil have women to be my frend;
> Of there dewosyon they wold send
> A peny for to drynke at the end.

The change in the rhyme scheme indicates that this conclusion is not an organic part of the carol. The colophon perhaps indicates a lack of success with the appeal: 'Exsplycyt lytyll thanke.'

l. 67. *muscadell*: the strong wine of muscat grapes.

ll. 94–95. Compare Chaucer's *Nun's Priest's Tale*, l. 100: 'Have ye no mannes herte, and han a berd?'

87. *Fill the Bowl, Butler*

E.E.C., No. 421; E. Flügel, *Anglia*, xxvi. 282; C. & S., p. 227; Robbins, *Secular Lyrics*, p. 10; B.–R. 903.

burden, l. 1. *Bevis a towt*: Beuvez à tous; drink to everyone.

l. 1. Compare the refrain of the cumulative drinking song reprinted from *Deuteromelia* (1609) by E. F. Rimbault, *A Little Book of Songs and Ballads* (London, 1851), p. 120; 'Sing, gentle butler, *balla moy*'.

l. 21. A good pun, as 'Walter' was pronounced 'water'.

88. *Bring Us in Good Ale*

E.E.C., No. 422A; *E.B.M.* ii. 184 (music wrongly associated); F. J. Furnivall, *The Babees Book*, p. 363; Rickert, p. 245; Robbins, *Secular Lyrics*, p. 9; Kaiser, p. 311; &c.; B.–R. 549.

(Other text: B.M., MS. Harley 541, f. 214 v.; *E.E.C.*, No. 422B.)

The carol is preceded in the MS. by a pleasantly simple modal melody, under the notes of which are written the burden and first stanza of No. 53. This is followed by the gloss: 'Thys is the tewyn for the song foloyng yf so be that ye wyll haue a nother tewyn it may be at yowr plesur for I haue set all the song.' This has been taken to indicate that 'Bring Us in Good Ale' was to be sung to the tune given, but the melody neither fits the stanza of the drinking-song nor suggests a convivial air. A difference in the ink with which 'Bring Us in Good Ale' begins (see facsimile in *E.B.M.*, No. c) shows that some kind of break occurred just at that point in the writing of the manuscript. The words of No. 53 are given in full ten leaves farther on, in accordance with an annotation written by another hand ('fo 10') directly after the words 'the song foloyng'. Apparently they should have followed the music directly but through mistake were entered elsewhere, and the space left vacant was filled with the words of the drinking-song, which undoubtedly had a very good tune of its own but was never meant to be sung to the 'Nowell, nowell,' melody. The note on this question in *O.B.C.* (p. 43) is misleading and gives as the source of the tune B.M. MS. Sloane 2593, which has no music.

ll. 4, 13. Compare the 'Proverbial Rhyme' quoted by John Ray (*A Collection of English Proverbs*, Cambridge, 1678, p. 293):

> He that buys land buys many stones,
> He that buys flesh buys many bones,
> He that buys eggs buys many shells,
> But he that buys good Ale buys nothing else.

l. 19. *al Godes good*. This is an East Anglian term for barm or yeast, which housewives sometimes came to a monastic kitchen to obtain, as at Mettingham College, Suffolk, where they managed to get some of the ale as well (A. Jessopp, ed., *Visitations of the Diocese of Norwich, A.D. 1492-1532*, Camden Society, 1888, p. 46). But barm is an unlikely constituent for puddings. The meaning here is probably 'God knows what', close to *O.E.D.* 2: 'Applied to what is considered to be without human owner, and therefore open to be appropriated by any one.' There is no culinary or other reason for Robbins's unattractive emendation to 'gotes blod' (pp. 10, 232).

89. *Of the Effects of Ale*

E.E.C., No. 423; *pr.* W. Sandys, 'Festive Songs', *P.S.* xxiii. 17, &c. B.-R. 163.

> The vigorous disapproval expressed in this carol of the nearly universal English beverage is surprising, especially in view of the convivial associations of carol-singing. It marks the piece as certainly the work of a moralizing religious, probably, to judge from its realistic observation of drunkenness in humble life, a friar.'

The above note on this carol in *E.E.C.* has roused some dissent, particularly from John Speirs (*Medieval English Poetry: The Non-Chaucerian Tradition*, London, 1957, p. 88), who calls it 'unbelievable' and accuses the editor of 'apparently having missed the kind of humour the song expresses'. He adds, 'The rollicking rhythm alone should have saved

Greene.' Utley (p. 165) remarks: 'But surely "Doll [*warm, mull*] thy ale" is a burden which destroys the sting of the serious charges in the stanzas proper, which go to the extreme length of threatening the ale-drinker with the gallows.' On the other hand Arthur K. Moore (*The Secular Lyric in Middle English*, Lexington, Kentucky, 1951, p. 171) accepts the piece as 'a prohibitionist carol', though he calls the burden 'lively'.

E.E.C. may have helped to suggest these comments by glossing 'doll' as 'warm, mull', citing *Promptorium Parvulorum*: 'Dollyn, as alle or oder lyke: Tabefacio', a meaning which does imply some conflict between burden and stanzas. It should rather be glossed as 'weaken; cause or permit to become flat or "dead"', as in *Catholicon Anglicum*, p. 103: 'Dollyd as wyne or ale; *Defunctus, vapidus; vapiditas, vappa,* dollyng [B.M. MS. Addit. 15562]' Note also *The Babees Book*, part ii, p. 79: '*dowld*, dead, flat (Yorkshire), Halliwell; not *dollyd*, sum what hotte, *tepefactus.* Prompt.' The contradiction then disappears.

There is every reason to believe that the carol is the work of a religious, though we may give up the friar, for it appears in a manuscript from the monastery of Bury St. Edmunds. That it was written down in the MS. at a different time from other carols is shown by the difference in ink and appearance of the hand in comparison with the matter preceding and following, so that it may well have had a different source from that of 'Bring us in good ale'. There is no arguing about a sense of humour, but other medieval literature gives no warrant for assuming that all warnings against drunkenness are ironic or that the misadventures mentioned here are to be regarded as mirth-provoking, singly or in a cumulative list. Chaucer's Pardoner speaks some serious words about drunkenness although under an ale-stake with tankard in hand (*Pardoner's Tale*, ll. 549–72). In the Chester play of Christ's Descent into Hell some manuscripts give a humorous addition to the scene in which Secundus Demon cries to 'mulier', the ale-wife:

> welckome, dere ladye, I shall thee wedd!
> for many a heavye and droncken head,
> cavse of thy ale, were broughte to bed,
> farre worse then anye beaste.

(Ed. J. Matthews, E.E.T.S., Ex. Ser., No. cxv, 1914, p. 331.)
The situation is humorous, but the words are not ironic. For an abundance of warning against the effects of ale in sermons rather than songs, see G. R. Owst, *Literature and Pulpit in Medieval England* (Cambridge, 1933), pp. 425–41. Owst comments: '. . . from the beginnings of Mendicant oratory, nay, for centuries before, the follies of the inebriate, both ludicrous and tragical, were held up to audiences in all their grim reality—

to audiences, moreover, that we happen to know were often all too ready, like Chaucer's Friar, to laugh and "gale" at the wrong moment' (p. 426). A bit from a sermon in B.M. MS. Addit. 41321, f. 97 v., is a good counterpart to l. 2 of this carol: 'And ofte as thei goth homward toward hire beddes, thei drencheth hemself in dichis bi the weie' (p. 429). Or note the translated mnemonic verses in B.M. MS. Lansdowne 762, f. 99 r. (*pr. Rel. Ant.* i. 288):

> Who that drynketh wele, mych is he the gladder;
> Who that drynketh to moch, more is he the madder;
> Whan he goth to his bed, his slepe is the sadder;
> At morowe whan he waketh, his brayne is the bradder;
> Whan he loketh in his purse, his sorowe is the sadder.

Any reader who thinks the rhythm 'rollicking' is advised to recite aloud first No. 88 and then this carol and compare the effects.

burden, l. 2. *doty poll*: stupid head, *O.E.D.* does not record this use, but gives '*doddy poll*', as transferred to the possessor of the head.

l. 1. *styk at a brere*: Probably figurative and proverbial rather than literal: to get into trouble. Compare the *Vulgaria* of Robert Whittinton, printed by Wynkyn de Worde, 1520 (ed. Beatrice White, E.E.T.S., Or. Ser., No. 187, 1932), p. 98, ll. 14–16:

> Thou art a sure spere at nede. that leues a man stykkynge in the breres.
> Fidus es / vbi opus est: hominem malis impeditum deficies.

l. 21. *falows*: ploughed land. Compare the proverb using the three rhyme-words of this stanza in Chaucer, *Wife of Bath's Prologue*, ll. 655–8, and the variant of it in *Rel. Ant.* i. 233.

90. *The Agincourt Carol*

E.E.C., No. 426a; with music; *pr.* Robbins, *Historical Poems*, p. 91; &c. with music: Thomas Percy, *Reliques of Ancient English Poetry* (London, 1765), ii. 24, music at end of volume; Charles Burney, *A General History of Music* (London, 1776–89), ii. 383; B.–R. 2716.

(Other text: T.C.C. MS. O. 3. 58; with music; *pr.* with music, Stevens, p. 6.)

This stirring song, perhaps the best-known carol in English not concerned with the Nativity, was probably composed and sung by clerics rather than by minstrels and thus may be regarded as not directly in defiance of Henry V's famous interdict (R. S. Wallace and A. Hansen, eds., *Holinshed's Chronicles, Henry V*, Oxford, 1917, p. 43): '... neither would he suffer any ditties to be made and soong by minstrels of his glorious victorie, for that he would wholie have the praise and thanks altogither given to God' (*E.E.C.*, p. 439, suggests such defiance). The burden of the carol reflects the King's often-recorded insistence on the divine agency in the victory, and the religious sentiment of the piece might have saved it from his disapproval. Both writings of the carol are later than Henry V's lifetime.

'Deo gratias' was displayed on the tower of a conduit near St. Paul's during the splendid celebration of the King's homecoming. Extracts from the descriptions of the ceremonies in the *Brut* and in a priest's diary printed by Sir Nicholas Harris Nicolas are conveniently found in Robbins, *Historical Poems*, pp. 296–7. But there is no reason to believe that this carol was actually sung on that occasion, to which ll. 17–20 refer as in the past. Neither can the carol be regarded, as Robbins states (p. 297), as 'clearly processional'.

Compare the long poem on Agincourt in B.M. MS. Harley 565, f. 102 r. (*pr.* [Sir Nicholas Harris Nicolas and Edward Tyrrel], *A Chronicle of London*, London, 1827, p. 216). This, though not a carol, has inserted at intervals the couplet:

> Wot ye right well that thus it was
> Gloria tibi, Trinitas.

Although F. M. Padelford (*Anglia*, xxxvi. 84) thought the verbal variants of the two versions to be such as showed evidence of oral transmission, the likeness of the two musical settings is such as to indicate MS. transmission, as with many other carols.

l. 23. Robbins pertinently quotes from the chronicle of Jehan de Waurin the cry of Henry's troops on the battlefield: 'Sire! Dieu vous doinst bonne vye et victore de vos annemis!'

91. *The Rose on Branch*

E.E.C., No. 427; *pr.* Rickert, p. 142; Robbins, *Historical Poems*, p. 92; B.-R. 3457.

The end of the carol is missing, as two leaves have been torn from the MS.

The phrasing of the first two stanzas shows strong influence from the symbolism and poetic convention of the rose as emblem of the Virgin. Not until the third stanza does it become clear that an English king is meant, as in *E.E.C.*, No. 431, 'The Rose of Rouen'. The allusion here is to Henry V and the Agincourt campaign. The fleur-de-lis, of course, France. Compare the song from oral tradition on the battle in Sir

Nicholas Harris Nicolas, *The History of the Battle of Agincourt* (London, 1832), Appendix, pp. 78, 79, in which the French king is made to say:

> And the fairest flower in all French land
> To the rose of England I will give free.

l. 16. Compare *E.E.C.*, No. 428, John Audelay's carol on Henry VI, stza. 6, ll. 3, 4:

> At Agyncowrt, at that patayle,
> The floure of Frawnce he fel that day.

92. *The Loveliest Lady in Land*

E.E.C., No. 440; *pr.* Wright, 'Specimens of Lyric Poetry', *P.S.* iv. 51; G. L. Brook, *The Harley Lyrics* (Manchester, 1948), p. 48; Kaiser, 5. 294; &c.; B.–R. 1395.

The title given to this carol by Brown (*English Lyrics of the XIIIth Century*, Oxford, 1932, p. 148) is adopted here. There are significant discussions of the piece in Böddeker: *Altenglishe Dichtungen des MS. Harl. 2253*, Berlin, 1878, pp. 167–8, Brown, and Brook, and also in Arthur K. Moore, *The Secular Lyric in Middle English*, pp. 65–68. It is the earliest preserved secular carol in English and is the only piece among the contents of the important MS. Harley 2253 which is in the full carol-form, although *Alysoun*, 'Bytuene Mersh ant Aueril', has a lively burden after all stanzas (Brook, p. 33). The contrast in style between the burden and the rest of the lyric is immediately apparent and has been much commented on. To the present editor it seems obviously, as to Sir Edmund Chambers (*Early English Lyrics*, p. 277), to Brook (p. 6), and to Moore (p. 65) it seems probably, derived from another song, folk-song or popular song as you will, but in any event from a piece quite outside the courtly rhetorical tradition of the stanzas. Robbins (*Stud. Phil.* lvi. 577) seems to reject this view for lack of 'evidence'; but it is not to be expected that Middle English scribes will attach a label 'folk-song' or even acknowledge a source in a footnote. The difference in the rhythm of the burden and its use of natural imagery connected with a simple and direct expression of love-longing are evidence enough. The same image is found in the refrain of a surviving folk-song, 'The Loyal Lover' (S. Baring-Gould and H. Fleetwood Sheppard, eds., *Songs of the West*, 5th ed., London, [1913], pp. 188–9):

> Blow summer breeze, o'er the sea
> Bring my pretty love to me,

not to mention the universally known 'My Bonnie Lies over the Ocean'. It is quite probable that here, as elsewhere, we have a poem not originally designed as a carol which has been later put into carol-form by either the original author or another. It seems more likely that the stanzas were written before and independently of the burden than that, as R. M. Wilson suggests, 'In all probability the refrain of a popular *carole* has been taken as the theme of a courtly lyric, a practice found elsewhere during the Middle English period' (*Early Middle English Literature*, London, 1939, p. 262).

Carleton Brown (*English Lyrics of the XIIIth Century* (Oxford, 1932), pp. xxxix, xl) regards this and three other poems in the manuscript (Brook, pp. 31, 34, 37) as 'the work of the same person, a poet of the Welsh border'. The others are *Annot and John*, 'Ichot a burde in a bour ase beryl so bryht'; *The Lover's Complaint*, 'Wiþ longyng y am lad'; and *The Fair Maid of Ribblesdale*, 'Mosti ryden by Rybbesdale'. He lists the many parallels between this piece and *Annot and John* and *The Fair Maid of Ribblesdale*. Brook dissents: 'There are no two lyrics in the manuscript that we can with certainty assign to the same poet' (p. 26).

An elaborate literary analysis of the poem with special attention to its syntax and rhetoric was given by Leo Spitzer, '*Explication de Texte* Applied to Three Great Middle English Poems', *Archivum Linguisticum*, iii (1951), 2–22. Spitzer, who did not appear to have seen either *E.E.C.* or Brook's edition, was emphatic about the character of the burden as folk-poetry. He also saw significance in the poem's having ten stanzas—'the perfect number!' In *E.E.C.* the following carols on different religious subjects have ten stanzas: Nos. 53, 78, 102, 124B, 167, 170, 204, 269, 297, 303. So has No. 81 in this collection, a satire on women.

Moore thinks ill of the poem (p. 66): 'This lyric is a patchwork of redundant images and hackneyed phrases.'

l. 39. *fi*[*th*]*ele*. Brook points out that the emendation may be unnecessary, as *fiele* is a possible form of Old French *viele*. For a full account of the crowd or 'crwth' see Hortense Panum, *The Stringed Instruments of the Middle Ages*, revised by Jeffrey Pulver, (London, n.d.), pp. 239–45.

l. 44. *baner*. Dickins and Wilson (loc. cit.) call this 'difficult to translate' and suggest emendation to something like '*burde* "lady"' which would then balance the *ledy* of [l. 48]'. There is no difficulty in translating it as 'standard bearer, one in the van', which gives a personal noun to balance 'ledy'.

ll. 49–72. In these allegorical stanzas Love is conceived as a masculine judicial personality to whom the speaker complains how Sighing, Sorrowing and Care, three 'knights' of the lady's retinue, have threatened him in spite of a similarly personified Peace. In l. 65 'Hire' gives some trouble. Böddeker removes it, and Brook says that perhaps it should be removed. Spitzer reads it as 'love for her', a personification of a more

special emotion than love in general. Perhaps a better interpretation is
that even Love as judge is also in the lady's service.

l. 70. *fen of fote*: mud from the foot.

ll. 71. 72. 'That she will deal honourably and helpfully with you.'

What seems to be a late parody of this kind of alliterative love poetry
is found in the Digby Play of Mary Magdalene (ed. F. J. Furnivall,
E.E.T.S., Ex. Ser., No. lxx, 1930, pp. 90–91, ll. 942–9, 958–60):

> [Kyng of Marcylle speaks]
> I have a favorows fode, and fresse as the fakown,
> she is full fayer In hyr femynyte;
> whan I loke on þis lady, I am lofty as the lyon; [&c.]
>
> now godamercy, berel brytest of bewte!
> godamercy, rubu rody as þe rose!
> ye be so ple[s]avnt to my pay, 3e put me from peyn.

93. *Green Groweth the Holly*

E.E.C., No. 448; with music for burden; *pr.* W. Chappell, *Archaeologia*,
xli. 374–5.

This famous composition, of which the words as well as the music have
been generally accepted as by King Henry VIII, shows a courtly adaptation of the old folk-theme of the holly and the ivy. The identification of
holly and ivy with man and woman persists, but the symbolism here is
of amity and not of opposition. Holly appears in the refrain of a love
song of similar spirit in B.M. MS. Addit. 5465, ff. 99 v.–100 v., 'Who
shall have my fayre lady?'

In two of the parts we find written 'undir þe levis grene' instead of the
preceding refrain 'undir þe holy grene'. The phrase forming the first two
lines of the burden enjoyed currency as a folk-saying in the sense of
'forever'. Compare the method of laying a ghost by tricking it into
agreeing to stay away 'while hollies are green' (E. M. Wright, *Rustic
Speech and Folk-lore*, London, 1913, p. 193).

ll. 15, 16. Compare the love poem in Bodl. MS. Rawlinson C. 813, ff.
3 r.–4 r. of about 1500 (*pr.* Robbins, *Secular Lyrics*, pp. 124–6), ll. 21, 22:

> She hathe my harte & euer shall,
> & neuer to change hur for no newe.

94. *Now Springs the Spray*

E.E.C., No. 450; *pr.* Sandison, p. 47; B.–R. 360.

This graceful *chanson d'aventure* is one of the very earliest texts preserved in the carol-form. The memorandum in the same hand which follows it is dated 1302-3 (31 Edward I). On its similarity to an Old French poem beginning 'L'autrier defors Picarni', *pr.* K. Bartsch, *Altfranzösische Romanzen und Pastourellen* (Leipzig, 1870), No. II, 7, see Brown, *English Lyrics of the XIIIth Century*, p. 214, and Sandison, pp. 47-48. R. M. Wilson comments: 'For all that the English lyric reads much more like a popular *carole* than a literary composition based on a French original' (*Early Middle English Literature*, London, 1939, p. 263).

R. H. Robbins (*Stud. Phil.* lvi. 577) mistakenly refers to this carol as from MS. Harley 2253 and denies, without offering evidence, that it derives from popular dance.

burden, l. 1. 'Nou' is best taken as a conjunction rather than as an adverb, so that the first line can be rendered 'Now that the shoots are sprouting (i.e. now that spring is here)', as suggested by C. T. Onions, 'Two Notes on Middle English Texts', *Medium Ævum*, xvii (1948), 32-33.

l. 5. May the clod cling to him! i.e. may he be buried (Skeat).

ll. 8, 9. *Son*: as soon as (conjunction). This sense is suggested by C. T. Onions (loc. cit.), who points to the parallel lines in the Old French poem:

> Si tost com j'oi le cri,
> celle part tornai;

(Brown, loc. cit.)

l. 21. *Bi this dai*. Skeat glosses 'If I can (contrive it), it shall repent him concerning this day', and does not think the line an expression of emphasis or affirmation (*M.L.R.*, v. 105). But compare *E.E.C.*, No. 415, burden:

> Ay, ay, be this day,
> Y wyll mak mery qwyll Y may.

95. *The Serving-maid's Holiday*

E.E.C., No. 452; *pr.* Robbins, *Secular Lyrics*, p. 24; B.-R. 225.

The holiday in this carol is probably Midsummer Day, as in No. 96. There is nothing to prevent our supposing that Jack is the same young man in both.

burden, l. 1. *Rybbe*: scrape the flax with an iron tool. Robbins reads 'Wybbe' and glosses 'to weave', but the 'R' is clear in the manuscript and is repeated after each stanza. This house-and-dairy-maid would not be carrying on the man's trade of weaving. The alliteration with 'rele' is effective.

l. 2. *werve*: The wharve, or whorl, the small pulley or flywheel of a spindle. (*O.E.D.* cites Elyot, 1538: 'a wherue, whyche is a rounde thynge

of stone, or wodde, or leadde, put on a spyndell to make it runne round'.)
vond: found. She has been mislaying everything.

ll. 18, 19. 'All this scattering [of the milk] gets the bread out for me,
except for the dough which stays under the nail.' The girl is, of course, a
'wet-hand' milker and like most old-time dairy people no doubt believes
that the cow will not yield her milk unless some is first spilled on the hands
('outh' from 'outen'; 'schayl' = 'skail', scattering, spillage). Thus the
dough would be rinsed off her hands, which she has not otherwise
washed in her scatter-brained haste.

96. *Jack and the Dancing Maid*

E.E.C., No. 453; *pr.* Robbins, *Secular Lyrics*, p. 22; Kaiser, p. 310; B.–R.
1849.

Midsummer Day (Nativity of St. John the Baptist, 24 June) and its eve
were the occasions of so much popular custom and celebration that a
separate treatise on the subject could be produced. In this carol the gathering is for the dancing of a *carole*, a 'ryng', and its sequel is sexual indul-
gence. Not much documentation is needed, but two references may be
given in illustration. An Augustinian canon of Barnwell, Camb., alleging
a mistaken etymology for the place-name, writes in 1295 of the 'wakes'
of the young people on St. John's Eve:

> ... eo tempore appellati, eo quod pueri et adolescentes semel per
> annum, in vigilia scilicet Nativitatis sancti Johannis baptiste, illic
> convenientes more Anglorum luctamina et alia ludicria exercebant
> puerilia, et cantilenis et musicis instrumentis sibi invicem applaudebant.
> Unde propter turbam puerorum et puellarum illic concurrencium et
> ludencium mos inolevit, ut in eodem die illic conveniret negociandi
> gracia turba vendencium et emencium.

(John Willis Clark, *Liber Memorandum Ecclesie de Bernewelle*, Cambridge,
1907, p. 41, quoted by F. Liebermann, *Archiv*, cxxxi (1913), 429, and in
part by Arthur K. Moore, *English Studies*, xxxii (1951), 59). A Yorkshire
parallel to the episode of this carol, in which the principals, John Dogson
and his serving-maid Alice Tomson, commit their sin while the St.
John's fires are being kindled, is reported in the *Acts of Chapter of the
Collegiate Church of SS. Peter and Wilfrid, Ripon, A.D. 1452 to A.D. 1506*
under date of 1454 (Surtees Society Publications, No. lxiv, 1875, p. 39):

> Interrogata an eam carnaliter cognovit, respondit quod sic. Inter-
> rogata de tempore, respondit quod in festo nativitatis Sancte (*sic*)

Johannis Baptistae. Interrogata de tempore respondit quod in nocte quando ignes erant illuminati. Interrogata de loco, respondit quod primo eam carnaliter cognovit in domo praedicti Jo. Dogeson in camera basa juxta Richarson et alia vice eam cognovit in coquina dicti Jo. D. Interrogata an fama erat publica quod haberat [*sic*] eam in uxorem, respondit quod sic.

l. 3. *haly-water clerk.* The carrier of the holy-water vessel, often regarded as one of rather low position.

l. 18. White gloves were apparently associated with leading the *carole*; compare the homily 'De Dominica in Passione Domini Nostri' in Mirc's *Festial* (p. 113); where St. Bernard 'yn Crystis person' says:

'Thow man for vanyte syngyst and rowtes, and I for þe crye and wepe; þou hast on þy hed a garland of flowres, and I for þe on my hed suffyr a wreþe of stynkyng þornes; þou hast on þy hondys whyt gloues, and I for þy loue haue blody hondys; thow hast þyn armes sprad on brode ledyng carallys, and I for þy loue haue myn armes sprad on þe tre, and tachut wyth grete nayles; thow hast þy cloþe raggyd and pynchyt smale, and I haue my body for thy loue full of great walus'.

The Glossarial Index offers 'carallys, *sb. pl.*, coral'! See also *A Stanzaic Life of Christ*, ed. Frances A. Foster, E.E.T.S., Or. Ser., No. 166, 1926, pp. 200–1, ll. 5925–44, which uses the same passage from St. Bernard, who has 'gloues' only (cyrotecas). In a *carole* danced at night, white gloves would be of real advantage to the gesturing leader as to a modern traffic patrolman. Gloves were also a conventional gift in courtship.

l. 31. *rong the bell*: This phrase can hardly have its usual meaning of 'reveal the secret' or 'spread scandal'. It is probably sexual slang and a borrowing of a term from the context of a religious service to indicate repetition. Or it may have the more modern meaning of 'succeeded'.

l. 33. *the reaggeth devel*. The Devil was often described, pictured, and represented on the stage as ragged or shaggy. Compare the instructions to the butchers in the Banns of the Chester Plays, ll. 121–2:

set out as Accostomablie vsed haue yee,
the devill in his fethers, all ragger and rente.

l. 34. *burdus*: Tricks or sports, here, of course, with sexual meaning

l. 41. *Ever by on and by on*: Over and over again.

l. 44. A proverb: 'Ill-spun yarn will always ravel.' Compare the Towneley Plays, 'The Killing of Abel', l. 435: '*Garcio.* Yey, ill spon weft ay comes foule out', and 'Shepherds' Play II', l. 587: '*ijus pastor.* Ill spon

weft, Iwys/ ay commys foull owte' (ed. George England and A. W.
Pollard, E.E.T.S., Ex. Ser., lxxi, 1897, 21, 135). Robbins notes (p. 236)
The Proverbs of Hendyng, l. 272: 'Euer out comeþe euel sponne web'.

97. *A Forsaken Maiden's Lament*

E.E.C., No. 455; *pr.* Robbins, *Secular Lyrics*, p. 17; B.–R. 1330.

The line prefixed to the burden of this carol appears to be the burden
of another carol, possibly on a similar theme, to the air of which this
piece is written. As pointed out by Robbins (p. 234), this air cannot be
that of 'Bryd on brere, brid, brid on brere!' written with music in King's
College, Cambridge, Muniment Roll 2 W. 32, verso, which is not a
carol (*pr.* Robbins, pp. 146–7, and previously by John Saltmarsh, *The
Antiquaries Journal*, xv (1935), 3–4, and *Two Medieval Lyrics*, Cambridge,
1933, p. 6). 'Bird on briar' is a proverbial phrase. Compare 'Ane deuoit
orisoun To oure Lady The Virgin mary', B.M. MS. Arundel 285, ff.
193 v.–196 v., ll. 11–13 (*pr.* Brown, *R.L. 15 C.*, pp. 38–41);

> Haill! cumly cristell cleir
> Aboue þe ordouris nyne
> Als blith as bird on brer,

and the burden of No. 10.

The scrap of song here written is in the same metre as the burden of the
carol and has the same rhymes:

> Bryd on brere y tell yt to
> none othur y ne dar.

It is quite possible that these are the first two lines of a four-line burden
which has been shortened, especially as the first words are again written
and deleted after the first stanza. Compare the treatment of a four-line
burden in No. 11.

This carol, to which it would be pedantic to deny the term 'popular',
is, of course, on a theme familiar in the medieval French lyric, and there
are many parallels to the bird-confidant of the 'Bryd on brere' lines. It
undoubtedly comes from the same milieu as Nos. 95, 96. Compare
E.E.C., No. 454, where a clerk is the betrayer, and No. 456, where Sir
John (probably a priest) sins with the speaker of the carol at a well-
waking.

98. *Jolly Jankyn*

E.E.C., No. 457; *pr.* T. Wright, *Songs and Carols* (London, 1836), No. xx; C. & S., p. 220; Robbins, *Secular Lyrics*, p. 21; Kaiser, p. 312; W. H. Auden, *The Oxford Book of Light Verse* (1938), p. 53; B.-R. 377.

The speaker in this lively and irreverent dramatic monologue of a flirtation during the procession and Mass on Christmas and of its consequences is one of 'þeos prude maidenes þat luuieþ Ianekin', who, according to 'A lutel soth Sermun' (*An Old English Miscellany*, ed. R. Morris, E.E.T.S., Or. Ser., No. 49, p. 188), are among the persons destined for hell. It has elements of parody of the Mass, its refrain being the solemn formula of the *Kyrie*, but it is more essentially a kind of sacrilegious trope of parts of the sacred text. Compare its burden with the opening lines of an actual trope of the *Kyrie*:

> *Kyrie*,—Rex pie,—Da nobis hodie,—
> Veniae—Munus et gratiae:—*Eleison.*

(quoted by Léon Gautier, *Histoire de la poésie liturgique au moyen âge. Les Tropes*, i, Paris, 1886, p. 148 n. II E). The piece is in much the same vein as such humorous parodies of the services as are found in Paul Lehmann, *Parodistische Texte* (Munich, 1923), pp. 59–69. In the burden there is probably a pun on the girl's name 'Alison'.

Eileen Power (*Medieval English Nunneries*, Cambridge, 1952, p. 610) quotes a 'very ribald Italian folk-song of the fourteenth or fifteenth century . . . founded upon Boccaccio's famous tale of the Abbess and the breeches', which has for burden and refrain 'Kyrie, kyrie, pregne son le monache!'

Robbins's note (p. 235) is confused. He attributes the Latin headings of the 'Venus Mass' to 'The Cuckoo and the Nightingale' (*pr.* W. W. Skeat, *Supplement to the Works of Geoffrey Chaucer*, Oxford, 1897, pp. 347–58), in which the birds say their Hours and not Mass, and in which there is no Latin. The 'Venus Mass' itself (*pr.* Thomas Frederick Simmons, *The Lay Folks Mass Book*, E.E.T.S., Or. Ser., No. 71, 1879, pp. 390–5) is divided into parts corresponding to *Introibo, Confiteor,* &c., but it bears no resemblance to the trope-like carol.

Margit Sahlin (op. cit., p. 57) attempts to use this carol in support of her theory of the derivation of '*carole*' from *Kyrie eleison* and of the form from processional songs. It is impossible to consider this carol a processional piece: only the first stanza refers to a procession, the others recounting Jankyn's part in the Mass, during which the parishioners would be kneeling and standing: 'on myn fot he trede'. What is being 'farced' is definitely the *Kyrie* of the Mass, not, as Dr. Sahlin would have it, 'le cri processionel'.

l. 3. 'Kerieleson' appears as the refrain of a Nativity song in B.M. MS. Harley 2942, f. 4 r., possibly a carol which has lost its burden, to which my attention was first directed by Mr. Geoffrey B. Riddehough.

ll. 13, 14. Compare the line from a song in the same MS. (*pr.* Wright, op. cit., p. 93): 'Therfore smale notes wil I crake'. The reference is to the rapidly sung short notes of polyphonic vocal music as opposed to the long notes of plainsong. Wycliffe and his followers objected violently and at length to this kind of 'newe song'. Compare particularly with this carol a passage from the tract 'Of feyned contemplatif lif [&c.]' (*pr.* F. D. Matthew, *The English Works of Wyclif Hitherto Unprinted*, p. 192):

> & þanne strumpatis & þeuys preisen sire iacke or hobbe & williem þe proude clerk, hou smale þei knacken here notis; & seyn þat þei seruen wel god & holy chirche, whanne þei dispisen god in his face, & letten oþere cristene men of here deuocion & compunccion, & stiren hem to worldly vanyte; & þus trewe seruyce of god is lettid & þis veyn knackynge for our iolite & pride is preised abouen þe mone (&c.).

In 'The First Shepherds' Play', ll. 305–6 and 413–19 the shepherds admire the 'small noytys' of the angels: 'I dar say that he broght/foure & twenty to a long'; in 'The Second Shepherds' Play' the angel 'crakyd it' only 'Thre brefes to a long' (pp. 110, 113, 137). On the simile Robbins (p. 236) cites *Liber Cure Cocorum*, l. 46: 'Hakke smalle þy wortis and persyl'.

l. 16. *pax-brede*: the disk of silver or gilt with a handle and a sacred symbol used in giving the 'kiss of peace' to the congregation. Its introduction is attributed to the Franciscans. See John S. Bumpus, *A Dictionary of Ecclesiastical Terms* (London, n. d.), s.v. 'Pax'.

l. 19. The exclamation is a sterotyped expression; it occurs, for example, in the opening lines of the romance *Sir Gowther* in Nat. Lib. Scot. MS. Advocates 19. 3. 1 (erroneously included as part of burlesque poem, *Rel. Ant.* i. 84).

99. *A Lover's Sad Plight*

E.E.C., No. 470; *pr.* Robbins, *Secular Lyrics*, p. 34; B.–R. 1280.

This carol is an amusing example of the use of a humorous device which has survived to modern times in such minor classics as Goldsmith's *Elegy on Mrs. Mary Blaize* or Gilles Ménages' 'Le Fameux la Gallise' (*Menagiana*, Paris, 1729, iii. 384–91). The latter has the lines:

> Tandis qu'il ne dormoit pas,
> On tient qu'il veilloit sans cesse.

A longer and more literary, but less effective, song on this same theme is found in Balliol MS. 354, f. 252 r. (*pr.* Dyboski, p. 119) and in MS. Porkington 10 (*pr.* J. O. Halliwell[-Phillipps], *Wart. Club*, ii, London, 1855, p. 6; combined text of the two in C. & S., p. 217). This is probably the work of a later poet inspired by the more informal carol.

burden. The burden of this carol, adopted as the burden of a later song of good riddance to a shrew, has the distinction, according to the note in the Hunt. Lib. reference copy of the *Short Title Catalogue*, of being probably the first English printed music. It appears in a fragment of which a photostat is catalogued as Hunt. Lib. R197862. The words which appear under the musical setting are:

no lenger morne I may
wey a wey mornyng a wey I am forsake Another ys take no lenger.

The song, printed in four stanzas of four long lines each, begins:

Now she that I Louyd trewly. Beryth a full fayre face

The supposed author and printer, whose device with the 'word' 'Iusticia Regat' appears below the text of the piece, is John Rastell, the author of the interlude *The Four Elements*, and brother-in-law of Sir Thomas More. See Arthur W. Reed, 'John Rastell, Printer, Lawyer, Venturer, Dramatist, and Controversialist', *Transactions of the Bibliographical Society*, xv (1917–1919), 59–82. This piece gives an interesting and clear example of the borrowing of a burden from an earlier carol for use with newer stanzas. It may be dated between 1516 and 1533. Since Rastell came to London from Coventry and one of the names written in the MS. of the carol (from Oxfordshire) is 'Thomas de Halton marchand de couentre', we may assume that 'Mourning away' was indeed a song in general circulation in that part of the country.

The phrase survives into the seventeenth century. Thomas Dekker's *Lachrymae Londinenses* (1626) warns the reader:

If you expect in these ensuing Lines any scarce credible or feigned matters of wonderment, made in some Taverne or on some Ale-bench, to tickle your Eares and helpe you to sing Care-away, you will be deceiued: . . .

(Quoted by Louis B. Wright, *Middle-Class Culture in Elizabethan England*, Chapel Hill, N.C., 1935, p. 447.) It is the key phrase of the song which Coridon the countryman sings after the supper of trout in chapter iii of *The Compleat Angler* (London, 1653, pp. 85–88; in later editions ascribed to John Chalkhill):

Then care away,
and wend along with me.

A song in Bodl. MS. Ashmole 36–37, f. 128 r. begins: 'Sing care away, let us be glad' (William Henry Beach, *A Catalogue of the Manuscripts Bequeathed . . . by Elias Ashmole*, Oxford, 1845).

l. 3. Robbins (p. 238) points to the scrap of song written in Worcester Cathedral MS. F. 64, a copy of Peter Lombard's *Libri Sententiarum*, f. 8 r.:

> He may cum to mi lef bute by þe watere wanne me lust
> slepen þanne mot i wakie wnder is þat hi liuie

(*pr.* Bruce Dickins, *Leeds Studies in English*, iv. 44; text from MS.). We probably have here a bit of the song of love-sickness of which this carol is a satirical reworking.

100. *A Nonsense Carol*

E.E.C., No. 473; *repr.* W. H. Auden, *The Oxford Book of Light Verse*, p. 87; Denys K. Roberts, *Straw in the Hair*, London, 1938, p. 190.

The words of the burden and first stanza occur in a round or canon in Ravenscroft's *Pammelia* (1609) as follows (Sir John Hawkins, *A General History of Music*, London, 1776, ii. 379–80):

> My heart of gold as true as steele,
> As I me leant into the bowers,
> But if my Lady love me well,
> Lord so Robin lowres.
>
> .   .   .   .   .   .
>
> My Lady's gone to Canterbury,
> St. Thomas be her boote,
> She met with Kate of Malmesbury,
> Why weep'st thou maple Root?

See Reed, pp. xlix, 78, where full text is given.

The nonsense of this delightful piece is free-ranging, and it is hardly to be classified as a 'lying-song', as Utley suggests (p. 203). For a carol of the 'lying' or 'impossibilities' type see *E.E.C.*, No. 471, with its burden alluding to the whetstone as the traditional 'prize' for a liar:

> Hay, hey, hey hey!
> I will haue the whetston and I may.

burden, l. 2. *me lened*: *O.E.D.* records the reflective use of 'lean' at the end of the sixteenth century.

l. 2. *the Saynt*: St. Thomas.

l. 15. *Jacke Napes*: a monkey. The line is apparently a current and stereotyped expression. The *Vulgaria* of John Stanbridge, printed by Wynkyn de Worde in 1519, includes it:

> Iacke napes maketh a mowe. Simea os distorquet.

(ed. Beatrice White, E.E.T.S., Or. Ser., No. 187, 1932, p. 26; see also note on p. 132.)

l. 25. *Saynt Katheryn of Kent*: I am not acquainted with any records of this saint.

INDEX OF LATIN PASSAGES, WITH
TRANSLATIONS

GLOSSARY

In this glossary vocalic *y* is treated alphabetically as *i*. Words identical in spelling but different in meaning are given separate entries. Words explained in the notes are omitted.

a, they.
a, have.
abey, atone for.
abone, aboun, abown, above.
ae, always.
aga, gone.
agast, afraid.
ale-schoch, scot-ale, where all present contribute.
alle(le) and sum(me), all and some, together.
allon, lonely.
among, together.
and, if.
anon, anonne, at once.
apeir, impair, make worse.
aray, condition.
arn, are.
as, has.
asay, try, test.
aspye, find out.
asyse, mode, fashion.
at, that.
aune, awen, own.
avise, consideration, argument.
avowries, patron saints.
ayeyn, against.

bale, ball, evil, hardship.
baly, jurisdiction.
band, bound.
bar, bore.
barn, infant.
bate, abate.
be, by.
bealte, beauty.
bed, offered.
beh, bent.
behest, promise.
beme, beam.
ben, were.
bende, bondage.
bene, are.

bere, bier.
berie, berry-bush.
beryng, birth.
beshrew, curse.
best(e), beast.
betake, entrust.
bethe, both.
betyde, bytyde, happen(ed)
betoken, betokyn, signify
betwene, in the midst.
by and by, at once.
bydyng, dwelling.
bihot, promised.
byrd, youth.
bleo, face.
blynketh, shines.
blys, bless.
blysse, comfort.
blo(o), livid.
blokkes, stones, obstructions.
boystous, overbearing.
bone, boon.
bord, jest.
bore, born.
bo(o)te, bothe, help, remedy; **to —** in payment.
boure, bower.
bouth, bought.
bowrd, table.
brayd, broyd, short time.
bred, breadth.
breder, brothers.
breme, bright.
brent, burny.
brer, briar, thorn.
brest, break.
bryd, child.
bryth, bright.
broth, browth, brought.
burd(e), maiden.
burion, burgeon, blossoming.
but, bott, but if, unless.

cakke, drop excrement.
carke, sorrow.
cease, cause to cease.
cence, incense.
cete, city.
cewre, cure, charge.
challes, chalice.
chalonus, blankets.
chamyd, shamed.
chanon, canon.
che, she.
chene, beautiful.
chent, injured.
chere, look, expression.
cherrus, chores, domestic work.
ches, took.
chesone, for the — of, because of.
chyld, give birth (to).
chongy(n), change.
clennesse, purity.
close, enclosed, held.
clot, blow.
clot, clod, the earth.
coynt, quaintly pretty.
compasse, consider.
comprysyd, compared.
con, know.
con, did.
coppud, in ill humour.
coste, country.
cote, coat.
crave, ask favours.
croppe, top of a plant.
crouth, crowd, stringed instrument.
crown, top of the head.
crownecle, chronicle.
cuces, excuses.
cumbers, cumbrous, troublesome.
cussynge, kissinge.

dare, crouch, hide timidly.
dawe, dawn.
day, die.
ded, dead, death.
ded(d)e, deed, work.
degre, rank.
delicte, sin.
dell(e), bit; **most del,** for the most part.
deme, judge.
demonyacle, possessed by demons.
den, deign, condescend.

denaye, deny; **without —,** without doubt.
dereworthe, glorious.
dest, doest.
deth, dieth.
dych, dish.
dyche, ditch.
dyght, direct.
dyspytously, without pity.
disstens, condescension.
dombe, dumb.
domynacyons, dominations, the angelic order.
domysman, judge.
done, put.
doo, doe.
dowge, douce, soft.
dowte, fear.
dray, draw near.
dredde, were afraid.
dresse, prepare.
drogh, drew near.
droupne, droop.
duk(e), leader.
dume, dumb, silent.

eche, same.
efere, together.
ey, eternity.
eyghe, awe.
eysell, vinegar.
ek(e), also.
eld(e), old.
ender(s), endurs, other, recent.
enfors, resolve.
ens, hence.
ensammple, ensampil, example.
entent, intention, purpose.
eor, their.
esylye, quietly.
eslayn, slain.
evene, heaven.
evereche, every.
everychon(e), every one.
expresse, made manifest.

fa(yy)rly, fair.
faytur, begging impostor.
falyid, failed.
faunt(e), infant.
fawe, fain, glad.
feld, field.

fele, many.
fend, fynd, fiend, devil.
fer, fire.
fere, companion, neighbour; **in —**,
　together.
fer(r)e, far.
fers, fierce.
fersly, fiercely.
feschun, fetch.
fey, faith.
fylyd, defiled.
fyllyn, fell.
fynkyll, fennel.
flagat, flageolet.
flayled, beat, clubbed.
fleysch, flesh, meat.
fleys, fleece.
flyng, hasten.
flyt, quarrel.
flytte, remove, transport.
fod, child.
fod, food.
fon, foes.
fond, attempt.
fonde, take.
for and, moreover.
forght, forth.
formest, first.
fote, foot.
fow, fool.
frale, thrall.
fraught, entrusted.
fray, assault.
frere, friar.
frynd, friends.
frount, forehead.
ful, foul.

gaff, gave.
galow-claper, gallows-bird.
gan(e), gunne, did.
gelofir, gillyflower.
gent, gentle.
gestes, guests.
gy, guide.
gyff, if.
gyn, begin.
gise, custom.
go, walk; **so mot I —**, so may I be able
　to walk.
go(o)d, goods.
gomyn, sport, fun.

gon, go.
goy, joy.
grad, proclaimed.
gramercy, thanks (to).
grane, seed.
greive on, scorn.
gryth, security, peace.
grundid, grounded, established.
gunne, began.

haght, hath.
hakke, cut.
hale, draw.
halwen, saints.
hammard, homeward.
han, have.
hape, wrap.
hard, heard.
hat, am called.
haylsyng, embracing, salutation.
he, they.
he, high.
heder, hither.
hem, hym, them.
hende, beautiful.
hent, struck, seized.
hent, until.
heo, hue, she.
herber, arbour.
here, hair.
here, their.
herte, heart.
herth, earth.
heste, vow.
heved, head.
hewe, hue, colour.
hy, hyghe, hasten.
hye, high,
hight, is called.
hym, it.
hyng, hang.
hode, hood.
hol, whole, well.
hon, one.
hondes, hounds.
hondul, fondle.
hope, hop.
hors, horses.
hos, whoever.
hoved, waited.
howlat, howlet, owl.
huerte, heart.

ibe, been.
ibore, iborn, yborne, born.
ichot, I know.
icome, come.
ierachy, hierarchy.
yfere, together.
yheryd, honoured.
yk, every.
ilk, same, every.
ilkon, everyone.
ilorn, lost.
ymong, ever —, continually.
ynde, end.
inow, enough.
yplaunte, planted.
ysched, shed.
yspunne, spun.
iwent, gone.
iwys, iwos, ywys, ewys, certainly.
ywraht, made.

jonkers, junkets, merrymakings.
Jury, Jewry, Judea.

kaght, caught.
keme, conceive.
kemyn, came.
kend, known.
kery, kyrie eleison.
keyn, keen, cruel.
kybe, chilblain.
kyd, known.
kynd(e), nature.
kyrchers, kerchiefs.
kun, cun, can.

lang, belonged.
lappe, flap of a gown.
largesse, generosity.
lasteles, blameless.
laudes, praises.
laverocke, lavyrok, lark.
law, low,
lay, belief, religion.
laye, customary usage.
leal, loyal.
lealte, loyalty.
led, lead, large kettle or cauldron.
lefe, dear.
leflich, lovely.
left, stopped.
legge, lay.
lekyng, liking.

lely, lily.
leme, shine.
lemman, lemmon, lover.
lene, (v.) lean.
lengest, longest.
lere, teach.
les, less; it is non —, it amounts to this.
les, lost.
lesyng, falsehood.
lesyng, lessening.
lest, least.
lesten, last, endure.
let, let go.
leve, believe.
lever, rather.
libben, live.
lyght, glad.
lyght, come.
lyght, lies.
lyth, listen.
lynne, cease.
liste, please.
loft, on —, high up.
long, belong, adhere to.
lore, teaching, company.
lossom, lovable.
low, laughed.
lure, frown.
lussomore, more lovable.
luste, pleasure, will.

mad, meyd, maid.
maden, mayden, maydyn, maydon, maiden.
mak(e), mate.
may, maid.
meane, cause, agent.
meche, much.
mede, meyd, reward.
medylmest, middle.
meyny, mene, company, herd.
mekil, mekyl(l), mykyll, much.
mene, middle.
menskful, graceful.
mer, pond.
mere, merry.
mery-go-down, strong ale.
mych(e), much, very.
myere, mire.
mis, amiss, wrong.
mysse, fail.
myth, might, power.

mo(o), more.
mody, angry.
moke, mockery.
mone, many.
monge, mingle.
morwe, morning.
most(e), greatest.
mot(e), may.
mouth, might,
mow(e), grimace.
mow(e), may.
mowlde, top of the head.
mow(u)n, may.
murgest, murgust, merriest.
muskilles, mussels.

namely, especially.
nay, hit is no —, it is certainly true.
necessyte, hardship.
ner, nearer.
nes, was not.
noll, head.
nome, taken, joined,
nother, neither.
nowbyll, noble.
nower, nowhere.
nowth, not.
nuste, did not know.

oblacion, offering.
oder, other.
on, one.
ontyll, unto.
or, before.
orayson, orison.
ordent, ordained.
ost, host.
outh, out.
owersette, put off.
owght, anything.

pair, payr, peyr, impair, make worse.
pall, rich fabric.
panter, pantryman.
parvenke, periwinkle.
pay, pey, satisfaction; to —, acceptably; to his —, to his liking.
per(e), peer.
perdone, pardon.
pese, pea.
pese, pece, peis, peys, peace.
pete, pity.
phinne, fiend.

pyght, fixed.
pyne, pain.
poll, head.
potestates, powers, the angelic order.
predele, adorn, trim.
preve, prove.
prevytes, secrets.
princypates, principalities, the angelic order.
prys(e), worth.
pryse, price.
privy, secret, secluded.
prouesse, virtue.
pusyn, poison.

quan, when.
quat, qwat, what.
quere, choir.
quityn, repay.
qwede, bad.
qweder, whither.
qwens, whence.
qwer(e), where.
qwer, wherever.
qwi, qwy, why.
qwyte, white.
qwoso, whoever.

rather, sooner.
ravyghth, rages.
rech, reach.
rede, advice.
rede, reed.
rede, advise.
redy, sound, healthy.
reych, rush.
ren(n)e, run.
rent, rend.
repayre, refresh.
repyn, reaped.
reprefe, reproof, shame.
res, rash or impulsive action.
reven, cracked.
rewe, pity.
rewful, sad.
rewit, saddens.
rewly, sorry,
reych, rush.
ryght, directly.
ryghtwessnesse, righteousness.
rynd, rend, tear off.
ryne, run.

ryng, circle of the carole.
ryse, branch.
ryth(e), right, very.
rywe, rue.
roke, rock.
rowght, go round.
rowne, whisper.

sad, sober, serious.
salsecle, heliotrope.
saltu, shalt thou.
salvoure, healer.
sauter-booke, psalter.
saw, save.
saw, sowed.
sawes, wise sayings.
sawus, promises.
schayl, spilling.
scheld, schilde, schylde, shield.
schene, beautiful.
s(c)hent, badly injured.
Scher Thursday, Holy Thursday.
schylderin, children.
schone, shoes.
schorges, scourges, whips.
schryf, shrive, be confessed.
schulle, shall.
schwln, shall.
scoth, shot, scot, share of reckoning for drink.
scrype, scrip, pouch.
se, episcopal see, city.
secrete, quiet, discretion.
secutoures, executors.
seek, sick.
seke, seek.
sekerly, sekyrly, surely.
sel, good fortune.
selcouth, wonder, marvel.
semly, seemly.
sen, since.
send, ascend.
sequence, prose, antiphonal sacred song.
sesse, seysse, cease.
seth, since.
sew(e), follow, pursue.
shen(e), bright.
shent, punished.
shyll, shrilly.
sick, sych, such,
syde, side; **be —**, moreover.

syghthy, sits.
sykke, sigh.
sinke, sing.
sytes, sights.
siwed, pursued.
skylle, reason, judgement.
skyrte, man's kilt-like garment.
skuses, excuses.
slake, fail.
sle, slay.
sleder, slippery.
slent, sly dealing.
slon, slay.
slober, feed untidily.
slow, slew.
smater, prate, chatter.
smert, stinging, painful.
snew, snowed.
snyb, correct sharply.
socour, succour, help.
sofer, suffer.
solas, joy.
solas, make easy.
son, as soon as.
sonde, gift, bounty.
soote, sweetly.
soth(e), true, truly.
sother, truer.
sothfast, truthful.
sowce, pickled pork.
sowse, soak.
space, opportunity.
spares, ceases.
spille, injure, punish.
spyn, stock of a plant.
spone, chip.
sprink, spring, bloom.
stal, stole.
stauns, dissension.
stefve, stiff, staunch.
stey(e), rise, ascend.
sterdyn, stirred.
ster(r)e, sterne, star.
sterte, started up.
sterve, die.
steven, voice.
stint, stynt, stop, check.
stoke, piece of wood.
stout, stately.
strake, struck, flowed.
streytly, tightly.
streme, beam of light.

stryfe, strive,
suyre, neck.
suld(e), should.
swaryd, squared, as by a mason.
swych, such.
swythe, quickly.

take, betake oneself, go.
tayd, tied.
talent, intention.
temperalte, secular power.
tene, sorrow.
then, thine
ther, thereas, where.
these, this.
thewes, usages.
thynk(e), seem.
tho, those.
tho, then.
thoght, care.
thoght, seemed.
thorugh, certain.
thorw, thurgh, through.
thowth, thought, purpose.
thral, captive.
thristilcok, male thrush.
thunder-dent, thunderbolt.
tide, tyd(e), time, season.
tyler, tiller, cultivator.
tyll, to.
tirtyll, turtle-dove.
tythyngis, tidings.
to, till.
tomorn, tomorrow morning.
tone, toes.
too, two.
to-torn, torn to pieces.
tour, tower.
tour, turn; on her —, in their degree
  or order.
traye, betray.
tretour, traitor.
trippus, dancing steps.
trones, thrones, the angelic order.
trow, trew, believe,
tunykes, tunicles, choir-vestments.
turmentowres, torturers.
twel, dwell.
tweye, two.
twinkel, wink.

umble, humbly.

811418

unbech, unmended.
unlahfulliche, unlawfully.
unrepe, unprepared.
unswope, unswept.
untille, unto.
unto, until.
unwysse, unwise.
upneme, uphold.

verray, verre, true, real.
vertues, virtues, the angelic order.
vise, advise.
vlech, floor.

wai, woe.
walaway, welaway, alas
wam, spot, stain.
wanne, when.
wappyd, wrapped.
war, careful.
ware, were.
warn, take heed.
watt, hare.
wed, clothing.
wem(e), wemmb, spot, stain.
wende, go.
wende, thought.
wene, think.
wepping, weeping.
wer, where.
wer, wher, wither.
wern, were.
werr, war.
wes, was.
wex, wexed, grew.
whereas, where.
wherso, wherever.
whylom, formerly, once upon a time.
who, how.
whot, hot.
wyde, far separated.
wyll, well.
wysse, wise.
wyst, knew, known.
wyth, white.
wod, wood.
wod(e), wood, mad.
wol, well, very.
wole, will.
won, country.
won, wan, pale.
wond, shrink, hesitate.

T

wonder, wonderful, wonderfully.
wondys, wounds.
wone, dwell.
wonynge, dwelling-place.
woode-colver, wood-pigeon.
worhliche, noble, excellent.
worschep, worchepe, woschyp, honour.
worschip, worschyp, pay honour to.
wortes, worton, herbs.
wost, knowest.
wot, know.
wow, woe.
wretyn, written.
wryng, suffer.
wroch, tunic, outer garment.

xal(l), xuln, shall.
xalt, shalt.
xulde, should.

ya, yes.
yech, yet.
yede, went.
yeffe, yeve, yyf, give.
yeman, yeoman, servant.
yerd(e), rod.
yyfte, gift.
yyng, young.
yitt, yytte, yet.
yode, went.
yore, long ago.

INDEX OF FIRST LINES

(First lines of burdens are in italics)